THE VIKING SAGA

In Ireland, Scotland and the Isles

Páll Thormod Morrisson

Sídh Chailleann Press
Ireland & Scotland

Formatting by Orla Kelly Publishing, Cork

Cover by Babs Burnett of Wolfpack Design, Edinburgh

Author's Photo by Kára Morrisson

Cover Illustration *Hrafnsmerki (Raven Banner)* by Páll Thormod Morrisson

For Kára

Also by the Author and available through Amazon:

The Viking Runes

The Celtic Heroic Tradition in Myth & Legend

Dionysos in Myth, Drama & Comedy: Bacchic Elements in Greek & Celtic Culture

SÍDH CHAILLEANN PRESS

Nú er ógurlegt um at litaz
er deyrug ský dregr með himni
mun lopt litat lýda blóði
er sóknarvaðr syngja kunnu.

An awful sight the eye beholds
as blood-red rack passes overhead.
Warriors' gore bloodies the welkin
whene'er the shield maids
take to singing.
Darraðarljoð

CONTENTS

CONTENTS Cont.

After this came the massive royal fleet of the Clann Ímair to Átha Cliath, and they pillaged the greater part of Erinn…

- Cogadh Gáedhel re Gallaibh

A NOTE ON LANGUAGE & NAMES

The main languages spoken in Ireland, Scotland and the Isles during the period covered in this book were Old Norse and the early Irish and Scottish versions of the Gaelic. Many people would have spoken both Norse and Gaelic tongues, either through having blood links to the two cultures or for social interaction, trade and alliance.

Most people at this time were illiterate, so languages would have been learned purely by ear.

Contrary to what some people believe, Gaelic was spoken widely throughout those areas of mainland Scotland that were later to come under Norse influence, such as Caithness and Sutherland, and before Gaelic, Pictish was the tongue.

Caithness, though considered part of the Orkney jarldom by the Norse, was still considered part of the realm of Moray by its rulers. During the reign of Máel Coluim mac Cináeda, High King of Alba in particular, Norse jarls were expected to hold it under Picto-Scottish overlordship or not at all.

The Northern Isles were originally inhabited by the Picts, so Pictish was the language and culture there long before the arrival of the Norse. The vikings did not invade uninhabited lands. In addition, Gaelic would continue to have been spoken by the earlier inhabitants of these areas even after Norse settlement. Furthermore, Gaelic was eventually to become pre-eminent as the everyday language among the Norse in both Ireland and Scotland.

English as we know it today was a thing unknown and would have been quite alien to the people featured in our sagas. This might seem obvious, but it is easy to forget.

There is an index toward the rear of the book, listing all personal names, tribal and group names, god and saint names, place names and terms with pronunciation and meanings in brackets, together with some historical background on the main people featured in the book.

Certain letters the reader will encounter repeatedly throughout the book are the Old Norse and modern Icelandic characters *thorn* and *eth.* These are written þ (capital Þ), pronounced *th* as in *thwack* and ð (capital Đ), pronounced with a softer *th* as in *mother.*

So, for example, Old Norse names that are often given an anglicised form such as *Thorfinn* or *Gudrod* are presented in their authentic, original forms of Þórfinnr (pronounced Thorfinn-ur), and *Guðrøðr* (pronounced Gooth-rith-ur).

Introduction

This book explores the viking presence in Ireland, Scotland and the Isles through the saga sources. Though largely based on historical events that are the subject of contemporary annals from the 9th to 11th centuries CE, the sagas also include material drawn from the rich store of Icelandic family and folk traditions, of which there are supernatural and mythological elements. The sagas and chronicles featured in this work were put to paper from the early 1100s to the late 1200s in the main.

The usual understanding is that the Viking Age lasted from 800 to 1066 CE, but the vikings didn't know about that and continued throwing their weight about in Ireland until after 1150 CE and in Scotland and the Isles up to the 1260s. Later yet, the *gall óglaigh* or foreign warriors of the Norse Gaelic Hebridean and West Highland kindreds hired themselves out as elite mercenaries in Ireland until the late 16th century.

We use the term *viking* here in the introduction without the capital V that has become generally popular, but inaccurate. In the sagas themselves the term has no capitalisation, and indeed, the original term in its proper form never had. The word *víkingr* meant pirate, freebooter, and was never a national term, as many people have come to see it. Rather it is to be understood more in the sense of a pursuit or trade. This was often carried out in between farming, though some made a profession out of it by regularly raiding or hiring themselves out as mercenaries.

Embarking on a viking expedition was not restricted to any particular section of society. The karls or freemen farmers composed the bulk of the raiding crew with the aim of grabbing whatever booty and silver they could lay their hands on. Professional warriors would be looking for pay as well as plunder. Warlords and kings leading an expedition – the biggest thieves yet – would sieze the lion's share of the spoils and distribute a proportion of it among their *hirð* or retinue to reinforce loyalty.

To whatever degree a warrior honour code was observed, the plain truth of the matter was that this was robbery with violence of the most brutal kind, in which heads were split to the teeth or breastbone and bashed in with axe blades, throats were cut, bodies gutted with spears, and limbs hacked off. No discreet cat burglary here, but a shock attack accompanied by the blare of battle horns and the roar of flames.

In those cases where areas were taken over and settled, tribute in the form of protection money, produce or goods in kind were extorted through intimidation and the threat of more violence. Those subject to this were not only the ordinary local population, but also weaker rival warrior factions not strong enough to defend themselves effectively. The Norse did not have the monopoly on extortion, however. In Ireland, viking leaders were themselves often forced to pay tribute to powerful Irish kings and warlords. Before the vikings ever arrived in Ireland or Scotland, the tradition of raiding for plunder, by sea or land, was an ancient one. Cattle raiding was particularly common, a custom commemorated in such heroic epics as *Táin Bó Cúailnge* and *Táin Bó Flidhais.*

Fame and glory were also pursued, for a grand reputation as a warrior would gain admiration and be celebrated, but praise poems were usually reserved for warlords and kings only, as they had the wherewithal to pay for them. Amlaíb Cuarán, a Norse Irish King of Dublin, was a noted patron of both Norse and Irish poets. This praise poetry, packed full of bloodthirsty motifs, was composed by the *skáld,* or northern bard, to exalt his patron before the eyes of the world.

As it will be seen from the introductory sections on Ireland and Scotland (or Pictland and the later Alba as it was earlier known), it would be wrong to imagine that the vikings had it all their own way. Both Ireland and Pictland put up stout resistance in which the invaders often suffered multiple defeats. Viking groups in Ireland, for example, who took tribute or protection money from the Irish were just as likely to be forced to pay it themselves to powerful Irish warlords, as the Norse Irish king Sihtric Silk Beard was forced to do on several occasions. Amlaíb Conung, King of Dublin tried to exact tribute from the Picts in 874 and was killed for his trouble. Viking chieftains not strong enough to stand alone sought alliances with Gaelic leaders sometimes just to survive.

The Uí Ímair

The Uí Ímair (or *descendants of Ímair* as the name translates from the Gaelic) was the preeminent viking dynasty in Ireland and Britain. Named after its founder Ímar (Norse Ívarr) and established in the middle of the ninth century, this Norse Irish dynasty would go on to dominate the Irish Sea regions. The Uí Ímair measured its strength against the rival branches of the

Uí Neill dynasty of Ireland and the Mac Ailpín dynasty of early Scotland among others and offered a persistent challenge to the House of Wessex, the main power in Saxon England, as well as opposing its Norse, Danish and Norse Gaelic rivals. Dublin, which would become one of the most important trading centres in the Norse world, was its main power base, from which it would plunder not only territories in Ireland, but Pictland and the later early Scottish kingdom of Alba. The Uí Ímair would also invade southern Britain, raiding the coast of Wales, conquering East Anglia and establishing its rule at York.

Though Ímar, from whom the Uí Ímair derives its name, is said to have been the son of one Gofraidh mac Ragnaill (Guðrøðr), ruler of Lochlann according to Irish sources, there are those who support the theory that he was one and the same as the famous Ívarr hinn Beinlausi or Ívarr the Boneless, son of the legendary Ragnarr Loþbrók. Among the scholars that support this theory are Kim Hjardar and Vegard Vike, who argue that Ímar was indeed Ívarr the Boneless, a leader of the Danish forces that defeated and came to rule the Norwegian vikings already settled in Ireland.

Professor Donnchadh Ó Corráin is unconvinced that any representative of a Danish dynasty was ever preeminent in Ireland and believes that Ímar, rather than being Danish, belonged to a Norse dynasty based in Scotland. The *Lochlann* or *Laithlind* Ímar's father was said to rule is a Gaelic word that has been applied to Norway or the Norse areas of Scotland and the Isles, depending on your point of view, although the latter is probably more likely.

Whether or not it can be proved that Ímar was Ívarr the Boneless, it does nevertheless appear that he was one of the leaders of the Great Heathen Army that invaded England CE 865, conquering Northumbria, East Anglia and Mercia and attempting to do the same to Wessex.

Ímar's brothers are given in the Irish annals as Amlaíb Conung (the nickname deriving from the Norse *konungr* or king, identified by some scholars as Óláfr the White) and Auisle (Auðgísl), but it is by no means certain that they were all actual brothers. Hjardar and Vike are more inclined to think that Ímar and Amlaíb were sworn brothers in the sense of loyal battle comrades rather than coming from the same family.

(Hálfdanr Ragnarsson, referred to as Albdann in the *Annals of Ulster*, may have been another brother or sworn brother, though any blood link to

Ímar would only be likely if he was indeed one and the same as Ívarr hinn Beinlausi).

The brothers are referred to in Irish sources as Ímar, Amlaíb and Auisle or Óisle, the Gaelic versions of the Norse names Ívarr, Óláfr and Auðgísl. It is a matter of conjecture whether they themselves used the Gaelic versions other than perhaps when involved in activities such as trading, but their descendants, through intermarriage and cross-cultural influence were increasingly Gaelicised, with Norse Gaelic names and the Gaelic tongue becoming the norm. As Clare Downham points out, by the tenth century at least, the vikings in Ireland were both Scandinavian and Gaelic in culture.

While the native Irish called the vikings *gall* or foreigners, Norsemen who had settled in Ireland were often referred to as *Írskr* or Irish by their cousins in Norway, and therefore outlanders, just as Icelanders, speaking the same Norse tongue, were also considered outlanders by those in Norway. This would be even more the case if they had Gaelic blood. The Gall Goídil or Foreigner Gael (Norse Irish or Scots mixed blood population) are described as apostates by Christian sources for having adopted viking heathenism, though many would have been born heathen. Whereas the full-blooded Norse were bad to the churches, the Gall Goídil were said to have been far worse.

The *Annala Rioghachta Eireann* or *Annals of the Kingdom of Ireland by the Four Masters* refers to the Dublin Norse as *Muintir Tomar* or *Tribe of* Þórr (Thór) from their devotion to that deity.

Ériu (Ireland) 849-1042 CE

The Uí Ímair are mentioned repeatedly in the Gaelic saga *Cogadh Gaedhel re Gallaibh* as invading Ireland and making a constant nuisance of themselves, killing, burning and plundering. The ring of Þórr and the Sword of Carlus were passed down from ruler to ruler as symbols of their power.

According to the *Fragmentary Annals of Ireland,* Amlaíb Conung came to Ireland in 849 (the sixth year of the reign of Máel Sechnaill) *with a proclamation of many tributes and taxes* from his father Gofraidh. His younger brother Ímar then *came after him to levy the same tribute.* Any tribute or plunder clearly did not go all one way, as in that same year the Irish kings Máel Sechnaill mac Máele Ruanaid, ruler of the Southern Uí Néill (mentioned above) and Tigernach mac Fócartaig pillaged Dublin, although the following year their own lands were raided by the Norse in alliance with Cináed mac Conaing, King of the Cíanachta Breg.

Amlaíb and Ímar had rivals not only among the native Irish, such as Máel Sechnaill, but also among the Norse and Norse Gaels in other parts of the country. For 857 the *Annals of Ulster* have the entry: *Great conflict between the heathen and Máel Sechnaill, supported by the Norse Irish.* Warlords who might be natural enemies most of the time were often willing to share common cause against a third party that threatened them both. For example, in 858 Ímar allied himself with the indomitable Irish ruler of Osraige, Cerball mac Dunláinge, against Máel Sechnaill and the Norse Gael of Munster, and in 859 Amlaíb was also in league with Cerball to pillage Máel Sechnaill's territories in Meath, although Cerball later pledged his allegiance to Máel Sechnaill. In 860 Máel Sechnaill and Cerball were in conflict with Máel Sechnaill's rival, Áed Findliath of the Northern Uí Néill, who had Amlaíb as his son-in-law. Before becoming *Ard Rí* or High King of Ireland, Áed made an alliance with Amlaíb and the Dublin Norse to plunder Meath in 861, after which he was beaten by Máel Sechnaill again, and in 862, the year Máel Sechnaill died. Laughably, in 863 one of Máel Sechnaill's successors as King of Meath, Lorcán mac Cathail, had Ímar, Amlaíb and Auisle as his allies when he raided Brega, Southern Uí Néill territory.

In 865, as a leader of the Great Heathen Army, Ímar invaded England and wintered in East Anglia, and in 866 York fell under viking control. Also, in 866 Amlaíb and Auisle invaded Pictland and took hostages and tribute. Meanwhile Áed Findliath, incited by his wife Land, trounced the vikings at Lough Foyle and burned all the viking *longphorts* or fortified ship harbours along Ireland's northern coast. In 866 and 867 *The Annals of Ulster* and *The Fragmentary Annals* tell of serious reverses for the vikings in Ireland, with defeats inflicted on them by Cennétig mac Gaethíne, King of Loíches and by the northern Osraige, and by the tribes of the Déissi and the Fir Maige, former foes who allied themselves against the common enemy. Amlaíb's stronghold at Clondalkin was also burned by Cennétig and the Leinster leader Máel Ciaraín mac Rónáin and a hundred viking heads taken and displayed after the slaughter there. In another encounter, Congal, King of the Ciarraige defeated the forces of one Tomrar (Þórir) who had plundered Clonfert, and during that clash a few of the raiders escaped, leaving behind *great quantities of gold and silver and beautiful women.*

An entry for the year 867 in *The Fragmentary Annals* mentions the hatred of Amlaíb and Ímar for their younger brother Auisle, who surpassed them in both valour and fighting skills. Amlaíb in particular nursed a fierce enmity and plotted with Ímar to have Auisle killed. The entry goes on to describe a meeting during which Auisle made a proposal to Amlaíb to the effect that if Amlaíb's wife did not love him, Auisle would be glad to have her, after which Amlaíb stuck his sword into Auisle's head in a jealous rage and a fight between their respective followers ensued.

Amlaíb's wife is referred to as *the daughter of Cináed* in *The Fragmentary Annals of Ireland.* Alfred P. Smyth identifies her father as Cináed mac Ailpín, King of the Picts. Irish sources also mention Amlaíb as the son-in-law of Áed Findliath. It was not unusual for the heathen Norse to have more than one wife, though we have to allow for remarriage after divorce or death of a spouse. In Icelandic sources Óláfr Hvíti (whom some scholars believe is one and the same as Amlaíb) is given as the husband of Unnr or Auðr the Deep Minded, daughter of Ketill Flatnefr.

In 868 Amlaíb's son Carlus was killed at Killineer, opposing Amlaíb's father-in-law and former ally Áed Findliath, who had a great victory there. And in 869 Máel Ciaraín mac Rónáin, who had burned down Amlaíb's stronghold together with Cennétig, was slain by his rivals in Leinster and his head given to the Dublin Norse, who threw it into the sea after using it as a target for sport.

By 870 the rulers of Leinster continued to fight amongst themselves and Ímar and Amlaíb were in Strathclyde, besieging Dumbarton, the capital of that kingdom. They arrived back in Dublin with their large fleet and a great many Britons, Picts and English loaded with slave-chains.

As has already been said, Auisle was killed in 867. Ímar died in 873, hailed in the *Annals of Ulster* as *king of the Northmen of all Ireland and Britain.* Also, in 873 *The Fragmentary Annals of Ireland* report the *death of Gothfraid the King of Lochlann of a sudden and horrible fit. Thus, it was good before God,* which makes it plain the Irish couldn't wait to get rid of him. And in 874 Amlaíb was slain in Pictland fighting King Causantín mac Cináeda.

Following the death of Ímar, the dynasty would continue with his descendants, among whom Ragnall ua Ímair (Rögnvaldr), Sihtric Cáech (One Eyed), Amlaíb Cuarán (Óláfr Kváran) and his son Sihtric (or Sigtryggr Silk Beard as he is known in *Njáls saga* and *Orkneyinga saga*), were particularly notable.

Their chief areas of operation outside Ireland were Pictland (later known as Moray and Alba), Northern England and Wales.

In 875, the year after Amlaíb's death, his son Oistín was killed by Hálfdanr, referred to as Albdann in *The Annals of Ulster,* in what was probably a struggle over control of the Uí Ímair territories.

In 877 Causantín mac Cináeda, King of the Picts, against whom Amlaíb died in battle, was himself slain fighting the warband of Albdann (Hálfdanr). Albdann was later killed fighting the Findgaill at Loch Cuan (Strangford Lough). In 879 Áed Findliath also passed away, as did Cerball mac Dúnlainge in 888, both formidable Irish leaders who successfully opposed general viking expansion, often using alliances with rival viking groups in the process.

In 902 the vikings were driven out of Dublin by the Irish kings Máel mac Flannacán and Cerball mac Muirecáin. The next year the grandsons of Ímar were in Pictland, plundering Dunkeld, and in 904 Áed, King of Pictland was killed in battle against two grandsons of Ímar. Ímar, grandson of Ímar was then killed by the Pictish Men of Fortriu along with a great many other vikings.

Ragnall ua Ímair came to the attention of the chroniclers in 914 when he defeated his rival Bárid mac Oitir in a sea fight off the Isle of Man. That same year he also defeated the Scots and Bernicians at the first Battle of Corbridge. In 916, together with Sihtric Cáech, he was raiding in Ireland and in 917, after the Battle of Cenn Fuait, Sihtric took back Dublin.

In 918 the forces of Ragnall ua Ímair opposed the Scots and Bernicians again in the second Battle of Corbridge. The first three columns of the Norse Gaels were beaten by King Causantin mac Áeda's Scots, who were then ambushed by Ragnall leading another column out of concealment. The result of the battle was indecisive, but Ragnall took York in 919 and became ruler of Northumbria. That same year Sihtric was triumphant at the Battle of Islandbridge in Ireland, where the *Ard Rí* Niall Glúndub fell along with several other kings, and in 920 he was in England, plundering Cheshire. In 921 Sihtric succeeded Ragnall as king in York when the latter died. Sihtric married a sister of Æþelstan, King of the Saxons in 926 and temporarily became a Christian, returning to the heathen faith not long afterwards. He died in 927.

Sihtric's son and Ímar's great-grandson Amlaíb Cuarán became King of Northumbria from 941-944 and from 949-952. He was also King of Dublin from 945-947 and from 952-980. Amlaíb had two Irish wives, Dúnlaith and Gormflaith, both king's daughters, and his marriage alliances forged links with both Norse Gaelic and Irish dynasties, though he faced challenges as well as support from factions on either side hungry for power.

The Battle of Tara took place in the final year of his Dublin reign. Máel Sechnaill mac Domnaill, High King of Ireland and Amlaíb's stepson, defeated the latter's forces that included Amlaíb's sons and Norse Gael mercenaries from the Hebrides and Man. Amlaíb's son Ragnall fell in the battle. Máel Sechnaill afterward laid siege to Dublin and set all the slaves free when his enemies surrendered and took a large tribute from the Dublin vikings. Amlaíb later abandoned the kingship of Dublin to become a monk on Iona, where he died.

Amlaíb's son Glúniarainn or Járnkné (Iron Knee) was made client King of Dublin by Máel Sechnaill and they were in close alliance thereafter. Glúniarainn and Máel Sechnaill were half brothers, sons of Dúnlaith. Glúniarainn is said to have been drunk at the time when he was killed by a slave called Colban in 989.

Sihtric (Sigtryggr Silk Beard), known as *Mac Amlaíb* in *Cogadh Gaedhil re Gallaibh,* succeeded his half brother Glúniarainn. Sihtric was the son of Amlaíb Cuarán and Gormflaith, daughter of Murchad mac Finn, King of Leinster. He appears in *Njáls saga, Orkneyinga saga,* and *Gunnlaugs saga ormstungu* and is apparently referred to in the skaldic poem *Darraðarljóð.* Although Dublin appears to have thrived as a trading centre during his reign and he was noted for his wealth, Sihtric's military endeavours were generally less successful, in particular his repeated failures in opposing the rise of Brian Bóruma, whose daughter Sláine he married.

In 995 Sihtric desecrated the church at Donaghpatrick in Meath. That same year Máel Sechlainn mac Domnaill plundered Dublin and took the Ring of Þórr and the Sword of Carlus, the symbols of Sihtric's authority. By 998 Máel Sechnaill mac Domnaill and Brian Bóruma forced Sihtric to hand over hostages.

The next year, at the Battle of Glen Máma, the allied forces of Sihtric and Máel Mórda mac Murchada, King of Leinster were trounced by the combined armies of Brian Bóruma and Máel Sechnaill, who had been the nemesis of Amlaíb Cuarán, Sihtric's father in 980.

Sihtric would have been further humiliated when Brian plundered Dublin in the year 1000, burned his stronghold and forced him to flee. Sihtric later submitted to Brian and again gave hostages. Brian married Sihtric's mother Gormflaith, although he later divorced her.

Brian Bóruma became *Ard Rí* or High King of Ireland in 1002 and in 1014 at the Battle of Cluain Tarbh (Clontarf), the allied forces mustered by Sihtric were heavily defeated, resulting in the deaths of Sigurðr Digri, Jarl of Orkney and the Manx viking leader Bróðir, who killed Brian Bóruma. Brian's sons Murchad and Toirdelbach also died. Many of the vikings perished by drowning as they fled into the sea after their ships were swept back by the rising tide.

Though forced to pay tribute to the victors, Sihtric was to remain in power after Clontarf. However, it would appear that he was driven to recoup his losses with raids for plunder. In 1018 he was pillaging another church, this time at Kells, in which he *carried off innumerable spoils and prisoners, and slew many persons in the middle of the church,* according to the *Annals of the Four Masters.* The captives were probably later sold as slaves.

Considering Sihtric's habit of targeting churches for plunder and desecration throughout his career, it is remarkable that he later established the bishopric at Dublin as well as Christ Church Cathedral. And in 1028, like Þórfinnr the Mighty, Macbeth and other notables, he also went on pilgrimage to Rome. Nevertheless, two years after that, he was plundering Wales in alliance with Knútr, King of Denmark, Norway and England.

A disastrous raid into Wicklow in 1021 saw Sihtric beaten by Augaire mac Dúnlainge, King of Leinster. According to the *Annals of the Four Masters,* Augaire wreaked *a dreadful slaughter among the foreigners.* A raid against Ulster the next year was equally ill-starred. The Dublin vikings were beaten in a sea battle by Niall mac Eochaid, King of Ulaid, and the survivors and their ships captured.

In 1025 Sihtric was forced to give hostages to King Flaithbertach ua Néill and again in 1026 to his own half brother, Donnchadh, son of Brian Bóruma. And as if things couldn't get bad enough, Niall mac Eochaid then swept down from Ulster to plunder Dublin in reprisal for Sihtric's failed raid of 1022. Sihtric's run of bad luck continued in 1027 when, allied with Donnchad of Brega, he was beaten by Roen ua Máel Sechlainn, King of Meath.

In 1029 Mathghamhain ua Riagain, King of Brega captured Amlaíb (Óláfr), Sihtric's son. Sihtric paid a huge ransom to free him, including the Sword of Carlus, the Irish hostages of Leinster and Leath Cuinn, over one thousand cows, one hundred and forty British horses and sixty ounces of gold and silver, plus eighty cows for the man who negotiated the deal with Mathghamhain, according to *The Annals of the Four Masters.*

In 1032 Sihtric was victorious at the Battle of Inbher Boinne against the allied forces of the Conailli, the Uí Tortain and the Uí Meith, but in 1036 Sihtric was forced to stand down as King of Dublin by Eachmarcach mac Ragnaill, King of the Isles. He died in 1042.

Pictland & the later Kingdom of Alba 843-1065 CE

Pictland or Pictavia, said to have been composed of seven realms in early sources such as *De Situ Albanie, Duan Albanach* and the *Pictish Chronicle,* took in most of what is now Scotland, with the Kingdom of Fortriu, centred in Moray, being preeminent. To the west the Gaelic Kingdom of Dál Riada was established, at first spanning the North Channel between Antrim in Ulster and Scotland's rugged west coast, it later became centred solely on Argyll. Indeed, Argyll itself means *coast of the Gael.* The two neighbouring realms of Pictland and Dál Riada were sometimes at war and sometimes in alliance, a situation that was to continue until the gradual merging of the Picts and Scots ultimately led to Pictland being renamed the Kingdom of Alba, with the rival realm of Moray to the north.

The Picts had a long and bloody history of confronting invaders, particularly the Romans, then later the Scots, Britons, Angles and the Norse.

Pictland was a target for the Uí Ímair and other viking raiders from early times, as has already been shown. The later realms of Alba and Moray also had to deal with viking aggression. As in Ireland, marriage and military alliances were made that might forge peaceful relations between two specific warrior dynasties, but of course that would not stop attacks and raids from enemies to both.

Cináed mac Ailpín was King of the Picts from 843 until 858. He is called *Cionaith chruaidh* or Cináed the Hardy in the early poem *Duan Albanach.*

The Prophecy of Berchán refers to him as a *man who shall feed ravens, fight battles,* and gives him the name *Ferbasach* – slayer or conqueror.

An entry in the *Annals of Ulster* for 839 has a disastrous defeat for the Pictish elíte at the hands of the vikings – Eóganán mac Óengusa, the then King of the Picts, his brother Bran, Áed mac Boanta, King of Dál Riada and *others almost innumerable* being slain. According to *The Chronicle of Huntingdon,* this led to a struggle for the kingship of the Picts in which Cináed *turned his arms against them, and having slain many,* eliminated all his rivals.

There is a record in *The Chronicle of the Kings of Alba* of viking incursions deep into Pictland in which land was laid waste during Cináed's reign, but Cináed also *harassed the Gaill* (or vikings), according to *The Prophecy of Berchan.* Indeed, he was secure enough in his power to invade *Saxonia six times, capturing Melrose and burning Dunbar,* as stated further in *The Chronicle of the Kings of Alba.* Saxonia here refers to Northumbria, Melrose and Dunbar being English-held settlements at the time.

With a view to protecting the relics of Colum Cille or Columba from viking raiders, Cináed had them brought from Iona to Dunkeld in 849.

Like other Gaelic and Pictish warlords of the time, Cináed's relationship with the Norse involved alliance as well as war. An entry in the *Annals of the Four Masters* has Cináed requesting reinforcements from Gofraid mac Fergusa, chief of Airgíalla in Ulster to strengthen Dál Riada in 836. Gofraid is of course the Gaelic form of the Norse Guðrøðr, which suggests that Gofraid mac Fergusa was of the Gall-Goídil or Norse Gael.

Cináed's rise to power as King of the Picts after the slaughter of the Pictish elite by the Norse caused the distinguished historian Skene and more recent scholars to speculate on whether Cináed had been acting in concert with the vikings. Alfred P. Smyth and John Marsden in particular suggest the Hebridean Norse, with whom Cináed would have had constant interaction as ruler of Dál Riada. In addition, Domnaill, Cináed's successor and brother or half brother is referred to as the *wanton son of the Gaillsigthe* or Norse wife, according to the *Prophecy of Berchán,* indicating the possibility of a marriage alliance between their father Ailpín and the Gaill or vikings. Cináed himself established important alliances by marrying his daughters to powerful warlords, among whom was Áed Findliath, who became High King of Ireland and, significantly for our study here, Amlaíb Conung (Óláfr the White), according to *The Fragmentary Annals of Ireland.*

Smyth goes on to suggest that the Mac Ailpín dynasty rose to pre-eminence either directly allied with the Hebridean and Dublin Norse, or at the very least by gaining advantage from repeated viking assaults on its rivals. The fact that Cináed and his successors also fought the vikings during their respective reigns does not necessarily contradict this theory. Pictish and Gaelic warlords might ally themselves with certain viking leaders, but they still had to defend their territories against viking factions they were *not* allied with.

Cináed died at the palace of Cinnbelachoir in 858.

In 980, Hloðvér, son of Þórfinnr Skull Splitter, became Jarl of Orkney and married Eithne, daughter of the Irish King Cerball. Their son was Sigurðr Digri (The Stout), who features in *Njáls saga, Orkneyinga saga* and *Gunnlaugs saga ormstungu* among others as a powerful jarl with control over not only the Northern Isles but also territories in the north of Scotland, though claims to these were no doubt disputed by the Kings or Mormaers of Moray. His forced conversion from heathenism to Christianity at the hands of King Óláfr Tryggvason and the death of his young son Hvelp, who was subsequently taken as a hostage to Norway, hardened Sigurðr against further recognising royal authority.

His other sons were Einar, Brusi, Sumarlidi and Þórfinnr.

Sigurðr married Olith, a daughter of Máel Coluim, Árd Rí *Albann* or High King of Alba and this appears to have forged an alliance between the Orkney Norse and the Mac Ailpín dynasty.

In 1014 Sigurðr was persuaded by Sihtric (Sigtryggr Silk Beard), King of Dublin to go against Brian Bóruma, offering the high kingship of Ireland and his mother Gormflaith as reward. Unbenownst to Sigurðr, Sihtric made the same offer to the Manx viking leader Bróðir to enlist his support also. Before sailing to Ireland with his forces, Sigurðr left his youngest son Þórfinnr with the boy's grandfather, Máel Coluim, High King of Alba.

At the Battle of Clontarf Sigurðr died at the end of a spear after taking up the ill-starred raven banner that had been the bane of all his standard bearers, according to the *Orkneyinga saga*. The jarldom was divided between Sigurðr's sons. As well as his share of this, the young Þórfinnr was given Caithness by his grandfather.

Máel Coluim mac Cináeda was *Ard Rí Albann* or High King of Alba from 1005 until 1034. According to the *Prophecy of Berchán,* he was the son of a Leinster woman. The *Prophecy of Berchán* also gives him the epithet *Forranach,* The Destroyer, reflective of his fighting skills and military power. He took the kingship after slaying his rival Cináeda mac Duib in Strathearn in 1005, according to the *Annals of Ulster.* The chronicler *John of Fordun* has Máel Coluim triumphing over a Norse force at Mórthlach in Moray shortly after coming to power that same year. So, his long reign was blood-soaked from the outset.

The dynastic marriages of his three daughters appear to have helped stave off threats from other potential rivals – Crínán of Dunkeld, who married Bethóc; Sigurðr Digri of Orkney, who wed Olith; and Findláech mac Ruaidri, ruler of Moray, who married Donada. Findláech was the father of Macbeth, the future High King of Alba. The *Orkneyinga saga* has a fight between the forces of a *Jarl Finnlekr* and Sigurðr with his raven banner, in which Sigurðr got the victory. The Jarl Finnlekr here was probably Findláech mac Ruaidri.

Máel Coluim invaded Bernicia in 1006 and mounted an unsuccessful siege of Durham, being beaten by Uhtred the Bold of Bamburgh. The heads of slain Scots, with their long, braided hair, were spiked on the walls.

In 1012 Máel Coluim inflicted another defeat on the Northmen, this time Danes, at Cruden Bay in Aberdeenshire. And in 1014, as we have said, the future Jarl of Orkney, Þórfinnr Sigurðarson was left in his care. The boy grew up at the court of his grandfather, who gifted him Caithness, where Þórfinnr later spent a lot of his time.

Máel Coluim is referred to as *King of the Mounth* in the early poem *Duan Albanach,* and as Alexander Grant points out, this clearly indicates that his rule extended across the Grampians, outside what would usually be considered the limits of the Kingdom of Alba's territory. The marriage alliances already mentioned with Sigurðr of the Orkney Norse and Findláech mac Ruaidri, ruler of Moray would have gone a good way toward securing that rule in areas traditionally independent of, and often, opposed to it. Findláech is referred to as *rí Alban* in the Irish annals, i.e. King of Scotland (or at least the northern territories, as far as the people of Moray would have been concerned).

Grant further notes that Dingwall, though normally understood as a Norse settlement under Norse control, was considered a thanage of the Kingdom of Alba in the territory of Ross under Máel Coluim. And with regard to Caithness and Sutherland, the fact that Máel Coluim could make his grandson Þórfinnr jarl or mormaer of these lands demonstrates the extent of his power.

After the death of Þórfinnr's father Sigurðr at the Battle of Clontarf, the jarldom of Orkney was shared out between his sons – Einar Rangmunnr or Wry Mouth, Brúsi, Sumarliði and of course Þórfinnr himself. One share was not enough to satisfy the young Þórfinnr's rapacious nature however, and when his brother Sumarliði died, he demanded his share too. Einar Rangmunnr, *ruthless and grasping,* according to *Orkneyinga saga,* took it and Þórfinnr then threatened him with his grandfather Máel Coluim's army. Their peace-loving brother Brusi settled things between them before it could come to blows, and the upshot was that Þórfinnr, with greater military resources than Einar, got what he wanted.

In 1018 Máel Coluim, in alliance with Owen the Bald, King of Strathclyde, invaded Bernicia a second time to avenge his defeat there in 1006 and mauled the English at the Battle of Carham. He then took Lothian.

Þórfinnr's fosterfather and enforcer Þórkel killed Einar Rangmunnr in 1020, ending a bitter feud between them and largely paving the way for the boy to take complete power in the islands.

There was also trouble in Moray that same year, when Findláech mac Ruaidri, Máel Coluim's son-in-law and the father of Macbeth, was murdered *by his own people,* according to the *Annals of Ulster.* The *Annals of Tigernach* lay the blame on *the sons of Máel Brigte* in what appears to have been a power struggle. (These sons, Máel Coluim and Gilla Coemgáin, were the sons of a later Máel Brigte, not the Máel Brigte Tooth who appears in *Orkneyinga saga,* dying in battle against Sigurðr Eysteinsson the Mighty). Máel Coluim mac Máel Brigte then took the rulership of Moray until his death in 1029, when he was succeeded by his brother Gilla Coemgáin.

By 1021 Þórfinnr's bullying attitude over land acquisition drove his remaining older brother Brúsi to seek the help of Óláfr Haraldsson, King of Norway. Þórfinnr sailed to Norway after him to argue his own case before the king and both brothers were presented with an ultimatum by Óláfr to do homage to him for the islands or lose them altogether, to which the young Þórfinnr replied that he was already allied to King Máel Coluim, with the implication that he couldn't make any other promises. However, as he was at the Norwegian court at the time and in Óláfr's power, he had no choice in the matter, and at the urging of his fosterfather Þórkel, he took the oath. But with no intention of honouring it, as it was made under duress, Þórfinnr returned to Orkney. Óláfr kept Brúsi's young son Rögnvaldr to ensure his father's loyalty. Þórfinnr was given one third of the islands, while Brúsi was given two as the king's personal agent in the west, each of the brothers to rule as vassals of the king. Þórfinnr spent most of his time in Caithness and Alba, with his stewards running things in his lands on Orkney.

Around this time Orkney became such a target for Norse and Danish vikings that Brúsi was forced to seek Þórfinnr's help as he couldn't cope with the task of defending the islands. So Þórfinnr proposed that he take charge of two thirds of the islands and handle its defences, to which Brúsi agreed.

In 1030 King Óláfr was killed at the Battle of Stiklarstaðir fighting the Peasant Army loyal to Knútr inn ríki (Knútr the Great). Kálfr Árnason, the uncle of Þórfinnr's future wife Ingibjörg, was among those who gave the king his death wounds.

In 1031 Knútr inn ríki, King of Denmark, Norway and England advanced into Alba with his forces for reasons that are open to question, one of them possibly being Máel Coluim's acquisition of Lothian in 1018 and another Knútr's desire to secure his northern border as a result. Knútr may also have been keen to neutralise any factions in Alba and the Isles siding with his enemies in Scandinavia. Ralph the Bald, a Burgundian chronicler, referred to a protracted conflict between Knútr and the High King of Alba and described Máel Coluim as *powerful in both resources and arms.* Sigvatr Þórðarson, the skald, mentions that a meeting took place between the kings in Fife in his poem *Knútsdrápa.* Macbeth mac Findláech was in attendance as well as Eachmarcach, King of Dublin, Man and the Isles. Through the negotiating skills of Knútr's wife Emma and her brother Richard, Duke of Normandy a peaceful settlement was reached between the two kings and Knútr returned south, honour apparently being satisfied on both sides.

The presence of Eachmarcach at the meeting may intimate that he was a sub king of Máel Coluim, who may have been supreme ruler over the Inner Hebrides at this time, according to the *Prophecy of Berchán.* Mention is also made in the *Annals of Ulster* and the *Annals of Tigernach* of a king of the Gall-Goídil called Suibne mac Cináeda ruling in the Isles before his death in 1034. If he was a brother of Máel Coluim, as the name *mac*

Cináeda suggests, he may also have been a client ruler answering to the High King.

With regard to Macbeth being in attendance at the meeting, it would suggest that he had joined Máel Coluim after the murder of his father Findláech by the latter's nephews, who took over as rulers of Moray.

In 1032, according to the *Annals of Ulster,* one of these nephews, Gilla Coemgáin, the then Mormaer of Moray, was burned to death, along with fifty of his followers. The record does not make clear who was responsible for the killing, but Macbeth obviously had reason to avenge his father. Máel Coluim also had motive to get rid of Gilla Coemgáin, as there was a long-running feud between the House of Ailpín and the House of Loairn in Moray. Gilla Coemgáin had already killed one king and could attempt to kill another. Removing him as a threat made sense, as did supporting the rightful heir to the rulership of Northern Scotland. Whatever the case, Macbeth became Mormaer of Moray, married Gilla Coemgáin's widow, Gruoch, and adopted her son Lulach.

Máel Coluim died in 1034 in a fight with more foes from Moray, according to the *Prophecy of Berchán.* These enemies may have risen in revolt over the king's choice of successor. The short but epic tribute in the *Annals of Tigernach* reads *Máel Coluim mac Cináeda, the glory of the west of Europe, died.*

Máel Coluim had chosen Donnchad, the son of Crínán and his daughter Bethóc, to succeed him, as he had no surviving sons of his own. Not the best choice, Donnchad was soon to stand out as rash and determined to pursue an aggressive policy against his rivals without the military aptitude required to match his ambitions in that age of cut-throat dynastic violence.

Donnchad had previously ruled Strathclyde, which appears to have been a client kingdom of Alba by that time. He was married to a sister of Siward, the Danish Earl of Northumbria, forging a link with the latter's Anglo-Danish dynasty in Northern England.

One of his first mistakes was to demand that Þórfinnr pay him tribute for Caithness. By this time Brusi had died and Þórfinnr was sole ruler of Orkney as well as Caithness. In addition, his influence probably extended to the Hebrides. Dark maned and powerful, with scowling black brows, he had grown into a formidable warlord used to defying anybody else's authority.

Donnchad is identified by some scholars as the Karl Hundason of *Orkneyinga saga.* Donnchad's father Crínán being known as the Hound Earl would naturally make Donnchad *Hundason* or *Hound Son* in Norse terms. For the sake of simplicity, we will just refer to him as King Karl, with the understanding that he was probably Donnchad.

In 1035 Donnchad or Karl Hundason sent his nephew Moddan against Þórfinnr with an army from Sutherland, but the nephew turned tail when Þórfinnr and his fosterfather Þórkel confronted him in Caithness with a far larger force.

Þórfinnr then descended on Sutherland and Ross and overcame the opposition there, advancing south into Alba and *plundering far and wide* before returning north.

When King Karl got the news, he flew into a rage and sailed against Þórfinnr with a fleet of eleven ships. He also sent Moddan to Caithness again, this time with a larger army. The next day Karl surprised Þórfinnr at Dýrness with his eleven ships to Þórfinnr's five, but Þórfinnr gave the order to advance undaunted. After a fierce opening clash, Þórfinnr leapt aboard Karl's ship and started clearing it, soon followed by his men. Karl gave the command to cut the ropes holding the vessels together, jumped into another ship and fled the battle.

Still not inclined to give up despite these reverses, Karl landed in the Moray Firth, went ashore and mustered yet another army. Together with Þórkel and a strong force, Þórfinnr went after Karl. News of Moddan's arrival in Caithness came to them and Þórkel advanced on him in secret, surprising Moddan in the night and setting fire to the house he was in. Moddan jumped from an upper window and Þórkel took a swipe at him, cutting off his head as he landed. Moddan's men were killed in large numbers and the rest either ran for it or surrendered.

Þórfinnr then confronted the forces of King Karl at Torfness on the southern side of the Moray Firth in a final battle. Karl had the bigger army drawn from not only Moray, but also from the west and east of Alba. In addition, he had reinforcements from Ireland.

Þórfinnr directed his attack on the Irish first, routing them, and after another fierce clash with the remainder of Karl's forces, drove them to flight. Þórfinnr pursued them down into Alba, plundering and burning wherever he went and lauded by his personal skald Arnórr. Having defeated Karl repeatedly, Þórfinnr returned north.

In 1039, presumably in an attempt to replenish his treasury with plunder, Donnchad mounted a disastrous siege of Durham, during which much of his cavalry was cut down and he himself barely escaped.

According to the *Annals of Tigernach,* Donnchad once again directed his attention at his rivals in Alba and invaded Moray in 1040. He was mortally wounded in battle by Macbeth *Rí Deircc,* the Red King near Spynie and later died at Bothgobhann (Pitgavenny being the probable modern location). The distinguished historian Skene came up with the theory that the cousins Þórfinnr and Macbeth were allies during this time and brought about the downfall of King Karl or Donnchad together.

Triumph in another dynastic power struggle, this time against his nephew Rögnvaldr, son of Brusi, would see Þórfinnr finally reigning supreme in his northern and western territories. Macbeth took the high kingship of Alba, and contrary to the lurid fantasies of Shakespeare, was hailed as *Macbeth the renowned* in the *Duan Albanach* and in the *Prophecy of Berchán* as *the generous king of Fortriu, the red, tall, golden-haired one* during whose reign *Alba will be brimful west and east* – not exactly the description of a bloody-handed tyrant widely feared by his people.

Around 1040, Macbeth dealt with a Danish incursion in the vicinity of Kinghorn, Fife. The Danes are said to have paid a large sum in gold to have their dead buried on Inchcolm Island, the *Iona of the East.*

The following year Þórfinnr was raiding in the Hebrides and afterwards put in to land south in Galloway. The Galloway people cleared their livestock out of reach, so Þórfinnr then sent raiders into Northumbria after cattle, but they were attacked by the locals and most of them killed for their trouble. The survivors were sent back north to let Þórfinnr know that this was how they dealt with vikings. Too late in the campaigning season to retaliate, Þórfinnr promised to pay the English back for the killings and mockery and returned to Orkney.

In 1042 Þórfinnr raised an army from the Northern and Western Isles, Caithness, Alba and Ireland and together with his nephew Rögnvaldr, he invaded Northumbria, harrying and burning wherever he went. The English under their leaders advanced to meet him and were mauled by Þórfinnr's army.

In the words of his skáld Arnórr:

Hard blew the war horns –
battle bold through burgs
advanced the ruler,
his banner billowing bravely…
warriors fierce he routed;
weapons flashing –
wolves were fattened.

After the victory, Þórfinnr resumed his burning and plundering. According to *Orkneyinga saga,* he defeated the English in two pitched battles as well as other, more casual encounters, and stayed for the duration of the summer.

In 1045 Crínán the Hound Earl, Donnchad's father, led a revolt against Macbeth in Atholl and was slain. The suppression of a revolt against the High King, in this case spurred by the desire for vengeance, would naturally be the expected response.

In 1050 Macbeth went on a pilgrimage to Rome, where he *scattered silver like seed* to the poor, according to the Irish chronicler Marianus Scotus. Þórfinnr the Mighty, who also went on a pilgrimage to Rome, may have gone this same year. There has been speculation that it may have been in Macbeth's company.

In 1054 Siward, Earl of Northumbria, brother-in-law of the late Donnchad, invaded Alba with a very large sea and land force and was opposed by Macbeth with heavy losses on both sides, including Siward's son Osbjörn and his son-in-law. Though the Scots are said to have lost 3,000 men and the Northumbrians 1,500, according to the *Annals of Ulster,* Macbeth continued to reign as *Ard Rí Albann* until 1057, when he was slain at Lumphanan in Aberdeenshire by Donnchad's half Danish son Máel Coluim, who then took the kingship.

Þórfinnr died around 1065, immortalised by his personal skáld, Arnórr in the following verse:

Gloom shall gather over gleaming sun,
Earth sink beneath black billows,

Austri's burden burst asunder.
wild sea rear above the mountains,
'ere among the isles
a fairer chief be born –
true lord of thanes,
may God guard Þórfinnr.

The Isles 682-1030s CE

Pictish Orkney and Shetland, known as *Innse Orc* and *Innse Catt* (Isles of the Orcs and Isles of the Cats, named after their respective tribes), already had a long history of piracy before the vikings ever appeared on the scene. In 682 Bridei or Bruide mac Beli, King of the Picts attacked the Orkneys and *destroyed them,* according to the *Annals of Ulster,* which suggests the annihilation of the pirate bases there that were probably preying on the Pictish mainland. This may have helped open the way for later Norse settlement if the Pictish sea raiders there were either largely destroyed or at least so seriously weakened they never really recovered their original power. Archaeological excavations on Shetland suggest that Norse settlement had already started around the middle of the 7th century CE, well before written records.

Raids for plunder are first recorded in 793, especially in the islands and exposed coasts, with Iona a particular target. Iona, a place of repeated massacre, would later become venerated by the Norse and Norse Gael and chosen as a favoured burial place for their kings, following an already long-established Gaelic tradition. The Northern Hebrides were later wrested from Pictish control, while the Southern Hebrides were taken at the expense of the Gaelic Kingdom of Dál Riada. The Isle of Man was also added to this insular empire. The degree to which the Hebrides were settled by the Norse is apparent in a later Gaelic term *Innse Gall* or Islands of the Foreigners. *Lochlann,* another Gaelic term, is believed by some scholars, particularly Ó Corráin, to refer to Viking Scotland, both the islands and coastal mainland areas controlled by Norse and Norse Gaels.

The Norse called Orkney and Shetland *Orkneyjar* and *Hjaltland* and referred to the isles collectively as *Norðreyjar* (North Isles). According to the sagas, the islands came under Norwegian royal power when King Haraldr Hárfagri (Fair Hair) attacked his enemies there. This was around 875. Haraldr also appears to have taken control in the Hebrides (known in

Norse as *Suðreyjar* or South Isles), as the island leaders there challenged his authority. Ketill Flatnefr (Flat Nose), the man Haraldr sent on his behalf to sort matters out, ended up taking over the Hebrides for himself and assuming the title *King of the Isles.* This title would be applied to successive rulers of the Hebrides and Man.

Two prominent rulers of the Northern Isles featured in the sagas highlighted in the book were of course Sigurðr Digri and his son Þórfinnr the Mighty, already mentioned. Sigurðr added the Hebrides to his dominions in 990. Like Ketill Flatnefr, Sigurðr and Þórfinnr largely disregarded Norse royal claims to the islands and existed as independent warlords in their own right.

As has already been said, there is reason to believe that the power of the formidable *Ard Rí Albann,* Máel Coluim the Destroyer extended to the Hebrides, from at least the early 1030's if not before. This would have strengthened the later claim of his grandson Þórfinnr to the Western Isles.

It would be wrong to consider the Isles as being somehow of less importance than mainland realms such as Dublin or York. The Kingdom of the Isles was a major player, not only in the politics of the Irish Sea, but also a force to be reckoned with by the powers of mainland Ireland, Scotland, Norway and the southern kingdoms in Britain.

West Over Sea

There has been much speculation as to what exactly motivated the viking invasions, but it was most likely a combination of overpopulation at home with not enough land to go around, better land prospects abroad, as well as opportunities for trade and plunder. Another factor to consider is people fleeing from oppressive kings, as in the case of Ketill Flatnefr in *Laxdaela saga,* Kálfr Arnason in *Orkneyinga saga,* and Egill Skallgrímsson (and his father and grandfather before him) in *Egil's saga.*

Both Ketill and Egill are at odds with King Haraldr Hárfagri, whose tyrrany drives people to exile in Iceland, the Faroes, the Northern and Western Isles, and Scotland. The story goes that Haraldr vows to keep growing his hair until he has conquered all Norway, thus earning him the nickname Shaggy Haraldr. When he achieves his ambition after victory at the Battle of Hafrsfjörðr, he has his hair cut, and everyone realises what a fine head of hair he has. So, his nickname is changed to *Hárfagri* or Fine Hair.

According to the sagas, in forcing the unification of Norway under a single king, Haraldr naturally makes enemies of every regional ruler he goes up against, and once he has consolidated his power, he strips those nobles who have opposed him of their lands and titles, bringing about bitter ill will. The knowledge that Ketill himself faces the same fate if he remains in Norway drives him overseas to Scotland.

Others who have fled to the Orkney and Shetland islands and the Hebrides use these as a base from which to raid Haraldr's lands in Norway, prompting him to mount a retaliatory expedition against them. Defeating these enemies, he puts all the islands under his power. Another version of this expedition from *Eyrbyggja saga* has Ketill leading it as Haraldr's commander, but then taking control of the islands for himself. *Landnámabók* adds that Haraldr seizes Ketill's Norwegian estates because of this disloyalty.

Independent Warlords

There is more than one case in which saga characters nurse an antagonism toward the Norwegian royal house that lasts for generations. Apart from Egill Skallagrímsson and his family, the Orkney jarls Sigurðr Digri (the Stout) and his son Þórfinnr in *Orkneyinga saga* are unwilling to recognise royal authority. And in Þórfinnr's case, the antagonism extends toward the Scottish royal house as well when a certain Karl Hundason (Donnchad mac Crínán) replaces his grandfather Máel Coluim Forranach as king.

The Norwegian ruler Óláfr Haraldsson and the Scottish ruler Karl Hundason might lay claim to islands and territories under Þórfinnr's control through what they believe is their royal right, but to Þórfinnr these lands are simply his, passed down through his father and grandfather and won by the sword, and he defies the claims of both these kings and refuses to pay tribute or recognise their rule in his dominions. Furthermore, with the resources at his disposal, he also proves himself powerful enough to defeat the royal forces sent against him.

This defiance of royal power and ability to overthrow it by Þórfinnr at the height of his strength can be set against the examples of other leaders, dispossessed and exiled, relying on the support of Norway's kings to restore them to power under royal authority. Þórfinnr's own nephew Rögnvaldr is one of these.

Swordland

In *Orkneyinga saga* Haraldr's punitive expedition against his enemies in the Northern and Western Isles and Man results in him bestowing Shetland and Orkney on Jarl Rögnvaldr the Powerful as compensation for the death of his son Ívarr during the fighting. But Rögnvaldr gives the islands to his brother Sigurðr, who goes on to become an avaricious and dominant warlord. Sigurðr allies himself with Þórsteinn Rauði (the Red), another predatory chieftain, and together they take Caithness and a large part of Moray, Ross and Argyll by force. A parley is arranged between Sigurðr and Máel Brigte, one of the Scottish leaders. It is agreed that each will bring equal numbers to the meeting place. But Sigurðr decides the Scots are not to be trusted and then proves he can't be trusted himself by bringing along twice as many men. His treachery pays off and his enemies are massacred to a man.

The sagas are full of brawny bearded men regarding the world around them with narrow-eyed piratical speculation or the contemplation of murder, taking whatever they can by force and being on guard against anybody else wanting to do the same.

The appropriation of *sword land* as it is referred to in the Gaelic tradition, that is land taken by conquest, was a common practice, and that land would be defended to the death in many cases against enemies intent on taking it themselves by force or treachery. Warlord after warlord would go down in blood and fire in defence of that land and their descendants would carry on the fight for power and wealth fueled by the demands of clan honour and the sacrifices made by their forebears.

Thraldom

Thraldom or slavery was common before and during the Viking Age in Ireland, Scotland and the Isles. Saint Patrick was taken at about the age of sixteen, probably from Strathclyde, by Irish raiders and sold into slavery himself as a herdsman, though he later escaped. The vikings conducted an extremely lucrative business in slaves from their Dublin base, which was one of the most important trading centres in the Norse world.

A verse from the *Old Icelandic Rune Poem* on the rune known as *nauðr* or *need* refers to *wet work aplenty.* This was the lot of the þræll or slave – herding pigs, collecting peat, digging ditches and spreading dung on the fields. *Anauð* or bondage, a term associated with the word *nauðr,* means to be fettered, to be in shackles. So, it is easy to see how much of an everyday thing slavery was in the Norse world when it was even symbolised by a letter from the viking *fuþark* or alphabet.

Donald A. Mackenzie cites an instance from *Gesta Danorum* by Saxo Grammaticus in which a certain Starkaðr tells a young woman that she deserves to be sold for a price to foreign peoples and to grind at the mill. Grinding at the mill or working at the loom was one thing, but all too often the fate of a pretty girl would be one of sexual slavery, trapped in a distant land, never to see her loved ones or native soil again.

In the year 980 Máel Sechnaill mac Domnaill, High King of Ireland defeated Óláfr Cuarán, King of Dublin and his Norse Gael mercenaries from the Hebrides and Mann at Tara. He is then said to have freed all the slaves after laying siege to Dublin, although it is unlikely that this would have permanently halted the viking slave trade in Ireland.

In *Laxdaela saga,* the Icelandic chieftain Höðskuldr visits a Norwegian market where there are slave women for sale and one of these in particular catches his eye. The man who is selling her claims she is a mute, as she has never once spoken, but Höðskuldr buys the woman anyway and spends the night with her. Höðskuldr doesn't seem to give much thought as to how all this will be received back home in Iceland, and his wife is far from pleased about it, but the slave woman is taken into the household nevertheless and the tension is set to rise. Höðskuldr, apparently embarrassed by the situation now, no longer has sex with the slave woman, perhaps mindful of the possibility that his wife might put an axe in his head. The slave woman then gives birth to a son. As if things can't get bad enough, Höðskuldr's later discovery of the slave woman's true identity only complicates things for him even further.

Selling slave women to foreign peoples was one thing; bringing one home was quite another. The trade in women slaves, especially for pleasure, operated outside the domestic world of the conventional Norse homestead, with the wife in charge of much of the running of it and the expectation of being the only one sharing the man's bed. This story serves to illustrate the sort of things that would have happened if a man attempted to blur the lines between these two worlds.

Magic & Prophecy

Supernatural elements pepper the narrative throughout the early saga literature, in many cases heightening the drama. Prophetic dreams and visions, second sight, the use of runes to curse or heal and the casting of spells pierce the fabric of the everyday world, often at times of danger and crisis.

The eponymous hero of *Brennu Njáls saga* is very wise in matters of law, but also a seer. The warrior Gunnar consults Njál for advice regarding his future and Njál delivers some prophetic warnings - never to kill more than once in the same family, never to break a settlement made by good men between himself and his enemies, on pain of death. We are reminded here of the Gaelic *geasa,* taboos or obligations, placed upon a person in the early literature, violation of which would lead to their doom.

In *Orkneyinga saga* the mother of Jarl Sigurðr Digri is a sorceress. She fashions a raven banner for him, the quality of which is that it will bring victory to the one it is borne before but death to the one who bears it. The ancient heathen belief system has no victory without sacrifice – *a gift demands a gift*, as it says in the Old Norse poem *Hávamál,* attributed to the god Óðinn. The raven is a sinister motif throughout the early Norse and Gaelic folklore, associated with dark prophecy, grim omens and bloodshed. Two ravens bring Óðinn the news. The Irish goddess Badb takes the form of a carrion crow to feed on the slain. The raven banner represented a totemic association with the bird of Óðinn, the bird of battlefield slaughter, in the hope that victory would be bestowed on those advancing to the fray beneath it. But whatever the result, the raven or crow would often be the last thing that a dying warrior would see, and in the clash of sword and spear it would always be the winner.

In *Brennu Njáls saga* you have the viking leader Bróðir (who used to be a deacon but *turned to sorcery and heathen ways*) beset by scalding blood showers, furious ravens and his own weapons turning against him when he decides to go against the Christian Brian Bóruma, High King of Ireland. Bróðir's brother Óspakr, a heathen seer, tries to dissuade him from fighting against *such a good king,* but Bróðir does it anyway, despite all the omens, and earns a grim death for his trouble.

The titanic Battle of Clontarf, near Dublin, where the conflict takes place, results in marvels and horrible visions appearing to people in various places. A group of twelve horsewomen who turn out to be no less than the mythological *valkýrjur* or *choosers of the slain* are seen by a man called Dorruðr in Caithness. He follows them to a house, where he spies on them through a window, and sees that they have woven the outcome of the battle on a grisly loom made of severed heads and blood-spattered weaponry. Other visions are seen as far away as Iceland.

The supernatural elements in the sagas serve to reveal a strange world existing alongside the everyday one, continuing to manifest itself even after the spread of Christianity, and seemingly unaffected by it.

Blood Feud & Revenge

The blood feud is a major theme in the early literary tradition, especially in *Njáls saga.* A feud can start from as simple a thing as a snippet of malicious gossip being overheard and then be carried on by the opposing sides for generations, fuelled by tit for tat killings. Individuals who might never have been personally involved in the feud but have a blood link to someone who has are also considered fair game for those looking to even the score. Whatever the circumstances of men being killed, honour will demand that they be avenged.

The *þing* or legal assembly provides people with the means to seek redress for wrongs, woundings and killings perpetrated against them, usually in the form of *gjald* or compensation (known as *eíric* in Gaelic). *Duinethãide* or secret killing in Gaelic (the stealing of a man's life) had a far higher blood fine accompanying it than a slaying openly declared. The Norse system appears to have been similar in that honour and the law would expect the killer to make his deed publicly known. In the legal judgement that weighs up injuries on both sides, one wounding might be deemed to cancel out another if they are considered to be of roughly equal severity. If enough compensation is paid out for a wounding or killing the matter might be settled, at least for that particular offense. But there is no absolute guarantee that a feud will not carry on regardless, stirred up again at some future point in time. In some cases, a situation is inflamed by the constant nagging of a female character in the sagas, casting aspersions on the manhood of her husband or brother for not seeking vengeance for a slur on the family honour or the killing of a kinsman. Hallgerðr and Bergþóra in *Njáls saga* are classic examples of this.

The haughty Bergþóra offends Hallgerðr by expecting her to sit at a lower position during a family feast, which the latter considers beneath her dignity. This smear on Hallgerðr's personal honour sets off a feud between the two women that culminates in the deaths of the manservants the women send out to get revenge, and also ultimately in the deaths of their husbands. The hero Gunnar is killed by his enemies when his wife Hallgerðr refuses to give him a length of her hair to replace his broken bowstring. These enemies are attacking him because of the feud she helped stir up. Njál and his sons are burned in their house along with his wife Bergþóra also as a result of the women's feud.

This book takes up the narrative in the wake of the burning when Njál's son-in-law Kári Sólmundarson embarks on a bloody rampage as he hunts down the Burners, as they are referred to. After each killing, he customarily declares that he is responsible as the law demands, and the news that reaches the survivors of their comrades being wiped out one by one will have a growing psychological impact.

An all too common occurrence in the sagas (if a doomed man isn't speared or hacked to death with an axe) is to be incinerated in his house. Incidents of house burning occur in *Orkneyinga saga*, in which the aim is to get rid of an arch enemy as well as his followers all at one go. Þórfinnr's disaffected nephew Rögnvaldr tries burning his uncle alive only to have Þórfinnr burning down Rögnvaldr's place later on.

Poetry

Poetry was an important element in the warrior tradition and features prominently in the sagas. It most usually took the form of praise poetry glorifying the exploits of kings and warlords composed by the *skáld* or northern bard in return for reward, often in the form of silver arm rings. One such court versifier was Arnórr Þórdarson, known as *Jarlaskáld* or the Earl's Poet, who praised the deeds of Þórfinnr the Mighty, Jarl of Orkney. His poetry features prominently in *Orkneyinga saga,* with frequent reference to wolves gaping over battlefield slaughter and ravens' talons red with blood. The sanguinary nature of this verse appealed to the warrior spirit.

Not all viking verse had such a violent quality, however. In *Orkneyinga saga* the somewhat eccentric Jarl Rögnvaldr Kali Kolsson peppers many of his everyday experiences both at home in the Isles and on his expedition to the Holy Land with commentary in verse, often bearing a humourous slant. Indeed, the saga narrative with regard to Rögnvaldr and his famous journey is notable for its poetic content.

The jarl makes wry observation of running ashore on the islands in bad weather and jokes about the bearskin given to him by the mistress of the house he and his men take shelter in from the storm.

When the voyage is under way, they drop off in Valland or Gaul and enjoy the hospitality of the golden-tressed young noblewoman Ermingerda, whose beauty Rögnvaldr praises in verse as he sits beside her. She makes such an impression on the jarl and the two skálds accompanying him that repeated poetic reference is made to her throughout the journey. Even when storming a Galician fortress with fire and sword, the jarl thinks nothing of contrasting the romantic sentiment inspired by Ermingerda with the familiar skáldic motif of laying out dead foes for the eagles in his bardic commentary.

Rögnvaldr's propensity for humour is again reflected in a later verse about the hopelessly drunken Erlingr Skakkr in the town of Imbolum comically tumbling off a bridge into the mud below.

Born Viking

Svein Ásleifarson led a colourful life as an outlaw and a viking. A killer and plunderer, he was nevertheless something of a loveable rogue, in and out of trouble with the Jarls of Orkney and just about everybody else. He raided in the Hebrides, Scotland, Ireland, Wales, the Isle of Man, the Isle of May, and the Isles of Scilly.

Svein's crimes and exploits are covered to a considerable degree in *Orkneyinga saga,* but we have condensed them here for the sake of space. In the saga he is taken in and given hospitality by Jarl Páll Hákonarson after the murder of Svein's father Óláfr, and then outlawed by the same jarl for splitting the belligerent Svein Breast Rope's head open with an axe. Jarl Rögnvaldr Kali Kolsson provides ships at Svein's request when the latter plans to exact revenge for the killing of his father, and on another occasion when he wants to go raiding. The jarl also pays out compensation from his own pocket for Svein's killing of the bully Arni Stick Leg. Initially at odds with Svein, Jarl Haraldr Maddadarson later makes peace with him and attends one of the viking's lavish feasts.

Svein even manages to get on the good side of David, King of Scots after plundering the monastery on the Isle of May. Having landed on the island because of rough weather, Svein and his men claim that they are envoys from the Jarl of Orkney to the king but are (unsurprisingly) suspected of being robbers by the monks. Svein then decides that if they are going to be suspected of pillaging, they may as well do it, and afterwards they go to see the King of Scots, who entertains them at his court in Edinburgh. The king later compensates the monks out of his own treasury.

Like Sigurðr Digri and his son Þórfinnr the Mighty, Svein has little respect for so called higher authority, but will play the game of going along with it if it is to his advantage and will save his skin in a tight spot.

Svein has a regular routine. He stays at home through the winter, feasting eighty men in his huge drinking hall. In the spring he sows his seed, and after that goes plundering in the Hebrides and Ireland. Returning just after midsummer, he sees to the reaping of the fields and the storage of the grain. Then he goes pillaging again and does not get back until the first month of winter is over.

Svein lives the viking lifestyle until his violent fall in Ireland, like many another of his kind, on what is meant to be a last glorious raid, perhaps having neither wanted, nor known, how to live or die any other way.

Although this book is concerned with the viking presence in Ireland, Scotland and the Isles, parts such as the timeline also cover the impact of the Norse Gaelic Uí Ímair dynasty on England and Wales as well as significant Gaelic events in Ireland and Scotland that would have had an influence on the political world of the time and affected the operations of the Norse and Norse Gaels.

The Sagas

We will explore three Icelandic sagas with episodes set in Ireland, Scotland and the Isles – *Laxdaela saga* (c.1230-1260), *Brennu Njáls saga* (c.1270-1290), and *Orkneyinga saga,* also known as *Jarla Sogur Orkneyja* (c.1230). We will also look at *Cogadh Gáedhel re Gallaibh* (The War of the Gael with the Outlanders) c.1103/1111, found in *The Book of Leinster* c.1160 and the 14th century *Dublin Manuscript,* as well as other early traditional material and subjects from both Norse and Gaelic sources, together with commentary and analysis. *Cogadh Gáedhel re Gallaibh* is not part of the Icelandic saga collective, but nevertheless covers events and traditions in the viking west from an Irish perspective and is important to our study.

In the first part we include excerpts from *Laxdaela saga,* featuring the chieftain Ketill Flatnefr and his daughter Unnr the Deep Minded, who leave Norway for Scotland to escape the oppression of King Haraldr Hárfagri (Fair Hair), and the story of Melkorka, the Irish princess who gives birth to the flamboyant Óláfr the Peacock. We also include passages from *Orkneyinga saga* that cover the conflict between the Orkney jarls and the rulers of Moray.

In the second part we focus on *Brennu Njáls saga* and the deeds of the hero Kári Sólmundarson in his quest to avenge the burning of the Icelandic chieftain Njál, after whom the saga is named. We also include the sections pertaining to Sigurðr the Stout, Jarl of Orkney and his involvement in the Battle of Clontarf.

In addition, we feature the same battle from the Irish perspective, as told in the work *Cogadh Gáedhel re Gallaibh.*

The third part focuses on *Orkneyinga saga* and the rise of Þórfinnr the Mighty, who succeeds his father Sigurðr as Jarl of Orkney and becomes the scourge of the western seas. We also include the adventures of the poet-jarl Rögnvaldr Kali Kolsson on his pilgrimage to the Holy Land, and the exploits of the infamous viking Svein Ásleifarson.

Though the setting for most of the narrative is based in the Isles and the Gaelic West, interludes in faraway climes ranging from Russia to Rome give some indication of how widely travelled some of our saga heroes were.

Authors referred to in the book can be found listed in the bibliography, alongside their works.

Páll Thormod Mac Alpin Morrisson

Dún Éideann, Alba agus Baile Átha Cliath, Eire 2019

Edinburgh, Scotland & Dublin, Ireland 2019

VIKING TIMELINE IN IRELAND, SCOTLAND & THE ISLES

CE (Common Era)

793 -795 Raids on the monasteries of Rechru, Iona, and Saint Patrick.

795 and **801** Iona ransacked.

800 Wexford *(Veisafjörðr)* founded by vikings as a trading town.

802 Iona burnt.

806 Iona monks wiped out during another raid.

815 Plundering of Inis Cathaigh (Scattery Island) and slaughter of monks there.

825 Saint Blathmac, Abbot of Iona killed by vikings when he refuses to reveal the whereabouts of Saint Columba's gold shrine.

832 Large viking fleet appears in the north of Ireland. Armagh raided three times in one month.

833 Niall Caille mac Áeda, *Ard Rí* of Ireland, defeats a viking force in Derry at the beginning of his reign.

836 Guðfriðr mac Fergus, *toíseach* or chief of the Airgíalla in Ulster, supplies reinforcements to Dál Riada at the request of Cináed mac Ailpín.

837 Viking fleets sail up the Boyne and the Liffey, widespread raiding. The Uí Colgain of Brega kill Saxolb or Söxulfr, chief of the outlanders.

839 Ulster and Pictland invaded. Battle between Picts and vikings – Uuen (Eógan) mac Óengus, King of Picts and Scots killed along with a great many of the Pictish warrior elite. Kingship of Picts and Scots later passes to Cináed mac Ailpín.

841 A longphort is built near Átha Cliath and Dublin later founded as a trading settlement.

845 Niall Caille mac Áeda, High King of Ireland defeats the Norse at Mag Itha.

Shrine of Clonmacnoise desecrated by vikings as well as other ecclesiastical settlements such as Kildare, Monasterboice and Dún Masc, where the abbot is slain.

Viking leader Turgeis or Þórgest takes Armagh – captured by Máel Sechnaill mac Máele Ruanaid, King of Meath and drowned in Lough Owel.

846 Cerball mac Dúnlainge, King of Osraige besieges and defeats a viking raiding party.

847 Cerball mac Dúnlainge trounces a warband under a certain Hákon at a place called *Carn Brammit.*

848 Vikings beaten at Cashel, Cork, Kildare and Sligo.

Tomrair or Þórir, a chief of the Norse based in Scotland, killed in battle at Sciath Nechtain in Kildare opposing Ólchobor mac Cináeda, King of Munster and Lorcán mac Cellaig, King of Leinster.

Máel Sechnaill beats the Norse at Forrach in west Meath.

Norse also beaten at Dísert do-Chonna by Tigernach mac Fócartai, King of Loch Gabair.

849 Saint Columba's relics split between Kells and Dunkeld for protection.

Máel Sechnaill and Tigernach mac Fócartai plunder Dublin.

Viking fleet of 140 ships puts in at Dublin from the Norse settlements in Scotland and the Isles to enforce control over the foreigners already established there.

850 The lands of Máel Sechnaill and Tigernach mac Fócartai pillaged by the Norse in alliance with Cináed mac Conaing, King of the Cíanachta Breg.

851 Battle between Norse and Danes at Dundalk Bay.

852 Vikings lay waste to Armagh. Gall Goídil clash with Áed, King of Ailech and his forces near Derry.

853 Amlaíb Conung (Óláfr the White) and Ímar (Ívarr) rule in Dublin.

Viking settlement established at Waterford *(Veðrafjörðr).*

855 Cerball mac Dúnlainge wipes out the viking force of Rodolb and enlists Danish allies commanded by a leader called Horm against the Norse, beating them again. Horm (or Ormr) is killed in Wales by Rhodri ap Merfyn, King of the Britons.

856 Áed Findliath, Overking of the Northern Uí Neíll, gains victory over the Norse Gaels at the Battle of Glen Foichle.

Máel Sechnaill mac Máele Ruanaid, High King of Ireland, battles the heathen with Norse Gael allies.

857 Ímar and Amlaíb Conung beat the Norse Gaelic leader Caittil Find and his forces in Munster.

858 Cerball mac Dúnlainge allied with Ímar beats the Cenél Fiachach and the Norse Gael at Ara Tíre in what is now County Tipperary, Munster.

859 Cerball mac Dúnlainge, allied with Amlaíb Conung and Ímar, go against Máel Sechnaill and the Norse Gael and plunder Meath.

Máel Gualae mac Donngaile, King of Munster captured and stoned to death by the Dublin Norse.

860 Cerball mac Dúnlainge defeats a viking force in Osraige, and together with Máel Sechnaill, beats Áed Findliath, Flann mac Conaing of Brega and Amlaíb at Moy near Armagh.

861-862 Áed Findliath makes alliance with the Dublin Norse and plunders Meath but is beaten by Máel Sechlainn at Drumomuy. Máel Sechnaill dies later that year and Áed Findliath succeeds him as *Ard Rí.*

Cerball mac Dúnlainge triumphs over a Norse raiding fleet in 862.

863 Lorcán mac Cathail, King of Meath, allies himself with Ímar, Amlaib and Auisle and pillages Flann mac Conaing's territories in Brega and the ancient Boyne Valley tombs.

Muirecán mac Diarmata, King of Leinster slain by the Norse.

864 Lorcán mac Cathail is captured by Áed Findliath and blinded.

Amlaíb drowns Conchobar mac Donnchada, Lorcán's rival at Clonard Abbey.

865 Ímar invades England with the Great Heathen Army and winters in East Anglia.

866 Amlaíb and Auisle invade Fortriu in Pictland and take hostages.

The Great Heathen Army takes York.

Cennétig mac Gáethíne, King of Loíches and the northern Osraige inflicts a *slaughter of the foreigners* at Mendroichet.

Congal, King of the Ciarraige defeats a viking force at Clonfert.

Áed Findliath beats the vikings in battle at Lough Foyle, destroys viking longphorts along Ireland's northern coast.

867 Cennétig mac Gáethíne and Máel Ciaraín mac Rónáin, a chief of the Leinstermen, burn down Amlaíb's stronghold at Clondalkin. One hundred viking heads taken. Dublin also attacked that year.

Murder of Auisle.

868 Áed Findliath defeats the Uí Neíll of Brega, the Leinstermen and the Norse Gaels in a battle at Cell Ua nDaigri.

The Great Heathen Army invades Mercia. The Mercians make peace terms.

869 Vikings beaten near Drogheda by King of Connacht.

Máel Ciaraín mac Rónáin driven out of Leinster by his rivals and is slain mounting a later invasion of the province. His head is presented to the Dublin Norse, who throw it into the sea after using it for sport.

Amlaíb pillages Armagh.

King Edmund of East Anglia shot to death with arrows and beheaded by followers of Ímar and his brother Ubba.

870 The Great Heathen Army conquers East Anglia.

Danish raiding party sack Coldingham Priory. Tradition has it that the abbess, Saint Æbbe the Younger, and her nuns mutilate their faces to discourage rape and die when the peeved pillagers set fire to the building.

870-871 Amlaíb and Ímar lay siege to Dumbarton. Return to Dublin with a fleet of two hundred ships, much plunder and many Britons, Picts and Angles as captives.

Áed Findliath devastates Leinster *from Dublin to Gowran,* according to the *Annals of Ulster.*

Máel Sechnaill mac Néill, King of South Brega, slain by Úlfr, chieftain of the Dubgaill.

870-890 Numbers of Hebridean and Caithness Norse move to Iceland.

871 The Great Heathen Army under Guþrum moves against Wessex and is paid off by Ælfred the Great.

Amlaíb puts down an uprising in Scotland against his father Gofraid mac Ragnaill.

871-872 Ímar and Oistín, Amlaíb's son pillage all over Ireland.

873 Death of Ímar.

874 Amlaíb killed in Pictland fighting King Causantín mac Cináeda.

The Great Heathen Army conquers Mercia.

875 Haraldr Hárfagri, King of Norway leads a fleet against his enemies in the Northern and Western Isles.

Albdann (Hálfdanr) invades Dublin and slays Oistín, Amlaíb's son and successor. Áed Findliath drives Albdann out and puts Bárid (Bárðr), Ímar's son in power.

876 Norse Gaels in the Hebrides and Man revolt against Haraldr Hárfagri's rule.

877 Causantín mac Cináeda, King of the Picts slain fighting the warband of Albdann (Hálfdanr).

Albdann (Hálfdanr) killed fighting the Findgaill at Loch Cuan (Strangford Lough in today's County Down).

878 Ælfred the Great defeats the vikings led by Guþrum at the Battle of Ethandun, but after a treaty is drawn up, they still possess much of England.

879 Death of Áed Findliath.

880 or **890** Death of Þórsteinn Rauði in Northern Pictland.

881 Bárid pillages the oratory of Saint Cianán in Meath. Death of Bárid, possibly by drowning, at Dublin.

888 Death of Cerball mac Dúnlainge.

900 Domnall mac Causantín, King of Alba killed by vikings at Dunnottar.

902 Vikings driven out of Dublin by the Irish kings Máel mac Flannacán and Cerball mac Muirecáin. They cross over to Wales, England and France.

903 Grandsons of Ímar pillage Dunkeld.

904 Áed, King of Pictland killed in battle against two grandsons of Ímar.

Ímar, grandson of Ímar killed by Pictish Men of Fortriu along with a great many vikings.

914 Viking fleets at Waterford. Ragnall ua Ímair defeats Bárid mac Oitir in a sea fight off Man.

Battle of Corbridge in which Ragnall defeats Scots and Bernicians.

915-922 Settlement established at Cork.

916 The fleets of Sihtric Cáech and Ragnall raiding in Ireland.

917 Battle of Cenn Fuait between Dublin vikings and the forces of Augaire mac Ailella, King of Leinster, at which the latter is defeated and killed. Sihtric Cáech takes back Dublin and becomes king.

918 Second Battle of Corbridge at which the forces of Ragnall ua Ímair clash with those of Causantín mac Áeda and Ealdred of Bamburgh. The first three columns of the Norse Gaels are defeated by the Scots, who are then ambushed by Ragnall leading another column out of concealment. Indecisive result.

919 Ragnall takes York and is made King over Northumbria.

Sihtric Caech is victorious at the Battle of Islandbridge, where Niall Glúndub, Overking of the Northern Uí Néill and *Ard Rí* of Ireland is slain along with several other kings.

920 Sihtric Caech raids Cheshire.

922 Jarl Þórir Helgason of Limerick, known as Tomrair mac Ailchi to the Irish, pillages churches and settlements on River Shannon, Lough Ree, Meath and Connacht.

924 Gofraid ua Ímair ruler of Dublin moves against the rival viking port of Limerick and is soundly beaten by Þórir Helgason.

927 Waterford vikings defeated by Limerick vikings on River Maigue at Kilmallock in what is now County Cork.

928 Massacre of Irish at Dunmore Cave, Kilkenny by Gofraid ua Ímair.

933 Amlaíb Cenncairech, ruler of Limerick has a victory over the Uí Maine and some of their nobles killed at Duibhthir in what is now Athlone.

934 Æþelstan, King of the Saxons invades Alba (the Pictish Gaelic Kingdom of Scotland).

Limerick vikings pillage Connacht as far as Magh Luirg to the north and as far as Bádhbhghna to the east.

936 Amlaíb Cenncairech stays seven months on the Shannon and plunders Magh Aei in what is now Roscommon.

937 Amlaíb mac Gofraid (Óláfr Guðrøðarson), King of Dublin and his forces come to Lough Ree at Lughnasadh and captures Amlaíb Cenncairech and his men after smashing their ships.

Causantín mac Áeda, King of Alba, with Amlaíb mac Gofraid, King of Dublin and Owain, King of Strathclyde invade England and are defeated at the Battle of Brunanburh by Æþelstan and his forces.

939 Death of Æþelstan.

941 Amlaíb mac Gofraid plunders Saint Bealdhere's at Tyninghame.

944 Dublin sacked by Congalach Cnogba, *Ard Rí* of Ireland.

950 Máel Coluim mac Domnaill, King of Alba plunders the English as far as the Tees on the incitement of Causantín mac Áeda.

952 Alliance of the men of Alba, the Strathclyde Britons and the English battle the Norse Gael and lose.

954 Eiríkr Blood Axe slain at Stainmore.

Death of Máel Coluim mac Domnaill, King of Alba.

956 Congalach Cnogba, *Ard Rí* of Ireland slain in battle with the Laigin and the Dublin vikings at Dún Ailinne in what is now County Kildare.

Between **954** and **962** Indulfr, King of Alba takes Edinburgh.

962 Battle of Bauds. Indulfr, King of Alba defeats Norse raiders in the Bauds, Moray, but dies in the conflict.

968 Battle of Sulcoit. Mathgamain mac Cennétig and his brother Brian Bóruma defeat Ímar of Limerick and his forces, then plunder and burn the port.

971 Cináed mac Máel Coluim, King of Alba pillages England as far as Stainmore.

973 Norse Gaelic rulers of the Isles ally with Alba and Strathclyde.

976 Death of Mathgamain mac Cennétig.

977 Brian Bóruma kills Ímar, King of Limerick and his sons Amlaíb Cuallaid (Wild Dog) and Dubcenn (Black Head) in the monastery on Inis Cathaigh (Scattery Island).

980 Battle at Tara. Máel Sechnaill mac Domnaill, High King of Ireland defeats Amlaíb Cuarán, King of Dublin and his Norse Gael mercenaries from the Hebrides and Man. Lays siege to Dublin and frees all the slaves when the enemy surrenders. Amlaíb abandons the kingship of Dublin to become a monk at Iona.

Hloðvér, son of Þórfinnr Skull Splitter, becomes Jarl of Orkney, marries Eithne, daughter of the Irish King Cerball.

Cináed mac Máel Coluim, King of Alba plunders England to the River Dee by Chester.

983 Ívarr, King of Waterford and his ally Domnall Claen, King of Leinster beaten by Máel Sechnaill and Glúniarainn, King of Dublin.

985 The Njálssons raid the Hebrides.

Danish raid on Dál Riada suppressed and 140 viking prisoners hanged.

986 Danes raid Iona on Christmas night, killing the abbott and fifteen monks.

987 Slaughter of the Danes who raided Iona.

989 Guðrøðr Haraldsson, King of the Hebrides killed by Gael of Dál Riada.

995 Sihtric, King of Dublin desecrates the church at Donaghpatrick in Meath.

Máel Sechnaill mac Domnaill raids Dublin and takes the Ring of Þórr and the Sword of Carlus.

997 Sihtric, King of Dublin desecrates Kells and Clonard.

998 Sihtric, King of Dublin forced to give hostages to Máel Sechnaill mac Domnaill and Brian Bóruma.

999 Battle of Glen Máma. Brian Bóruma and Máel Sechnaill mac Domnaill with the forces of Munster and Meath heavily defeat Máel Mórda mac Murchada, King of Leinster and Sihtric, King of Dublin.

1000 Brian Bóruma pillages Dublin, burns down its stronghold and sends Sihtric into flight. Sihtric later returns, submits to Brian and gives hostages. Brian marries Sihtric's mother Gormflaith.

1002 Brian Bóruma *Ard Rí* or High King of Ireland.

Saint Brice's Day massacre of Danes in England.

1005 Máel Mórda mac Murchada at odds with Brian Bóruma.

Máel Coluim Forranach (The Destroyer), High King of Alba defeats the Norse at Mórthlach in Moray.

1006 Máel Coluim Forranach (The Destroyer), High King of Alba invades Bernicia and lays siege to Durham but is defeated. The raid may have been a *creach rígh* or royal prey customarily carried out by a new king on enemy territory.

1012 Danes defeated by Máel Coluim Forranach, High King of Alba at Cruden Bay in Aberdeenshire.

1014 Battle of Cluain Tarbh (Clontarf). Death of Brian Bóruma, High King of Ireland, Máel Mórda mac Murchada, King of Leinster and Sigurðr Digri, Jarl of Orkney.

Þórfinnr, the future Jarl of Orkney is raised by his grandfather, Máel Coluim Forranach, High King of Alba.

1018 Máel Coluim Forranach, High King of Alba defeats the English of Bernicia at the Battle of Carham. Takes Lothian.

Sihtric, King of Dublin pillages Kells for an immense booty and many prisoners probably later sold as slaves. A large number of people are killed in the church.

1020 Gilla Coemgáin, Mormaer of Moray involved in the murder of his uncle Findláech, the father of Macbeth.

1021 Sihtric, King of Dublin beaten in Wicklow by Augaire mac Dúnlainge, King of Leinster. According to the *Annals of the Four Masters,* Augaire wreaked *a dreadful slaughter among the foreigners.*

1022 Death of Máel Sechnaill mac Domnaill, *Ard Rí* of Ireland.

Niall mac Eochaid, King of Ulaid defeats the Dublin vikings in a sea battle and takes the survivors prisoner.

1025 King Flaithbertach ua Néill takes hostages from Sihtric, King of Dublin.

1026 Donnchadh son of Brian Bóruma takes hostages from Sihtric, King of Dublin.

Niall mac Eochaid, King of Ulaid plunders Dublin.

1027 Sihtric, King of Dublin, allied with Donnchad of Brega defeated by Roen ua Máel Sechlainn, King of Meath. In a second clash at Lickblaw, Roen and Donnchad both fall.

1029 Mathghamhain ua Riagain, King of Brega captures Amlaíb (Óláfr), Sihtric's son. Sihtric pays a huge ransom to free him.

1030 Sihtric, King of Dublin pillages Wales in alliance with Knútr, King of Denmark, Norway and England and a Norse Irish settlement is founded in Gwynedd.

1031 Knútr, King of Denmark, Norway and England in conflict with Máel Coluim Forranach (The Destroyer), High King of Alba. Peace negotiated between them by Knútr's wife Emma and her brother Richard, Duke of Normandy.

1032 Sihtric, King of Dublin defeats the allied forces of the Conailli, the Uí Tortain and the Uí Meith at the Battle of Inbher Boinne.

Gilla Coemgáin, Mormaer of Moray burned to death, along with fifty of his followers. Macbeth mac Findláech marries Gilla Coemgáin's widow, Gruoch.

1034 Death of Máel Coluim Forranach (The Destroyer), High King of Alba, in conflict with the men of Moray.

Death of Suibne mac Cináeda, King of the Gall Goídil.

1035 Sihtric, King of Dublin pillages the church at Ardbraccan in Meath, burns two hundred men inside and captures as many more.

1040 Þórfinnr the Mighty, Jarl of Orkney defeats Karl Hundason, King of Alba (probably Donnchad mac Crínán).

Donnchad mac Crínán, King of Alba killed in Moray, opposing Macbeth, who then takes the kingship.

Macbeth resists a Danish invasion force around Kinghorn, Fife. In Shakespeare's lurid play, the Danes pay a large sum in gold to have their dead buried on Inchcolm Island after the conflict.

1042 Þórfinnr the Mighty, Jarl of Orkney invades Northumbria and defeats the English in two pitched battles.

Death of Sihtric, King of Dublin.

1045 Crínán The Hound Earl, father of Donnchad, leads a revolt against Macbeth in Atholl and is slain.

1050 Macbeth goes on a pilgrimage to Rome, where he scatters silver like seed to the poor. Þórfinnr the Mighty, who also goes on a pilgrimage to Rome, may have gone this same year. There has been speculation that it may have been in Macbeth's company.

1054 Siward, Earl of Northumbria invades Alba and is opposed by Macbeth with heavy losses on both sides, including Siward's son and son-in-law.

1057 Macbeth slain at Lumphanan.

1065 Death of Þórfinnr the Mighty.

1158 Death of Rögnvaldr Kali Kolsson

1171 Death of Svein Ásleifarson.

THE SAGAS

PART ONE

WILL SEAFARERS HOLD SWAY THE LAND WHERE THE BATTLE BANNERS ARE BORNE FORTH…

LAXDAELA SAGA

(Saga of the Laxárdalr People)

Ketill Flatnefr, a powerful chieftain, decides to leave Norway for Scotland to escape the oppression of King Haraldr Hárfagri.

WEST-OVER-SEA

There was a man called Ketill Flatnefr, the son of Björn the Ungartered. Ketill was a powerful chieftain in Norway, well born and influential. He lived in Raumsdalr between Sunnmøre and Nordmøre. Ketill's wife was Yngvildr, daughter of Ketill Wether, a man of great standing. They had five children – two sons and three daughters. Their sons were Björn the Eastman and Helgi Bjólan. Their daughters were Þórunnr Hyrna (the Horned), wife of Helgi the Lean, son of Eyvindr Eastman and Raferta, daughter of Kjarval, the Irish king. Another of Ketill's daughters was Unnr Djúpúdga (the Deep Minded), wife of Óláfr Hvíti, the son of Ingjaldr, the son of that Fróði the Valiant who was killed by the Svertlings. Another of Ketill's daughters was Jórunn the Wit Breaker, mother of Ketill the Finn, who had a steading at Kirkby. His son was Asbjörn, father of Þórstein, father of Surtr, father of Sighvatr the Law Speaker.

In Ketill's latter days King Haraldr Hárfagri rose to power in such a manner that no folkland king or any other men of note could rely on keeping their title or prospering unless he said so. When Ketill found out that King Haraldr intended to give him the same option as other powerful men, and to put up with his kinsmen not being compensated for their losses, and himself being reduced to a mere attendant, he gathered his people together and made a speech:

'You all ken my dealings with King Haraldr, concerning which there is no need to elaborate here, as we are confronted with a greater need – to take counsel regarding the troubles now facing us. It appears that King Haraldr's enmity is real and that we can trust in nothing else from that quarter. It seems to me that there are but two choices left to us – either to flee the country or get killed, each in his own place. Now, as far as I'm concerned, I would rather end my days as my forefathers have done, but I would not wish to drag you into danger on my account. I ken well the mettle of my kinsmen and friends, that you would not abandon me, though it would take some courage to stand by me.'

Ketill's son Björn then said: 'I will make my own wishes clear at once. I will follow the example of other great men and leave this country. I see no sense in staying at home, waiting for King Haraldr's thralls to chase me from my land or kill me.'

There was a loud cheer of approval at these brave words, and it was agreed that they should quit the country, as Ketill's sons strongly urged it with no opposition. Björn and Helgi had it in mind to go to Iceland, as they had heard a lot of good things about it – good land to be had for the taking and plenty of stranded whales and salmon, as well as other fishing all year round.

Then Ketill said, 'I will not go to that fishing place in my old age,' and added that he would rather go west instead for the chance of a good living. He kent the lands there well, as he had plundered there far and wide.

Ketill then had a lavish feast, during which he gave his daughter Þórunnr the Horned to Helgi the Lean, as has already been said. After that, he prepared to sail west-over-sea. His daughter Unnr and many others of his kin accompanied him. That same summer Ketill's sons went with their brother-in-law Helgi to Iceland.

Ketill Flatnefr took ship to Scotland and the leading men there gave him a great welcome, as he was famous and well regarded. He was offered status and position best suited to him and he settled there with his kin, except for Þórsteinn Rauði, his daughter's son, who took to arms right away, harrying Scotland widely and overcoming opposition wherever he went. He later made a truce with the Scots and took half of the land into his power. His wife was Þúríðr, daughter of Eyvindr and sister of Helgi the Lean. The Scots were not for keeping the peace and treacherously broke the truce, killing him in Katanes, as told by Ari the Learned.

Unnr the Deep Minded was in Katanes herself then. On hearing of her son Þórsteinn's death and considering that her father had passed away as well by that time, she concluded that her prospects were now poor. She then had a ship built secretly in the forest, and when it was ready, she had it loaded with her valuables and great wealth. All of her kinfolk still alive accompanied her, and few could say that they had ever heard before of anyone, man or woman, getting themselves out of such a dangerous situation with so many riches and such a large following. It can be seen from this how remarkable a woman she was. Among the great men in her retinue was the chieftain Kollr and another man of noble renown called Hord. When all was ready, she sailed her ship to Orkneyjar and stayed there for some time. There she gave Gróa, daughter of Þórsteinn, away in marriage. Gróa was the mother of Greiloð who wed Jarl Þórfinnr, son of Turf Einar, son of Rögnvaldr Mere-Jarl. Their son was Hloðvér, father of Jarl Sigurðr, father of Jarl Þórfinnr, from whom descend all the kin of the jarls of Orkneyjar. Unnr then sailed off to Færeyjar, where she stayed for a while and married off another of Þórsteinn's daughters, Ólof, from whom sprung the race that came to be known as Gate Beards.

A jarl *is a Norse chieftain ranking next below a king.*

Katanes *is Caithness,* Orkneyjar *is the Orkney islands and* Færeyjar *is the Faeroes.*

Ketill Flatnefr (Flat Nose) was presumably so named either from having a broad nose or a broken one.

Haraldr Hárfagri became King of all Norway after his victory at the Battle of Hafrsfjörðr. Many who were unhappy with his rule, such as Ketill Flatnefr, left the country to settle in Ireland, Scotland, the Isles and Iceland. Haraldr later mounted a punitive expedition against his enemies in the Isles.

Helgi the Lean got his name from being in a starved state when left for fostering as a child in the Hebrides. He was afterwards raised by his blood parents, Eyvindr Eastman and Raferta in Ireland. Helgi's beliefs were a mixture of heathen and Christian, not unusual among people of mixed heritage at the time. He appeared to acknowledge Christ in good times but called on the god Þórr when things got difficult.

Helgi's father Eyvindr Eastman (Ostman/Austman) would have got his nickname from being one of the Austmen or Eastmen, the Norse Gael of Dublin. (The Gael themselves were referred to by the Norse as Vestmenn, or Men of the West). Helgi's mother Raferta (Rafertach, from which the surname Rafferty derives) was the daughter of Kjarvalr (which Irish and Icelandic tradition has as Cerball mac Dúnlainge) the Irish king.

Unnr the Deep Minded, daughter of Ketill, also referred to as Auðr, appears in Laxdaela saga, Njáls saga, Eyrbyggja saga, Grettis saga, Eiríks saga rauða and Landnámabók *as a woman of much wisdom and substance. She was the wife of Óláfr Hvíti (the White), according to the saga sources. If he was one and the same as the Amlaíb Conung of the Úi Ímair, Irish sources mention only two other wives – a daughter of Cináed (probably Cináed mac Ailpín, King of the Picts) and a daughter of Áed Findliath, High King of Ireland.*

Unnr later settles in Iceland at a place called Hvammr with her people and bestows on Óláfr Feilan, her grandson, the steading and all its wealth. After her death, Unnr is laid to rest in a ship surrounded by treasure, within a howe or burial mound, and the mound is closed up, a heathen funeral typical for one of high status.

The god Njörðr's symbol was the womb shaped galley. People were buried in vessels that resembled this divine ship. Others were interred in ship-shaped mounds. The ship womb probably represented rebirth in the afterworld.

The Scar boat burial on Orkney, dated between 875 and 950, unusually contained three bodies – that of a warrior, an old woman and a child. Among the grave goods was a plaque made from a whale's rib bone. The plaque is surmounted by two carved dragon heads and has been called the Scar Dragon Plaque, though the carved heads also look horse-like.

For more information on Norse heathen practices see the author's book The Viking Runes.

ORKNEYINGA SAGA

(Saga of the Orkney Jarls)

King Haraldr's punitive expedition against his enemies in the Isles concludes with the giving of Shetland and Orkney to Jarl Rögnvaldr the Powerful as compensation for the loss of his son Ívarr in the conflict. But Rögnvaldr passes the islands over to his brother Sigurðr, who goes on to become a ruthless and rapacious warlord.

THE POISONED TOOTH

Jarl Sigurðr established himself as a powerful chieftain. He went into alliance with Þórsteinn Rauði, son of Óláfr the White and Unnr the Deep Minded, and they took all of Katanes and much else of Scotland, Mýrhæfi and Ros. There he had a stronghold built south of Mýrhæfi.

Sigurðr and Máel Brigte Tooth, the Scottish jarl agreed to meet and settle their differences at a certain place, each of them with forty men. When the day came Sigurðr decided that the Scots could not be trusted, so he had eighty men mounted on forty horses.

When Máel Brigte realised this, he said to his men: 'Now Sigurðr has cheated us, for I can see the legs of two men on each horse's side, so the horses must be bearing twice as many men as we have. Let us now harden our hearts and each take one man with us before we die.'

They then prepared themselves for the fight.

When Sigurðr realised their intent, he addressed his men: 'Let half of our force dismount and take them in the flank when the battle starts. The rest of us will ride at them hard and break their array.'

And so, a fierce battle ensued, but it was not long before Máel Brigte fell along with all his followers, and Sigurðr had the heads hung from the horses' saddles as a sign of his battle prowess. And then they rode for home and bragged about their victory. And when they were come on the way, Sigurðr spurred his horse forward and struck his calf against the tooth sticking out of Máel Brigte's head, grazing it. The wound became painful and infected afterwards, swelling up, and he died from that.

Sigurðr the Mighty was buried under a howe at Ekkjalsbakki. Guðþormr was the name of Sigurðr's son. He ruled the lands for one winter and died without issue. When Jarl Rögnvaldr of Mæren got word of their deaths, he sent his son Hallad west and King Haraldr gave him the title of jarl. When Hallad arrived in the west, he stayed at Hrossey, and vikings were all over the isles and in Katanes, killing and robbing. But when the farmers complained to Jarl Hallad, he considered it too great a task to deal with and he got fed up with it all. So, he gave up the jarldom, took up his freehold right and cleared off back to Norway. His journey was deemed a great laughing stock.

Katanes *is Caithness,* Mýrhæfi *is Moray,* Ros *is Ross and* Ekkjalsbakki *is Oykel.*

Máel Brigte is referred to as a jarl here, but would be more properly known as a mormaer (Sea Lord or Great Steward), the ruler of a province.

The violent takeover of Pictish-Gaelic territory in the north by Sigurðr and his ally Þórsteinn Rauði initiated an ongoing conflict between the Norse and the rulers of Moray that would last for generations. It is however a matter of debate as to the extent of the territory taken. It was a common thing for hostile parties to lay claim to land they had not wholly secured. The leaders of the House of Loairn that governed the kingdom of Moray were distantly related to, and rivals of, the Mac Ailpín dynasty ruling Alba to the south.

LAXDAELA SAGA

(Saga of the Laxárdalr People)

Höðskuldr Dala-Kolsson is a chief character in both Laxdaela saga *and* Brennu-Njáls saga. *He was the son of that Kollr who accompanied Unnr the Deep Minded to Iceland, later known as Dala-Kollr or Kollr of the Dales. Höðskuldr inherits his father's farm after his death and grows to be an able man and widely popular both in Iceland and Norway, being a member of the court of King Hákon the Good (c. 920-961).*

In Laxdaela saga *it recounts his marriage in Iceland to a woman called Jórunn, capable and wise, though often hot tempered. She and Höðskuldr are said to have got on well and loved each another but were not given to show it much. On one of his visits to Norway, Höðskuldr attends a royal assembly with King Hákon in the Brenn Isles, southern Sweden, and at a market there purchases a slave woman for his pleasure, a woman who turns out to be not at all what she seems...*

THE SLAVE WOMAN

One day when Höðskuldr was setting out to join some friends for a get-together, he happened to spot an eye-catching tent situated away from the other market booths. He approached it, and on entering, saw a richly dressed man in a Russian hat. Höðskuldr asked him who he was.

'I'm called Gilli,' came the reply, 'but most people know me by my nickname – Gilli the Russian.'

Höðskuldr said that he had often heard the man's name mentioned, as he was considered the richest man in the merchant guild.

'There is little doubt then that whatever we want to purchase, you can provide,' Höðskuldr said.

Gilli asked what that might be, and Höðskuldr told him he wanted to purchase a slave girl, if he had one.

'You wouldn't embarrass me by asking for something you don't expect me to have,' Gilli remarked.

Höðskuldr's glance went to a curtain that Gilli then raised, revealing a dozen women sitting there in a row. Gilli encouraged him to go over and see if any of them took his fancy to buy. Höðskuldr looked them over, and his eye settled on a scantily dressed woman sitting at the edge of the tent. He thought she was very comely.

'How much would it be for this woman here,' Höðskuldr asked, 'if I was minded to buy her.'

'Three silver marks,' Gilli replied.

'That's a bit steep for a slave woman, is it not?' remarked Höðskuldr. 'It's triple the usual price.'

'Indeed,' answered Gilli, 'for I consider her of greater value than the others. You can have any of these for one silver mark and leave this one with me.'

'Let me check how much silver I have in my purse,' said Höðskuldr, and asked Gilli for the scales.

'I will not deceive you over this, Höðskuldr,' said Gilli. 'The woman has a major flaw, and I want you to know about it before we agree on this deal.'

When Höðskuldr asked what it was, Gilli told him the woman was mute. 'I've tried all sorts of ways of getting her to talk, but I've never managed to get a word out of her. It is my belief that she can't speak.'

Höðskuldr then asked for the scales again to weigh the silver from his purse, and it came to exactly three marks.

'It appears that we have a deal,' declared Höðskuldr. 'Here's the money, and I'll take the woman now.' He added that he considered Gilli's honesty over the matter very fair.

After that, Höðskuldr returned to his booth, where he spent the night with the slave woman. The next morning, he said to her: 'Gilli wasn't too free-handed with the clothes he had you wear, though it may have been harder for him to clothe twelve than for me to clothe one.'

He then opened a chest and brought out some fine clothing for her, which became her very well.

Höðskuldr sails home to Iceland with a cargo of building timber provided by King Hákon, as well as the gifts of a gold arm ring and a gold-adorned sword from the king. His ship lands at Salmon River Mouth and he has the timber unloaded and stored in a shed before being transferred to his nearby home. He then rides back to the farm with a few men, gets a warm welcome from his people and finds that all his possessions have been well maintained. His wife Jórunn, however, soon asks him who the woman is.

'You'll probably think I'm being funny when I tell you I haven't a clue what her name is,' says Höðskuldr.

'Well, it's either one of two things,' responds Jórunn. 'Either the talk that has reached my ears is lies, or you had to have spoken to her enough to have got her name.'

Höðskuldr could not deny it and so he told her the truth. He added that he wanted the woman treated well, and that she should take up service with them.

'I have no intention of locking horns with this fancy woman you've brought over from Norway,' said Jórunn, 'if she finds little joy staying here. And it should concern me even less if she is deaf and dumb'.

Höðskuldr slept with his wife every night after his return and had little to do with the slave woman. It was clear to everybody that there was something dignified and well-born about her, and that she was of no low intelligence. Towards winter's end she gave birth to a baby boy. Höðskuldr was summoned and it was his opinion, as it was of others, that he had never seen a comelier nor more noble looking child. When asked what the boy should be called, Höðskuldr named him Óláfr after his uncle, Óláfr Feilan, who had died a little while before. Óláfr stood out from all the other children, and Höðskuldr grew very fond of him.

The next summer Jórunn suggested that the woman should do some work or clear off. Höðskuldr said that she should wait on Jórunn and himself, while looking after the child. When the boy was two years old he had acquired full speech and dashed about like a child of four.

Early one fine, sunny morning, Höðskuldr went out to do the rounds of his farm when he happened to hear people talking. He followed the voices down to where a little stream ran past the slope of the home field, and he saw his little son Óláfr with his mother, who was talking in a lively way to the boy and was not mute at all. Höðskuldr then approached and asked her name. The woman replied that there was little point in concealing it now, and he sat beside her there in the field.

'If you want to know my name,' she said, 'it is Melkorka.'

When Höðskuldr inquired of her kin, she replied: 'My father is Mýrkjartan and he is a king in Ireland. I was taken from there as a prisoner of war when I was but fifteen winters.'

Höðskuldr said that she had kept quiet for far too long about such a high-born descent.

Höðskuldr later told Jórunn what he had discovered, but she questioned the truth of it, and declared that she had little love for the ways of mystery folk. So that was that. Jórunn was every bit as aloof with the woman, but Höðskuldr now had more time for her.

Soon after this, Melkorka was helping Jórunn undress before she retired to bed. She was putting her shoes on the floor, when Jórunn started beating her about the head with her stockings. Melkorka lost her temper and let Jórunn have it with her fist, giving her a bloody nose. Höðskuldr had to pull them apart.

After this, he arranged for Melkorka to stay at a place up in Salmon River Dale, later called Melkorkastaðr. Melkorka set up home there with her son Óláfr, and Höðskuldr provided her with everything she would need. It soon became clear that Óláfr was growing up to be a cut above other men on account of his looks and refinement.

Melkorka's name, given here in Norse, may be the Irish Gaelic Máel Curcaig, meaning hooded devotee, and suggesting a religious function. The word máel was often put before the name of a saint e.g. Máel Brigte *(devotee of the female saint Brigit, from the earlier Celtic goddess Brigantia or Brigindo).*

The saga does not make it clear why Melkorka pretended to be mute, unless it was basically a way of expressing hostility, by refusing to communicate with her captors.

When Höðskuldr purchases Melkorka, it seems to be on a whim and with little or no thought at the time as to how it will impact on his wife and home life. His flippant reply to Jórunn's question as to who Melkorka is displays a reckless lack of consideration, and on discovering Melkorka's true identity and regal status, he is left baffled with the realisation that he has quite literally got more than he bargained for. With this revelation, Jórunn's resentment of the mystery woman suddenly explodes into violence and she starts laying into Melkorka in a farcical attack with her stockings. Melkorka doesn't just stand there and take it, but like any proud and able Irishwoman of the time, knows how to use her fist.

Óláfr comes to be fostered by a wealthy man called Þórðr Goddi, and Höðskuldr gives him the nickname 'The Peacock' on account of his handsome, dignified bearing and flamboyant appearance. He is not only well built, but his clothes are the height of fashion and his weaponry also stands out.

As Höðskuldr starts getting on in years and his other sons are grown, he has less to do with Melkorka or her household, being of the opinion that Óláfr should be the one to see to her needs. Melkorka takes a very dim view of this and determines to do something that will really annoy him. Laxdaela saga *tells us that a man called Þórbjörn Skrjup had taken over Melkorka's household affairs. Melkorka, having previously turned down an offer of marriage from Þórbjörn, now reconsiders if it will help with her plans. She is sick of Óláfr being described as the son of a slave woman and wants him to visit Ireland to find his grandfather, King Myrkjartan. A deal is arranged in which Þórbjörn will provide Óláfr with ample trade goods to finance the journey in return for Melkorka's hand in marriage. The ceremony is conducted without Höðskuldr knowing anything about it, though he isn't best pleased when he does find out.*

When Melkorka was seeing her son off on his journey, she gave him a gold ring.

'This was a teething gift from my father,' she told him, 'and I know he will recognise it.'

She also gave him a knife and a belt, tokens that her childhood nurse would know.

'I have prepared you for home as best I could,' she added, 'and I've taught you Irish.' In this way, wherever he landed in Ireland, he'd at least know the language.

Despite being regarded as a slave and a concubine, Melkorka will not accept it and insists on making independent decisions, marrying Þórbjörn without Höðskuldr's consent and sending Óláfr off to see his grandfather with the trip fully funded. She is also resourceful enough to have concealed her father's ring as well as the knife and belt she gives to Óláfr.

Óláfr boards the ship of Orn, who is one of King Haraldr Grey Cloak's bodyguard, in the hope that he will get to Ireland. Their first port of call, however, will be Norway.

After that, Óláfr went on board ship, and sailed out with a fair wind, landing in Norway after a good voyage. Orn encouraged Óláfr to visit the court of King Haraldr, seeing that it was usual for men like Óláfr to be accorded honour according to their standing.

Whoever thinks of him as a slave's son in Iceland, Orn clearly sees him as suitable for an audience with the king.

Óláfr said he would take that advice and accompanied Orn to the court, where they received a good welcome. The king accepted Óláfr on account of his kin and gave him an invitation to stay.

King Haraldr's mother, Queen Gunnhildr, paid close attention to Óláfr when she found out he was Höðskuldr Dala-Kolsson's son and nephew of Höðskuldr's half brother Hrút Herjolfsson. But there were those men of the opinion that she would have relished the young man's company without the need for any formal introduction.

Queen Gunnhildr has a reputation as something of a man-eater. In Brennu-Njáls saga she seduces Hrút, Óláfr's uncle, when he visits the royal court, and sleeps with him for two solid weeks, even giving him her throne to sit on and warning her servants that if they breathe a word of what is going on, it will be their last. She is so infatuated with Hrút, that when he is about to leave Norway, she lays a spell on him to the effect that he will never enjoy the woman he is betrothed to back in Iceland. As Óláfr is Hrút's nephew, Gunnhildr shows a keen interest in him, though nowhere in Laxdaela saga is it said that she takes it any further than that.

As winter wore on, Óláfr grew sad and moody, and Orn asked him what was wrong.

'I have a voyage I need to make west-over-sea,' Óláfr explained, 'and it is my hope that you will assist me in this, so that I can set out on the journey this summer.'

Orn advised him not to build up his hopes, as he knew of no ships sailing west that year.

Gunnhildr then appeared and remarked that she had never heard them talk in this manner before, with each of them wanting their own way.

Óláfr greeted her warmly, meaning to carry on the talk, but Orn made himself scarce and Óláfr started discussing the matter with Gunnhildr instead. He told her of his wish and how important the trip was to him, and that he was sure King Mýrkjartan was his grandfather.

'I will give you my assistance for this trip,' said Gunnhildr, 'so that you can set out in as fine a style as you please.'

Óláfr thanked her for her offer.

Gunnhildr had a ship made ready and set about gathering a crew, asking Óláfr how many men he thought he'd need. Óláfr said he would need sixty, adding that they should be more like warriors than merchants. Gunnhildr said he would have all as he wanted. Orn was included in the number and is the only one of the crew mentioned by name. All of them were well equipped.

King Haraldr and Gunnhildr conducted Óláfr to his ship and wished him good fortune on his journey. King Haraldr told him that no worthier man had come out of Iceland in their days and confirmed their goodwill toward him. He then asked Óláfr how old he was and Óláfr replied that he was eighteen winters.

'Indeed,' remarked the king, 'men such as yourself surpass others in worth, considering also that you have left the age of a child not long behind. Be sure and come to visit us when you return.'

King Haraldr and Gunnhildr then bade him farewell and Óláfr boarded the ship with his men and sailed out. The weather was poor that summer, with heavy fog and no decent wind to speak of, and what there was of it was no help at all. The ship drifted about over the open sea and most of the crew couldn't tell which direction they were going. When the fog finally lifted and the wind rose, they raised the sail, but then started debating as to what direction Ireland was. Orn was convinced that it lay one way, but most of the crew disagreed with him and thought his judgement was befuddled, declaring that the majority should decide on the matter.

When the issue was put before Óláfr, he replied that only the wisest among them should have a say. 'The way I see it,' he added, 'a counsel of fools is all the more useless the bigger it is.'

So, the upshot was that Orn, as the more experienced, decided on the direction they should go. They sailed on with little wind for several days and nights. Then one night the watchmen called out for the crew to wake up, as they had sighted land so near that the prow of the ship had almost ran into it. The sail was up, with the usual light wind. They all roused themselves, and Orn directed them to steer the ship away from land if they could.

Óláfr said that, with all the breakers astern, that wasn't likely, and to get the sail down. He advised to wait for daylight and find out what land it was before they did anything else. They dropped the anchors and debated the matter through the night but recognised it in the light of day as Ireland.

But in Orn's view they had not landed at a favourable place, as it appeared to be nowhere near any of the harbours or marketplaces that offered safe conduct to outlanders.

'So here we are,' he said, 'stranded like sticklebacks on a beach. I'm pretty sure that they have the right to take our goods under Irish law, for they claim everything as flotsam even when the sea has ebbed less from the ship's stern than it has done here.'

Óláfr was sure this would not happen. 'I noticed a lot of folk gathering ashore there, and I have little doubt that they consider the arrival of this ship is a grand thing,' he remarked. 'During the ebb-tide I spotted an estuary round behind the headland that doesn't empty completely at low tide. Provided there is no damage to our vessel, we will lower the boat and tow the ship there.'

The ship's planking had been saved by a bottom of loam where it had lain at anchor, so now they towed the ship into the estuary and anchored there.

Later that day, people gathered in great numbers on the beach and two of them approached the ship in a rowing boat. They inquired as to who the masters of the ship were and Óláfr answered them in Irish. Despite this, the men could tell that the strangers were Norse, and told them that if they handed over their goods in accordance with Irish law, they would be safe until their king had given his judgement.

Óláfr answered that this only applied if merchants had no one to interpret for them, and he assured the Irish that they had come in peace, but if pushed into a fight, they would resist.

The Irish shouted out a war slogan at this and piled into the sea with the aim of dragging the ship ashore, crew and all. The water was up to the armpits of some and to the waists of the tallest among them, but the ship was in far deeper water.

At Óláfr's command, his crewmen armed themselves and stood all along the gunwales with the blades of their spears thrust out from between their overlapping shields. Óláfr advanced to the prow, wearing a gilded helmet and a coat of mail. Belted round his waist was a sword with gold on the pommel and guard, and in his hand a barbed spear, skilfully engraved. The shield he held was red, with a gold lion emblazoned on it.

This brave and determined show on the part of the strangers daunted the Irish, who soon realised that the ship would be harder to take than they had first believed. They withdrew to confer and murmured anxiously at the realisation that it was a warship and not a merchant ship that confronted them, and that it might be part of a fleet.

Word was sent quickly to the king, who was at a feast nearby, and he rode in force to where he could hail the ship, lying where it was, close to the shore. The Irish had been repeatedly casting missiles at it, but neither Óláfr nor any of his men were hurt. Óláfr was standing there in his battle gear as earlier described, and the folk there were fascinated by the imposing appearance of the ship's captain. However, when Óláfr's men witnessed the massive gathering of horsemen coming bravely towards them, they fell quiet, as it seemed to all a daunting force to deal with. Óláfr heard the nervous murmuring among his crewmen and encouraged them to take heart.

'Things are looking up for us now,' he said, 'the Irish are hailing their king, Mýrkjartan.'

The horsemen rode as close to the ship as they could get and each side had no trouble hearing the other. The king asked who the commander of the ship was. Óláfr identified himself as the leader and inquired in turn who the valiant warrior was addressing him.

'I am Mýrkjartan,' came the reply.

Óláfr then asked if he was King of the Irish, and Mýrkjartan answered that he was. Mýrkjartan asked him the news and Óláfr responded well to all his queries. The king then asked from whence they had sailed and whose men they were, questioning Óláfr in particular with regard to his lineage, for he knew that he was dealing with a proud man who would not reveal more than he was asked.

Óláfr informed the king that they had come from Norway and that the crew were retainers of King Haraldr Gunnhildarson. 'As for my lineage, my lord,' he said, 'my father bides out in Iceland, Höðskuldr by name, a man of good birth. But my mother's kin I believe you are more familiar with than I, for her name is Melkorka, and I have it in good faith, my lord, that she is your daughter. It is for this reason that I have undertaken such a long journey, and now it is of great importance to me the answer you give to what you have been told.'

The king grew quiet and took counsel with his men, some of whom questioned the truth of Óláfr's tale.

'It is plain to see that this Óláfr is a well born fellow, whether he be kin or not,' said the king. 'And in addition, of all men, his mastery of Irish is outstanding.'

The king then addressed Óláfr again, declaring that he would now give him his answer. 'I shall grant safe conduct to yourself and your men,' he said, 'but with regard to this claim of kinship, we need to talk further before I give comment on it.'

So, they put the gangways out to shore and Óláfr and the crew disembarked, with all the Irish impressed by their warrior-like demeanour. Óláfr gave the king a respectful greeting, doffed his helmet and bowed to him, and he in turn welcomed Óláfr warmly, and they fell straight away to conversing. Óláfr repeated his case with great eloquence and sincerity and then presented the ring Melkorka had given him before leaving Iceland.

'She said, my lord, that you gave her this as a teething gift,' he told Mýrkjartan.

The king took the ring and, on regarding it closely, his face grew deep red.

'This token is true,' he declared, 'and is all the more remarkable in that you bear your mother's looks, and this alone you would be known by. And on account of these things, I will indeed acknowledge our kinship, Óláfr, and may all here bear witness to this. Furthermore, you are invited to my court, together with your men, but your honour will depend on how worthy I find you when I try you further.'

After that, the king arranged for them to have horses and men to watch over their ship and goods. Now the king rode to Dyflin, and all the folk thought this a great matter, that the man accompanying Mýrkjartan was the son of his daughter, carried off captive in war when she was fifteen winters old. But most affected of all by the news was Melkorka's elderly foster mother, bed-ridden with ailing health and old age, though a walking staff was no consideration when she met Óláfr.

'Here is Melkorka's foster mother,' said the king, 'and she will want to know all about her.'

Óláfr welcomed the old woman warmly with open arms and placed her on his knee and assured her that the girl she had cared for was out in Iceland, settled and in a comfortable position. And when he presented her with the knife and belt, she knew them and cried out of happiness and said it was clear to see that Melkorka's son was a gallant one, because he came from such good stock. She was in grand spirits all winter.

Trouble was never far from the king's door, as there was incessant raiding by war bands in the western lands, and all through winter he fought off attacks by vikings and pillagers. Óláfr and his followers were on the king's ship, and whoever went against them found them a grim handful. The king looked to Óláfr and his men for advice on important matters, as he found Óláfr both wise and steady in the face of all perils.

Towards the end of winter, the king called an assembly, and it was attended by a great many people. Then the king stood up and spoke: 'You all know that last autumn a man came among us who is my daughter's son and also well born on his father's side. It strikes me that Óláfr is a man of such courage and ability that it is rarely found. I have it in mind to offer the realm to him when I am done ruling, as Óláfr is more suited to taking it over than my own sons.'

Óláfr thanked the king for his offer with many courteous and respectful words but said that he would not wish to risk how his sons would take it when he was gone. Swift renown was better than a lingering shame, and he would rather sail for Norway when it was safe for ships to set out, and that his mother would be far from happy if he did not return.

The king told Óláfr that he should do what he thought was best. After that, the assembly came to a close. When Óláfr's ship was ready for the voyage, the king bade him farewell and presented him with a gold-chased spear and a gold-ornamented sword as well as an abundance of money. Óláfr asked if he could take Melkorka's old foster mother with him, but the king said there was no need for that, and so she stayed on there. Then Óláfr boarded his ship and parted from the king with the greatest affection. Óláfr sailed out and had a good voyage to Norway and these travels of his became well known. When he had berthed his ship, he arranged for horses and set off with his men to find King Haraldr.

On arrival at the court, Óláfr received a warm welcome from the king and an even warmer one from Gunnhildr. They encouraged him with many a kind and friendly word to stay there and he accepted their invitation, along with Orn, to join the court. King Haraldr and Gunnhildr held Óláfr in such high esteem that no foreigner before him had enjoyed such honour at their court. Óláfr gave the king and Gunnhildr many a fine present that he had brought with him from Ireland. When Yule came around, King Haraldr gave Óláfr a set of clothes made of scarlet material, and Óláfr stayed through the winter. But in the spring, Óláfr requested the king's leave to return to Iceland that summer to see his family.

The king answered: 'It would please me better if you stayed here with us and accept whatever position best suits you.'

Óláfr thanked the king for all the honour being offered to him but insisted that he wished to go to Iceland if it was not contrary to the king's will.

'There will be no incivility between us in this, Óláfr,' said the king. 'You shall go to Iceland this summer, for I can tell your heart's set on it. But you shall have no trouble with the preparations, as I will see to it all.'

In the spring King Haraldr had a ship launched, a fine merchant vessel. The king had it loaded with building timber and fitted out with full rigging. When the ship was ready, the king informed Óláfr that it would be his, 'for I would prefer that you do not set out from Norway this summer as a passenger on someone else's ship.'

Óláfr thanked the king in fine words for his freehandedness.

Óláfr then prepared for the voyage, and once he got a fair wind, he sailed out to sea, parting from the king on the very best of terms. He had a fine voyage and landed at Bordeyri in Hrútafjörðr. News of the ship's arrival soon got around, as well as who the captain was. When Höðskuldr received word, he was well pleased, and rode with some of his men north to Hrútafjörðr for a happy reunion with his son. Höðskuldr invited Óláfr to come with him and Óláfr accepted. So, he set up the ship, but his goods were transported from the north, and when this was done, Óláfr rode with a dozen men to Höðskuldstaðr, where his father greeted him happily, and his (half) brothers welcomed him warmly, as did all his kin there. But between Óláfr and his brother Bárðr the love was strongest.

Óláfr's journey earned him high renown, and the word spread widely of his descent from Mýrkjartan, King of the Irish and the honour bestowed upon him by great men.

Melkorka soon came to see her son and Óláfr greeted her gladly. She asked him for all his news from Ireland, first of her father and then of her other kin, and Óláfr answered all her questions. She then asked if her foster mother was still alive, and Óláfr said that she was. Melkorka then asked why he hadn't brought her with him to Iceland, and Óláfr told her: 'The people there wouldn't allow me to take your foster mother out of Ireland, mother.'

'That may be so,' said Melkorka, and it was clear to see that she took this much to heart.

Melkorkastaðr *is Melkorka's Steading.*

Dyflin *is Dublin.*

ORKNEYINGA SAGA

(Saga of the Orkney Jarls)

Þórfinnr Torf-Einarsson, also known as Þórfinnr Hausakljúfr (Skull Splitter), was a renowned warlord and Jarl of Orkney. He married Grélaða (Gruaidh), a daughter of Jarl Dungad (Donnchad) of Caithness. Þórfinnr had five sons – Arnfinnr, Hávarðr the Fecund, Hloðvér, Ljótr and Skúli. After Þórfinnr's death in 963, his son Arnfinnr became jarl and was killed at the instigation of his wife Raghnildr, daughter of Eiríkr Blood Axe, who subsequently married his brother Hávarðr when he became jarl. She then had him killed in turn by his nephew Einar Kliningr (Buttered Bread) and denied having anything to do with it in the wake of public outrage. She next incited another nephew of Hávarðr, Einar Harðkjotr (Hard Mouth), to take revenge on his cousin Einar Kliningr for the killing of his uncle, by tempting him with the jarldom. And after that she married Hávarðr's brother Ljótr, who had Einar Harðkjotr put to death.

Skúli, another of Þórfinnr's sons, is said to have sailed over to Scotland from Orkney and was given the title of jarl by the King of Scots. Skúli raised an army in Caithness and sailed back to Orkney to confront his brother Ljótr but was beaten in battle and fled back to Scotland. He returned with Scottish forces and clashed with his brother in the Dales of Caithness. Skúli was defeated again and killed. Ljótr then took over Caithness, but the Scots were not at all pleased and went against him with a large army. They met at Skiðamýrr (Skitten), and despite being outnumbered, Ljótr won the victory, though the survivors on both sides were heavily wounded and Ljótr himself died of a battle wound later.

THE RAVEN BANNER

After Ljótr's passing, Hloðvér took over the rule of the jarldom and governed well. He wed Eithne, daughter of King Kjarvalr of Ireland and their son was Sigurðr Digri (the Stout). Hloðvér breathed his last in bed and was laid in a burial mound at Ham in Katanes.

Sigurðr then took over the jarldom after his father. He was a powerful chieftain and ruled over wide territories. He had the resources to defend Katanes against the Scots and used to go on regular viking raids in the summer, taking booty in the Suðreyjar, Scotland and Ireland.

One summer a Scottish jarl called Finnleikr dared Sigurðr to fight him on a certain day at Skiðamýrr. Sigurðr's mother knew a thing or two when it came to sorcery and so he sought her counsel on the matter, telling her that luck was against him, being outnumbered by around seven to one.

'If I'd thought you'd want to live forever,' she said, 'I'd have raised you in my wool basket. But our lives are shaped by what will be, not by where you are. I'll give you this banner. I've made it for you with all my craft, and this is my belief – that whoever it is carried before will get victory, but the one who carries it dies.'

The banner was grandly made, with very skilful needlework forming a raven, which gave the impression of being in flight whenever the wind caught it.

Jarl Sigurðr grew muckle angry at his mother's gibe. He gave back the land rights to all the farmers on Orkneyjar and gained their unswerving support. After that, he moved against Jarl Finnleikr, who waited for him at Skiðamýrr. The two armies then readied to fight, and as soon as they commenced the battle, the man bearing Sigurðr's banner got killed. When the jarl ordered another man to pick up the banner, he was also cut down. A third suffered the same fate before Sigurðr was victorious, and the farmers of Orkneyjar recovered their land rights.

Skiðamýrr *is Skitten in Caithness,* Suðreyjar *is the Hebrides,* Katanes *is Caithness, and* Orkneyjar *is the Orkney islands.*

Dungad, *also known as Dungal, was the Picto-Scottish mormaer of Caithness. He established good relations with the Norse through intermarriage and had his stronghold at* Duncansby *(Dungalsbaer in Norse), which was named after him.*

When Ljótr took over as Jarl of Orkney, his brother Skúli, obviously unhappy about it, decided to assert his own claim to Orkney and Caithness by gaining Picto-Scottish support and the title of jarl (or mormaer), thus becoming a client ruler.

The Irish King Kjarvalr or Cerball mac Dúnlainge, is the renowned ancestor of leading Icelandic families in both Irish and Icelandic traditions, here the father of Eithne, wife of Hloðvér and sorcerous mother of Sigurðr.

The jarl Finnleikr *who fights Sigurðr is Findláech mac Ruaidri, King of Moray and father of the famous Macbeth. Sigurðr and Findláech both married daughters of Máel Coluim Forranach (the Destroyer), High King of Alba, who sought to establish political leverage with both the Orkney Norse and Moray.*

The raven banner was typically associated with viking war bands. The raven as bird of battlefield slaughter, was the symbol of the heathen god Óðinn. It was also the bird of the Irish Gaelic goddesses Badb and Morrigan, who sometimes appeared in its form in the mythological sources. Those using the raven as an emblem sought victory through its association with the deities of battle, usually accompanied by blood sacrifice. In the early mythological poem Hávamál, *Óðinn uses the expression a gift demands a gift, with the meaning that everything gained is accompanied by a sacrifice of some sort. In the saga, Sigurðr gains the full support of his followers by giving them their land rights, but the supernatural power behind the sorcerous gift of his mother's raven banner claims the lives of each standard bearer as payment for his victory.*

PART TWO

SHAFTS WILL SHATTER, SHIELDS WILL BURST…

BRENNU-NJÁLS SAGA

(Saga of Burnt Njál)

The central theme of Brennu-Njáls saga is a fifty-year blood feud instigated by the vindictive Hallgerðr, daughter of Hoðskuldr Dala-Kolsson (whom we have already met in the story The Slave Woman*) and Bergþóra, the crotchety wife of the saga's eponymous hero Njál. Bergþóra offends Hallgerðr at a family feast by telling her to move down a place for another woman, which she considers beneath her dignity. This smear on the latter's personal honour sets off a feud between Hallgerðr and Bergþóra that results in the killings of the manservants the women send out to get revenge, and ultimately in the deaths of their husbands. The hero Gunnar is killed by his enemies when his wife Hallgerðr refuses out of spite to give him a length of her hair to replace his broken bowstring. These enemies are attacking him because of the feud she helped stir up. Njál and his sons are later burned in their house along with his wife Bergþóra also because of the women's feud.*

After Gunnar's death and in the course of the events leading up to the burning, two of Njál's sons, Helgi and Grímr, sail off in a merchant ship captained by Bárðr and Óláfr on a journey that takes them to the Northern Isles, where they join the retinue of Jarl Sigurðr Digri.

THE NJÁLSSONS

They got so forceful a northern wind that they were driven hard before it to southward into the main, and a mist descended so dense that they couldn't tell where they were. They were lost for a good while. Finally, they came to shallow seas and guessed that they must be near land. So Njál's sons put it to Bárðr, did he have any clue what land they might be near.

'There are many lands we may have reached on account of the weather we had,' said Bárðr. 'It could be the Norðreyjar or Scotland or Ireland.'

Two nights later, they spotted land to both sides of them and a muckle surf running up the fjord. They anchored outside the breakers, and that night the storm died down, followed by a morning calm. Then they saw thirteen ships advancing toward them.

'What are we going to do now?' asked Bárðr. 'These men look as if they're advancing against us.'

They then debated as to whether they should yield or put up resistance, but before they could decide, the vikings were upon them. Each side asked the other who their leaders were. Bárðr and Óláfr on the merchant side gave their names, and then asked who the viking captains were. These gave their names as Grjótgarðr and Snaekólfr, the sons of Moldan of Dungalsbær in Scotland and kin to King Máel Coluim.

'And now we offer you one of two choices,' said Grjótgarðr. 'Either you put yourselves ashore and surrender your goods, or we fall to and kill every man within our reach.'

Helgi then answered: 'The choice of the merchants is to fight.'

'Curse that wretched tongue,' the merchants rounded on Helgi. 'What kind of fight can we give them? Life is more precious than silver.'

Grímr started bawling and shouting at the vikings, so that they couldn't hear the merchants complaining.

Then Bárðr and Óláfr scolded them: 'Don't you see that the Icelanders are making fools of you slouches? Arm yourselves and fight.'

So, the merchants took up their weapons and vowed never to yield while they had the strength to defend themselves.

Then the vikings shot arrows at them and the fight was on, with the merchants defending themselves well. Snaekólfr leaped aboard the merchant ship and ran Óláfr through with a spear, and then Grímr thrust his own spear so powerfully against Snaekólfr that he was knocked overboard. Helgi then joined Grímr and they drove back any vikings trying to get on the ship, and wherever there was the most need, they were at hand.

The vikings called on the merchants to surrender, but they replied that they would never yield. Just at that moment somebody looked out to sea and spotted some ships rounding the ness from the south, ten in all, advancing swiftly toward them. Shields lined the gunwales, and on the leading ship a man stood by the mast, garbed in a silken tunic, and wearing a gilded helmet over his thick fair hair. He held a gold-inlaid spear in his hand.

'Who here plays such an uneven game?' he inquired.

Helgi gave his name and the names of the viking leaders.

'Who are your captains?' the stranger asked.

'Bárðr the Black, who is still alive,' replied Helgi, 'but the other, Óláfr, was slain. My brother here is Grímr.'

'Do ye hail from Iceland?' the stranger asked next.

'We do indeed,' said Helgi.

The stranger then asked who their father was, and when they told him, he knew who they were and said: 'Your names are well-kent, both father and sons.'

'Who are you?' Helgi asked.

'I am Kári Sólmundarson,' replied the stranger.

Helgi asked him where he had come from.

'From the Suðreyjar,' said Kári.

'You are welcome,' said Helgi, 'if you can lend a hand.'

'I'll give you all the help you need,' replied Kári. 'What would you like me to do?'

'Lay into the vikings,' said Helgi.

It seems a little obvious what Helgi wants him to do, so this appears to be an example of the quirky Nordic humour we find throughout the sagas.

So be it, was Kári's response. They rowed up alongside the viking ships and the fight started where it had left off. When they had struggled for some time, Kári jumped onto Snaekólfr's ship. Snaekólfr turned to meet him and swung at him with his sword. Kári sprang swiftly back over a beam lying athwart the ship and the sword bit down into it so hard that both lower and upper edges were buried in it. Kári smote at him in turn and his sword landed on Snaekólfr's shoulder with such force that it hacked straight through it and clove the arm clean off. Snaekólfr died on the spot.

Grjótgarðr then flung a spear at Kári, but Kári saw it flying toward him and sprang above it, so that it passed on. At that point Helgi and Grímr both joined Kári, and Helgi spitted Grjótgarðr on his spear and that was the end of him. After that, they worked their way round the ship and the enemy begged for quarter, which was given, but they were deprived of their goods. After that, they brought all the ships out under the islands.

Jarl Sigurðr Hloðvisson ruled Orkneyjar at that time. Kári was a retainer of his and had been collecting tribute for him from Jarl Gilli in the Suðreyjar.

Kári invited the Njálssons to Meginland in Orkneyjar and assured them of a welcome from Jarl Sigurðr. They agreed to accompany Kári to Meginland, where he introduced them to Jarl Sigurðr.

'How did they come to meet you?' asked the jarl.

'I came upon them in Skotlandsfjörðr,' answered Kári, 'fighting the sons of Moldan and offering stout resistance. They appeared to be everywhere at once on the ship and were ever ready where the need was greatest. I ask leave for them to be accepted at court.'

'As it pleases you,' replied the jarl. 'You have vouched for them so much already.'

They passed the winter with the jarl in high renown. Then Helgi became quiet as time got on. Unable to understand why, the jarl inquired of Helgi what was on his mind, and if he was discontent at court.

Helgi assured the jarl that he was happy there. The jarl then asked Helgi what was bothering him.

'Have you lands in Scotland to protect?' Helgi asked the jarl.

'So I believe,' the jarl replied. 'What about it?'

'Well,' said Helgi, 'the Scots have slain your steward and prevented any word of it from crossing Péttlandsfjörðr.'

The jarl asked him if he was prescient.

'It has never been put to the test,' said Helgi.

'I will increase your honour if what you say is true,' said the jarl. 'But if you are wrong, you will pay.'

Kári said: 'Helgi is not that sort. It must be right what he says, for his father has the gift.'

The jarl despatched messengers southward to Arnljótr, his steward at Straumey, and he in turn sent men across Péttlandsfjörðr, and they discovered that Hávarðr of Þrasvík, brother-in-law to Jarl Sigurðr, had been slain by Jarl Hundi and Jarl Melsnati. Arnljótr sent a message to Sigurðr, requesting that he come south with a powerful host to rid the realm of these two jarls. Sigurðr then mustered a large army from the islands.

Jarl Sigurðr advanced southward with his army, accompanied by Kári and the Njálssons. They reached Katanes. The jarl had these realms in Scotland – Ros, Mýrhæfi, Suðrland and Dalar. Men from these territories flocked to Sigurðr's banner and said that the jarls were near at hand with a strong host. Jarl Sigurðr advanced with his army against them and faced his enemies at Dungalsbær, where they met in a ferocious battle. The Scots had sent a separate division to assail Jarl Sigurðr's unprotected flank, killing a lot of men, until the Njálssons led an attack in turn and drove off the foe.

At the peak of the battle, the Njálssons returned to Jarl Sigurðr's banner and fought with distinction. Then Kári confronted Jarl Melsnati, who flung a spear at him. Kári snatched the spear out of the air and hurled it back, spitting the jarl through and through.

Jarl Hundi took to flight at that. Jarl Sigurðr went after him at first but decided against it when word came that King Máel Coluim was mustering large forces at Dungalsbær. The jarl retreated to Straumey, where he shared out the plunder, and afterward sailed over to Meginland, accompanied by Kári and the Njálssons.

The jarl held a grand feast and presented Kári with a fine sword and a gold-inlaid spear, gave Helgi a gold arm ring and a mantle, and a sword and shield to Grímr. After that, he appointed Helgi and Grímr as retainers and thanked them for their stout support.

They stayed the winter with Jarl Sigurðr and part of the next summer, and then accompanied Kári on a raid, plundering widely. They went against Guðrøðr, king of Mön and beat him, returning loaded with spoils. They stayed then with Jarl Sigurðr through winter in high esteem.

Norðreyjar *(the Northern Isles),* Dungalsbær *(Duncansby),* Meginland *(Mainland, Orkney),* Skotlandsfjörðr *(the Minch),* Péttlandsfjörðr *(Pentland Firth),* Þrasvík *(Freswick),* Ros *(Ross),* Mýrhæfi *(Moray),* Suðrland *(Sutherland),* Dalar *(Dales of Caithness) and* Mön *(Isle of Man).*

*Moldan or Moddan (*Máel Dúin *in Gaelic) of Dungalsbær i.e Duncansby appears to have been a mormaer in Caithness. The Norse names of his sons, Grjótgarðr and Snaekólfr, again reflect the dual culture so prevalent at the time.*

It is unlikely that the saga can be trusted with regard Sigurðr's control over the north of Scotland – in particular with regard to Moray, whose native rulers still appear to have been in power and offered repeated opposition. Caithness and Sutherland were also Picto-Scottish territories, themselves part of Moray, and tribute would be expected from Sigurðr if he governed these lands as a client ruler, in which case a refusal to pay tribute may have brought about a Picto-Scottish reprisal and the killing of Sigurðr's steward Hávarðr. Whatever the case, the Orkney jarl makes himself scarce when he receives the news that Máel Coluim Forranach is nearby, mustering large forces. Sigurðr clearly cannot enforce any territorial claim when he is up against the High King of Alba. In 1005, shortly after becoming king, Máel Coluim defeated a Norse force at Mórthlach in Moray, according to John of Fordun. Was the battle in the saga taking place during this campaign? It probably occurred at least before Máel Coluim gave his daughter in marriage to Sigurðr, which appears to have brought about an understanding with the Orkney Norse. Máel Coluim later made his grandson Þórfinnr, the issue of this match, Mormaer of Caithness and Sutherland after Sigurðr was slain at Clontarf in 1014.

Máel Coluim clearly extended his authority effectively into Northern Scotland, well beyond the reach of previous rulers of Alba. We should bear in mind however that the rulers of Moray, to whatever degree they may have come under the power of the High King of Alba and the House of Ailpín during Máel Coluim's rule, were of the rival House of Loairn and certain elements would most certainly not have been happy about it. One source, The Prophecy of Berchán, *has Máel Coluim slain during a fight with enemies from Moray.*

According to Skene, Jarl Hundi can be identified as Crínán, the warlike Abbot of Dunkeld and Mormaer of Atholl. He was known as the Hound Earl, hence his Norse nickname here – Jarl Hundi. He married Máel Coluim's daughter Bethóc.

Jarl Melsnati (or Máel Snechtai *in Gaelic) is probably a mormaer of Moray here, not to be confused with the later Máel Snechtai mac Lulach, grandson of Macbeth.*

Kári accompanies the Njálssons back to Iceland, marries their sister Helga and has a son by her named Þórdr.

***

We now take up the narrative in the wake of the burning of Njál and his family. Njál's son-in-law Kári Sólmundarson, whose son Þórdr also dies during the burning, escapes under cover of the smoke and embarks on a bloody rampage as he hunts down the Burners, as they are referred to. He is supported by his friends Kolbein the Black and David the White. After each killing, he customarily declares that he is responsible as the law demands, and the news that reaches the survivors of their comrades being wiped out one by one will have a growing psychological impact.

THE VENGEANCE TRAIL OF KÁRI SÓLMUNDARSON

Kári and Kolbein the Black put out to sea from Eyrar half a month after Flosi and his companions left Hornafjörðr. They had a fair wind and a short voyage. They made land at Friðarey, lying between Hjaltland and Orkneyjar. There that man called David the White welcomed Kári into his home, and he told him all he knew for sure about the doings of the Burners. He was one of Kári's closest friends and Kári stayed through the winter. They got tidings there of all that was going on in Orkneyjar.

Jarl Sigurðr invited his brother-in-law, Jarl Gilli from the Suðreyjar to his Yule feast. He was married to Sigurðr's sister Svanlauga. Also, to the feast came King Sigtryggr (Sigtryggr Silkiskeggi) from Ireland, the son of Óláfr Kváran.

His mother was Kormlöð, one of the most beautiful of women and well-endowed in everything not in her own power. But men said that in all the things she herself had power over, she was downright evil. She had been the wife of a king called Brian but had since parted the ways. He was a noble-minded and good-natured king and had his seat in Kunnaktir, in Ireland. He had as brother Ulfr Hreða, an outstanding champion and fighting man. Brian's foster son was Kerthjalfad, whose father was King Kylfi, who had often been at war with Brian, but later fled before him and became a hermit. When King Brian went south on a pilgrimage, he met King Kylfi and they made peace. King Brian took Kerthjalfad in fosterage and loved him more than his own sons. Kerthjalfad was now fully grown and the boldest of men.

King Brian had a son called Dungaðr, one called Margaðr and another called Taðkr – he was the youngest, and we refer to him as Tann. King Brian's older sons were full grown and full of courage.

Kormlöð was not their mother. She was so consumed with enmity toward King Brian after their divorce that she wanted him dead. King Brian would always be forgiving of outlaws, even after they committed the same crimes three times, but if they stepped out of line again after that, he let the law come down on them. From this it can be seen what manner of king he was.

Kormlöð was always egging on her son Sigtryggr to have Brian killed. With that aim, she sent him to Jarl Sigurðr to ask for his help.

King Sigtryggr arrived before Yule on Orkneyjar, and there too came Jarl Gilli, as was mentioned before.

The feasting hall where they gathered was full, with King Sigtryggr seated between Jarl Sigurðr and Jarl Gilli. To one side were arranged the following of Sigtryggr and Jarl Gilli, while on Jarl Sigurðr's side sat Flosi and Þórsteinn Hallsson.

King Sigtryggr and Jarl Gilli wanted all the news about the Burning and what had followed, so Gunnar Lambason was put forward to tell the tale and a seat provided for him.

While this was happening, Kári, David the White and Kolbein arrived in secret at Hrossey and left men to watch their ship. Kári and his companions made straight for Jarl Sigurðr's hall while the feasting was going on, just as Gunnar Lambason was in the middle of his story. Kári and his comrades stood listening outside. It was Christmas Day.

King Sigtryggr asked Gunnar how Skarp-heðinn had endured the burning.

'Bravely to begin with,' answered Gunnar. 'But towards the end he cried.'

His version of events was extremely skewed and peppered with falsehoods, and now and again he would laugh. To Kári it was beyond bearing. Bursting into the hall with drawn sword, he said:

These fray-craving fighters
brag of burning Njál.
But have they told you
how we made them run?
Their flaming ardour
has borne a heavy price -
ravens have been glutted
on servings of hacked flesh.

Kári lunged across the hall and smote Gunnar Lambason on the neck with his sword edge so that his head came off and went rolling across the table in front of King Sigtryggr and the jarls. The boards were splattered with a welter of blood and so was Jarl Sigurðr's clothing.

Jarl Sigurðr called for Kári to be seized and put to death for the killing, but Kári had been a popular retainer at the court there, and nobody made a move to obey the jarl.

Kári said: 'There are many who would be of the opinion that I have done you a favour, my lord, by avenging your man Helgi Njálsson.'

'Kári has not done this deed without reason,' said Flosi. 'He has not made peace with us, and he has only done what honour demanded.'

Kári left the hall then and nobody stopped him. He joined his companions and returned to the ship. They had fine weather and sailed south to Katanes, where they landed at Þrasvík and stayed for a good while with a reliable man called Skeggi.

Back in the hall, the tables were wiped clean and the dead man carried out. Jarl Sigurðr was then informed that Kari and his comrades had sailed down to Scotland.

'That was a bold man,' remarked King Sigtryggr, 'to behave so bravely, and without a second thought.'

'No one can match Kári for daring,' said the jarl.

Flosi then told his own version of the Burning and gave every man the credit he deserved. On account of this, his story was believed.

Friðarey *is Fair Isle,* Hjaltland *is Shetland,* Kunnaktir *is Connacht, and* Þrasvík *is Freswick.*

Jarl Gilli of the Hebrides was Sigurðr Digri's brother-in-law and appears to have been subject to him, as the saga has Kári collecting tribute from Gilli on behalf of the latter. His wife's name appears as Svanlauga in this version of Brennu-Njáls *saga, but Hvarflóð in another, which is the Norse version of the Irish female name Forbflaith.*

*Sigtryggr Silkiskeggi or Silk Beard (*Sihtric *in Gaelic) was the son of Óláfr Kváran (Amlaíb Cuarán) and King of Dublin. He is referred to as* mac Amlaíb *(son of Amlaíb) in the Irish* Cogadh Gáedhel Re Gallaibh (War of the Gael with the Outlanders).

Kormlöð, Sigtryggr's mother instigates the war against Brian Bóruma in Brennu-Njáls saga *in revenge for him putting her aside. Her name in Irish is* Gormflaith *or* Blue Sovereignty, *and like Queen Medb from the mythological epic* Táin Bó Cúailnge, *any marriage with her is equated with the right to rule and she uses this popular belief and her famed beauty to tempt all would-be contenders to the throne.*

Flosi Þórdarson, Þórsteinn Hallsson and Gunnar Lambason are three of the surviving Burners. After the Njálssons kill the chieftain Höðskuldr Hvítanessgoði, who is married to Flosi's niece Hildigunna, Flosi is goaded by her to seek blood vengeance. He leads the Burners, who surround Njál's house and set it on fire. Flosi lets the women leave and also extends the offer to Njál and his wife Bergþóra, who turn it down, perishing with their sons and grandson Þórdr. Conflict later breaks out at the Alþingi or legal assembly where the matter is brought to court and some of the Burners are killed. Flosi and other surviving Burners are forced to leave Iceland and sail to Orkney.

King Brian's sons are given here with the Norse versions of their names. Dungaðr is Donnchadh in the original Gaelic and Margaðr is Murchadh. Taðkr or Tann is Tadhg. The name of Brian's fosterson and favourite is given as Kerthjalfad in Norse, which does not appear to be easily identified in the Gaelic.

Jarl Sigurðr clearly does not appreciate his outfit being spattered with blood, nor his feast being violently interrupted, but Kári is defended by his enemy Flosi, who respects his courage and the deadly action that honour demands.

Cath Chluain Tarbh *or the Battle of Clontarf occurred on the 23rd April 1014 near viking Dublin. Brian Bóruma, High King of Ireland, with the Dál gCais from Munster, the men of Connacht and the Limerick vikings as allies, confronted the confederation of Irish and vikings fighting for Máel Mórda mac Murchada, King of Leinster and Sihtric (Sigtryggr Silk Beard), King of Dublin. It has popularly been celebrated as a conflict solely between the native Irish on one side and Norse invaders on the other, an Irish victory that broke the back of viking power on the island. However, it was not quite as straightforward as that. There were Irish and vikings on both sides, and of course a large proportion of those vikings had Gaelic blood from many years of intermarriage. The triumph of the Dál gCais did seriously damage Norse Irish power in Dublin but did not permanently break it. Sihtric or Sigtryggr, himself half Irish, was to survive as King of Dublin, but he would have a run of bad luck that would pretty much continue until 1036, when he was forced to stand down. Brian was killed, as was his son and heir Murchadh, leading to a renewed power struggle between his Dál gCais dynasty and its rivals, the Eóganacht. Máel Mórda mac Murchada also fell, as did Sigurðr Digri of Orkney, plunging his surviving sons into conflict over the jarldom. According to both Irish and Norse sources, the battle was ferocious. In* Cogadh Gáedhel re Gallaibh, *Máelsechlainn mac Domhnaill describes the killing being so fierce that the keen wind covered his division with a dense blood spray before it had even engaged the enemy.*

THE BATTLE OF CLONTARF

There was a king called Sigtryggr, the son of Óláfr Kváran. Sigtryggr's mother Kormlöð, a woman of outstanding beauty but of a wicked nature, had been married to Brian High King of Ireland, but was then divorced by him. Afterward, Kormlöð was not best disposed toward King Brian, whose death she actively plotted. She sent her son Sigtryggr to Orkneyjar with a view to enlisting the help of Jarl Sigurðr Hloðvisson in this enterprise. The jarl needed some persuasion and many of his men were against the idea, but he eventually agreed on the understanding that he would have Kormlöð for a wife and be High King himself if the expedition was successful.

Kormlöð was well pleased at the news her son brought back to her but made it plain that they would need greater forces yet to overthrow King Brian. So, she sent Sigtryggr off to negotiate with two infamous vikings, Óspakr and Bróðir, who lay off the Isle of Man with thirty ships. Sigtryggr was to promise them whatever it took to win their support.

Bróðir was no keener than Jarl Sigurðr had initially been to get involved until Sigtryggr offered him what the Jarl of Orkneyjar had agreed to as his price – to rule Brian's kingdom and have Kormlöð as his wife. All knowledge of this separate agreement with Bróðir was kept quiet for fear of it reaching Jarl Sigurðr.

Bróðir then asked his brother and ally Óspakr to join him on the expedition, but Óspakr, a cunning heathen, wasn't the least bit pleased about attacking King Brian, who was noble, generous and well-liked. The upshot was that they agreed to split their forces and parted on far from friendly terms, Óspakr anchoring his ten ships inside the sound, while Bróðir lay outside it with the other twenty.

Bróðir had been a deacon once, but then took to sorcery and heathen ways. Following his decision to oppose King Brian, several bad omens appeared to Bróðir, including a rain of blood, a mighty clamour, his own weapons turning against him and a frenzied assault by ravens.

Understandably disturbed, Bróðir went to see Óspakr about it. Óspakr was wary and would say nothing until Bróðir swore peace between the two of them. Also knowing that Bróðir wouldn't kill at nightfall, he put off interpreting the omens until dark. Óspakr then gave his explanation of the omens and it was far from cheery. The blood shower signified that Bróðir would shed a lot of blood, his own as well as that of others. The great din was the sound of the world splitting and meant the fall of Bróðir and his men. The attack on Bróðir by his own weapons was a clear sign that the battle would go against him. And the ravenous birds were the demons Bróðir had once believed in when he was a deacon dragging him down to Hell.

Afterward, Bróðir had the sound blocked with ships, as he didn't particularly like Óspakr's interpretation of the omens and planned to kill him in the morning. Óspakr saw the line of ships cabled to the shore, and it did little to improve his presence of mind. He knew that Bróðir was trying to prevent his escape. He then vowed to be a Christian and to follow King Brian.

Óspakr ordered his men to cover their ships and to pole them quietly along under darkness. They cut the cables of Bróðir's vessels and waited for them to drift from shore while their crews slept on board. Óspakr and his men were then able to escape and headed straight for Ireland, travelling to Kincora to warn the High King about the plot to overthrow him. King Brian took Óspakr under his protection and mustered forces.

Bróðir *means brother in Old Norse, but as he was a deacon at one time, it could have been the clerical form of address that he may ironically have continued to be called after he lapsed and became a heathen.*

Before Jarl Sigurðr set out for Ireland, he left his elder sons Sumarliði, Brúsi and Einar Wry Mouth in charge of Orkneyjar. The youngest boy Þórfinn was sent over to Scotland to be fostered by King Máel Coluim, his maternal grandfather.

Bróðir and his men were mustered ready for battle at Dyflin when Jarl Sigurðr arrived with his forces on Palm Sunday. As well as his own Orkneymen, the jarl had recruited warriors from Skýey, Ljoðahús, Sátíri and Dalar. Bróðir was curious to learn more about the upcoming battle and used divination and sorcery to find it out. He decided not to attack before Good Friday, as he had learned that he and all King Brian's enemies would die as a result. If the assault took place on the Friday, however, Brian would win the battle but lose his life.

King Brian refused to raise arms on Good Friday, but as the forces opposing him were drawn up in battle array, he had his army march out of Dyflin to meet them. On one flank was Ulfr Hreða, the king's brother, on the other Óspakr with the king's sons. In the centre was Kerthjalfad, King Brian's fosterson and the bravest of men. Behind his army, the king was guarded by a shield wall in respect of his wishes not to fight on that day.

The opposing forces were drawn up with Jarl Sigurðr in the centre, while Bróðir and King Sigtryggr held the flanks.

The battle started fiercely, with Bróðir slaying all before him until he came up against Ulfr Hreða. Ulfr attacked Bróðir with such force that he knocked him down twice, after which Bróðir retreated into the woods.

Meanwhile, Kerthjalfad cut through Jarl Sigurðr's army until he reached the standard bearer, whom he killed. Another man was then told to lift the banner and Kerthjalfad killed him too. The banner had been made by Jarl Sigurðr's Irish mother Eithne, a sorceress, and bore the figure of a raven in flight. Its quality was this – that it would bring victory to the one it was carried before, but death to the man who carried it, and that was certainly proving true.

Jarl Sigurðr told Þórsteinn Hallsson, an Icelander, to pick up the banner, but a man called Amundi the White warned him not to, as it was certain death to carry it. Jarl Sigurðr then turned to another man, Hrafn the Red, and ordered him to take up the banner, but Hrafn told him to carry his own devil.

The jarl tore the standard from its staff and tucked it beneath his clothing with the words: 'A beggar should carry his own bundle.'

He was killed by a spear shortly afterward.

Óspakr drove King Sigtryggr and what remained of the opposing army to flight.

As everyone else was running, Þórsteinn Hallsson suddenly stopped to tie the thong on his shoe.

Kerthjalfad asked him why he'd stopped.

'Because I can't reach my home in Iceland tonight,' said Þórsteinn, and Kerthjalfad took him under his protection.

Bróðir saw that King Brian's army was in hot pursuit of their fleeing foes and that the shield wall was now thinly manned around him. He burst out of the woods, hacked through the shields and attacked the king. Brian's youngest son Tann put out an arm to protect his father, but Bróðir's sword cut right through it and carried on to lop off the king's head.

When Ulfr Hreða and Kerthjalfad received the news that Bróðir had killed Brian, they turned back with their forces and had tree branches cut. They wanted Bróðir alive, and so they surrounded him and hemmed him in. Neither he nor his men could make any headway against the mass of branches, as their weapons couldn't break through the tangle, and so they were all overcome and slain.

Bróðir was taken to an oak tree, where Ulfr Hreða cut him open. He was then led about the tree with his entrails unwinding around it, and that's how he met his end.

Dyflin *is Dublin,* Skýey *is Skye,* Ljoðahús *is Lewis,* Sátíri *is Kintyre and* Dalar *is the Dales of Caithness.*

One of the most memorable scenes in Njáls saga *is the encounter between Þórsteinn Hallsson and Kerthjalfad. In the midst of bloody slaughter and widespread panic flight,* Þórsteinn's fatalistic *decision not to bother running and to tie the loose thong on his shoe instead persudes the curious Kerthjalfad to spare him.*

The brother of Brian Bóruma is referred to as Ulfr Hreða in the saga. Ulfr is the Norse name for wolf and Hreða means rowdy. A Norse name does not necessarily mean he had Norse blood, though there is a possibility. Rowdy Wolf *might simply have been a nickname given to him by the Norse. Canon John O'Mahony suggested that Ulfr was Brian's brother Cuiduligh.*

Bróðir's brutal death reminds one of the similarly gruesome viking execution known as the blood eagle that is described in Orkneyinga saga, Þáttr af Ragnars sonum *and other saga sources in which the victim's ribs are severed from the backbone and the lungs pulled out.* Orkneyinga saga *specifically refers to the practice as a sacrifice to the god Óðinn.*

In Cogadh Gáedhel re Gallaibh *Jarl Sigurðr Digri's death differs in that he perishes at the hand of Murchadh, Brian's son. Sigurðr's helmet strap is cut by a blow from Murchadh's right hand sword and his exposed neck slashed by a stroke of the sword in Murchadh's left hand.*

We take up the saga again, where disturbing visions are seen on Good Friday, on the day of the battle and in its aftermath…

In Katanes on Good Friday, a man called Dorruðr was outside when he happened to see twelve women riding towards a bower, where they dismounted and stepped inside. Approaching the bower, he peered through the window and saw the women gathered at a loom. It was weighted with the severed heads of men, while the warp and weft were formed of entrails. The shuttle was a sword and arrows were the battens. They chanted these verses:

Wide warped
boding slaughter,
blood rains on
the back beam's web.
Spread with spears
grey web of folk,
valkýrjur *fill the warrior weft*
with the red warp of Randver's
killer.

This web is woven of entrails
and hard weighted with dead men's heads.
Blood-spattered spears are the treadles,
iron-bound beams, arrows as battens –
let's weave this web of battle with our swords!
Goes Hilðr to weave, and Hjorðrimul,
Sanngriðr and Svipul, with swords bared.
Shafts will shatter, shields will burst,
hound-of-helms will bite the byrnies.

Wind we, wind we the web-of-darts
as the young king waged afore.

Forth shall we fare to the thick of the fray
where friends fight the foe.

Wind we, wind we the web-of-darts
where the battle banners are borne forth.
We shall not let his life be taken
the valkýrjur *alone select the slain.*
Wind we, wind we the web-of-darts
and faithfully follow the king to battle.
Men will see bloody shields
where Gunn and Göndul ward the thane.

Will seafarers hold sway the land
who erstwhile dwelt on outer nesses.
A brave king is doomed to die,
by point of spear the jarl now falls.

Will the Irishmen bear such bale
as ne'er to fade in the minds of men.
Woven now the web, reddened the wold,
the woe will travel far afield.

An awful sight beholds the eye
as blood-red rack passes overhead.
Warriors' gore bloodies the welkin
whene'er the shield maids
take to singing.

Well we have chanted many a charm
about the king's son: may it bring him luck!

Let he who listens learn them by heart
and speak the spells to spearmen after.

On bare-backed steeds we start out swiftly,
swords unsheathed and so away.

They ripped the woven cloth from the loom and rent it in pieces, each of them keeping the bit she tore off. Dorruðr came away from the window then and returned to his house. The women mounted their steeds and rode off, six to the south, six to the north.

Brand Gneistason witnessed a similar vision in the Færeyjar.

Blood spattered the priest's stole at Svínafell in Iceland on Good Friday so that he had to take it off. Also, on Good Friday at Þvatt River, the priest there is said to have seen an ocean abyss alongside the altar, full of frightening things, on account of which he could not say the prayers for a good while.

On Orkneyjar, a man called Hárekr appeared to see Jarl Sigurðr and some of his men. Hárekr mounted up and rode out to see the jarl, and he was spotted in the company of the jarl riding behind a hill, which was the last that was seen of Hárekr.

Jarl Gilli in the Suðreyjar had the dream of a man called Herfiðr, who told him he had just lately come from Ireland.

When the jarl asked him the news, he said:

I was there at the clash of warriors –
Swords keening in Ireland.
Sundered arms
in the struggle of shields.
Fierce the fray, I can tell –
*in the spear rain fell Sigur*ðr.
Blood from wounds unstaunched,
Brian won, but died.

Flosi and Jarl Gilli discussed the dream for a long time, and then a week later, Hrafn the Red came to them with news of the battle at Clontarf – the fall of King Brian, Jarl Sigurðr, Bróðir and the vikings.

'What news of my own men?' Flosi asked him.

'All slain,' answered Hrafn, 'but for your brother-in-law Þórsteinn Hallsson. He was spared by Kerthjalfad and is with him now. Hallþorr Gudmundsson was slain too.'

Flosi then told Jarl Gilli that he was leaving, as he had a pilgrimage to Rome to fulfil.

The jarl said that he could do as he pleased and supplied Flosi with a ship and everything else he required, along with a pile of silver. Flosi and his men sailed southward to Bretland and stayed awhile.

Færeyjar *is the Færoes,* Suðreyjar *is the Hebrides and* Bretland *is Wales.*

The twelve women in Dorruðr's vision are none other than the Valkýrjur, *daughters of the god Óðinn in Norse mythology, who choose the slain who will go to the warrior's afterlife in Valhöll. They are warrior women who signify different aspects of battle and control its outcome (see the author's book* The Viking Runes *for an in- depth study of the valkýrjur and other characters in ancient Norse belief).*

In the poem Darraðarljóð, *known as the* Lay of Darts *or* Lay of Dorruðr (Spear Fighter), *the valkýrjur weave the outcome of the battle on the sinister loom, each of them riding away with a ripped piece of the cloth when their work is done. They mimic the northern Fates or* Nornír *here, who are also described as literally weaving events. It is clear to see the significance of the loom, on which patterns are created, being linked with the unrolling of birth, life and death itself, the latter brought about by the cutting of the thread.*

Points of the poem explained:

The red warp of Randver's killer (a kenning for blood). *Hilðr and Hjorðrimul, Sanngriðr and Svipul, Gunn and Göndul (valkýrjur,* warrior women*). Hound-of-helms (*a kenning for axe*). Byrnies (ring mail hauberks). Web-of-darts (*the weaving of the battle. The *valkýrjur are weaving the battle's outcome on the macabre loom). A brave king* (Brian Bóruma, High King of Ireland). *The jarl now falls* (Sigurðr Digri, Jarl of Orkney). *Rack (*Cloud). *Welkin* (Sky, heavens). *Shield maids (*valkýrjur*).*

Hárekr's vision of Jarl Sigurðr and his men and his own disappearance while riding behind the hill in their spectral company is part of a familiar element in both Nordic and Gaelic belief in which the dead are seen accessing a hill or burial mound that serves as entry to the otherworld. In an earlier episode of Njáls saga, *a burial mound is seen open and illuminated and within it the dead hero Gunnar Hamundarson loudly chants a verse.*

Prophetic dreams are a regular feature in the saga material and usually have a gloomy, eldritch quality about them. That of Jarl Gilli is typical of the kind.

After the killing of Gunnar Lambason, Kári and his companions sail south to Caithness and stay with a worthy man called Skeggi at Freswick.

Kári Kills Kollr

Kári asked Skeggi to give him a vessel and Skeggi provided him with a longship and crew. Kári, David and Kolbein went aboard and sailed southward through Skotlandsfjörðr. They met men from the Suðreyjar there who gave them the news from Ireland, and of Flosi's departure with his men to Bretland. Kári was of a mind to go after them and said that anyone who was not happy about that could leave, but that his revenge on the Burners was not yet complete. Everyone chose to stay with him and they sailed southward to Bretland, putting in at an out-of-the-way creek.

That same morning Kollr Þórsteinsson went to town to purchase silver. Of all the Burners, he was a particular blow-hard. He had been courting a wealthy woman there in Bretland and looked set to wed her and settle down.

Kári went to town the same morning, and when he came upon Kollr, he knew him right away. Kári drew his sword and hewed at Kollr's neck. Kollr was counting silver at the time and he had just said 'ten' when his head was hacked from his shoulders.

Then Kári declared: 'Send the news to Flosi, that Kári Sólmundarson has killed Kollr Þórsteinsson. I give notice of his killing by my hand.'

Kári returned to the ship and told his companions of the deed. They sailed northward to Beruvík, where they laid up their ship, and then made their way to Hvítsborg in Scotland, where they stayed with Jarl Máel Coluim that year.

When Flosi got word of Kollr's killing, he had his body laid out and went to great expense over his burial.

Flosi never said one word against Kári.

Skotlandsfjörðr *is the Minch,* Suðreyjar *is the Hebrides,* Bretland *is Wales, Beruvík is Berwick and* Hvítsborg *is Whithorn.*

The saga does not go into any detail as to Kári's knowledge of exactly where to track Flosi and his men down in Wales, but we are to presume he got accurate information from the men he met in Skotlandsfjörðr.

Kári wastes no time with words but gets straight down to decapitating Kollr on the spot and then publicly declares his responsibility for the killing, as custom and the law requires.

Again, Flosi does not condemn Kári, who he respects as an honourable enemy doing what is expected of him.

Flosi's Pilgrimage

After that, Flosi sailed south to begin his pilgrimage and walked all the way to Rome. There he was shown such honour that he received absolution from the Pope, in return for which he handed over a large sum of money.

Then he returned by the east road, staying long in towns, and had great honour bestowed on him by powerful men. He was in Norway the winter after and stayed with Jarl Eiríkr until the time came around for him to sail, and the jarl provided him with much meal, and many other men treated him with generosity. He then sailed to Iceland and put in at Hornafjörðr, from where he set out home for Svínafell. He had then fulfilled all the terms of his atonement, both in his exile and payment in compensation.

Flosi was banished from Iceland after the Burning subject to satisfying certain conditions. Embarking on a pilgrimage to Rome became a common practice for those with a bloody past.

Kári and Flosi Reconciled

Now we have it to tell of Kári that the summer after, he boarded his ship and sailed southward to Normandy, where he began his pilgrimage, and fared on to southward, where he received absolution, returning by the western way. He sailed out from Normandy then, north over the sea to Dover, in England. After that, he sailed west, round Bretland, northward through the Scottish firths, and did not stop until he reached Þrasvík in Katanes, to Skeggi's house. There he gave the cargo ship to Kolbein and David, and Kolbein fared to Norway in it, while David stayed on in Friðarey.

Kári stayed the winter in Katanes, and out in Iceland that same winter his wife Helga died.

The next summer Kári got ready to sail for Iceland, and Skeggi provided him with a cargo ship and a crew. They were late setting out, but put to sea and had a long voyage, finally making Ingólfshöfði, where their ship was smashed to bits, though the crew survived. Then it started snowing fiercely.

Everybody then asked Kári what they should do, and he replied that they should make for Svínafell and test Flosi's hospitality. So, they set off for Svínafell in the teeth of the storm.

Flosi was there in the hall when they came in, and when he recognised Kári, he sprang up to embrace him and gave him the high seat beside him. He then invited Kári to stay there through the winter and Kári accepted. Things were then squared between them and they made peace. Flosi gave away his brother's daughter Hildigunna, once the wife of Höskulðr Hvítaness-Priest, to Kári, and they dwelt at Broadwater.

Men say with regard to Flosi's end that he sailed abroad when old to get timber for building a hall. He was in Norway that winter, but the next summer he was late in sailing, and folk told him his ship was not fit for sailing. Flosi answered that it was a fit enough vessel for a doomed old man, and when he got his goods on board, he put to sea and that ship was never seen or heard of again.

Bretland *is Wales,* Þrasvík *is Freswick,* Katanes *is Caithness and* Friðarey *is Fair Isle.*

Kári's wife Helga was the daughter of Njál.

The wrecking of Kári's ship and the rough weather forces him to seek shelter with his men at Svínafell, where Flosi resides, and it would seem that Fate brings about the reconciliation between the two men. Flosi welcomes Kári and strengthens the peace by giving his widowed niece Hildigunna to him in marriage. This closes the circle of revenge in a way, as it was the killing of Hildigunna's husband Höskulðr Hvítaness-Priest and the girl's bitter goading that had spurred on Flosi to move against Njál and his family in the first place.

In his last sea trip, returning from Norway, Flosi ignores warnings about the condition of his vessel and fatalistically sails out anyway, resigned to not getting back.

COGADH GÁEDHEL RE GALLAIBH

(War of the Gael with the Outlanders)

The following Irish text was written for the great grandson of Brian Bóruma, Muirchertach ua Briain, King of Munster between 1103 and 1113. It lauds the fame and exploits of Brian and the Dál gCais dynasty and interprets matters as a struggle with and ultimate triumph over the Gallaibh or vikings at Cath Chluain Tarbh *(Battle of Clontarf) in 1014. The manner of the narrative lionises the champions on the Irish side while presenting their enemies as all-round villains, in a similar manner to how the* Túatha De Danann *and their enemies the* Fomoire *are presented in the mythological texts* Cath Maige Tuired. *This has led to the battle being popularly viewed by many as a straightforward struggle between Gael and Norse, when in reality it appears to have been a mainly Irish conflict.*

Máel Mórda mac Murchada, King of Leinster and his nephew the Norse Irish Sihtric, King of Dublin opposed the Ard Rí Brian Bóruma and the Dál gCais of Munster together with his allies Máel Sechnaill of the Southern Uí Néill and the Norse-Irish Kingdoms of Limerick and Waterford, Dublin's rivals. Clearly there were vikings on both sides, and even those enlisted from the Isle of Man were split - Bróðir and his men fighting against Brian and Óspakr fighting for him. The Mormaer of Mar in Alba, Domnall mac Eimen mac Cainnech, was also fighting for Brian, suggesting a blood link or alliance. The conflict can therefore be seen as a battle for supremacy between Irish dynasties, the politics of which primarily involved native viking factions whose interests coincided with the side they chose to fight for. The term native can be justly applied to the vast majority of those vikings settled in Ireland who by 1014 would have been a blood mixture of Norse and Gaelic through generations of intermarriage, just like Sihtric, and in their own way part of Irish culture and society.

As with Brennu-Njáls saga, *the account of the battle in* Cogadh Gáedhel re Gallaibh *features supernatural elements and motifs, such as the appearance of Aoibhinn, the bean sídhe or fairy woman of the Dál gCais, who tells Brian of his coming death on the eve of the conflict, and the wild horde of sprites and furies hovering over the battle with screams and incitements. This is typical of early Irish heroic saga - the epic* Táin Bó Cúailnge *is a prime example - and it serves to heighten the drama by ramping it up to mythic proportions.*

CATH CHLUAIN TARBH (BATTLE OF CLONTARF)

'But there was one thing in particular that captured my attention there, when the armies first clashed and started piercing one another. There was a field and ditch between us and them, and the keen wind of the spring blowing over them toward us, and it was no longer than it takes to milk a cow or two that we bided there, when not one man of either host could recognise the other, though his son or his brother might be near him, unless he could tell him by his voice or knew where he was standing, we were so covered, both our heads and faces and our garb, with drops of bloody gore borne by the keen cold wind passing over them to us…'

- Máel Sechnaill mac Domnaill

The Sprites and Demons of Battle

Both the Icelandic saga and Gaelic heroic versions of Cath Chluain Tarbh *are peppered with supernatural battle visions. In* Brennu-Njáls *saga the grim manifestation of the valkýrjur at the bloody loom and other frightful imagery show the forces of the Otherworld involved in the conflict. Here in* Cogadh Gáedhel re Gallaibh *the sprites of the glens and demons of the air raise a cacophony over the contending armies.*

And there arose a wild, furious, headlong, frenzied, gloomy, dreadful, ravenous, grim, bellicose vulture shrieking and flapping over their heads. And there also arose the satyrs, the dimwits and maniacs of the glens, and the witches and sprites and the birds of primordial times, and the baleful demons of the air and sky, and the sickly cold-blooded spectral host, and they were screaming and matching the courage and contention of both sides.

The spectral host being referred to is probably what is known in Gaelic tradition as the Sluagh *(horde), a malevolent flock of restless spirits flying out of the west for the souls of the dead.*

The Badb or Irish battle fury, who often takes the form of a macabre witch or carrion crow also frequently haunts the fields of slaughter in the early Gaelic literature.

The Connachtmen Clash with the Outlanders

The battle is traditionally described as particularly fierce, loud and bloody. Here the warriors of Connacht attack a force of the Dublin vikings, with heavy losses on both sides.

The Connachtmen advanced against the outlanders of Áth Cliath, and each side set upon the other. And in the momentous destruction that ensued there on the plain, nearly all were slain, for of the men of Connacht, only one hundred survived, and of the outlanders of Áth Cliath, only twenty.

The Blood Fray of Murchadh and the son of Ebric

In this section two champions, the son of Ebric (probably Éirikr) *king of Lochlann* (Norway) *and the Irish hero Murchadh, Brían's son, who has killed Sigurðr Digri, Jarl of Orkney in the story, clash in the middle of the battle. The son of Ebric smashes his way into the battalion of the* Dál gCais, *tribe of King Brían, deals out numerous death blows and spreads disarray among them. On seeing this, Murchadh is heart-sore, and he fights his way through the vikings until he clashes ferociously with the son of Ebric in a bloody combat, and like dying animals still lethal, they deal death to one another.*

He grasped the top of the outlander's head and pulled his mail coat over it, and they fell to wrestling. Murchadh forced the outlander down under him, and taking up his enemy's sword, he thrust it three times through the ribs of his breast down into the ground. The outlander then dealt Murchadh such a cut with his knife that his innards tumbled out before him. Murchadh shuddered and collapsed, and they lay there, the outlander and Murchadh, until Murchadh severed the outlander's head.

The Route of the Outlanders

The battle rages all day until the resistance of the Leinster forces, the Dublin vikings and their overseas allies collapses in a disorderly rout. The viking ships, beached on the shore during low tide, are carried out to sea when the high tide returns, leaving many of the fleeing warriors floundering hopelessly after them in the sea, slaughtered by their pursuers or drowning as they are taken, exhausted, by the waves.

They continued in battle array, struggling from sunrise to evening. This is the same length of time it takes for the tide to go, to flood and to fill, for the outlanders came to the battle that morning when it was full tide, and at the end of the day the tide had returned again to the same extent when they were overthrown. And their ships had been swept away, so that they had no means of escape and only the sea to run to, after the Dál gCais killed all those in mail coats. A dreadful rout befell the outlanders and the Laighin, who retreated together. And they bawled out their pleas for quarter and howls of vanquishment and withdrawal and flight, but only the sea was open to them, as they had nowhere else to flee to, cut off as they were between the waters and Dubhgall's Bridge. So, they ran to the sea, like cattle in heat, from the sun and from gadflies, and they were closely and quickly pursued. And many of them drowned there in the waters, and lay floating in profusion by the hundreds, stupefied, after the sense and understanding left their bodies beneath the tremendous pounding blows and the bitter vehemence with which the Dál gCais and the Connachtmen, as well as many of the nobles of Erin, pursued them.

Toirdelbach, the son of Murchadh, son of Brian, chased them into the sea, and the force of the tidal wave threw him against the weir of Cluain Tarbh, and he drowned there, with an outlander beneath him, and while gripping an outlander in his right hand and another in his left, and a stake of the weir through him.

Then it happened that Brian's daughter, the wife of mac Amlaíb, remarked: 'It seems to me that the outlanders have won their inheritance.'

'What do you mean, woman?' asked mac Amlaíb.

'The outlanders are going into the sea, their natural inheritance,' she replied. 'I wonder if it is because of the heat that is on them, but if it is, they are not waiting to be milked.'

Mac Amlaíb then struck her.

Áth Cliath *is Dublin,* Dubhgall's Bridge *is a bridge of the River Liffey and* Cluain Tarbh *is Clontarf.*

Mac Amlaíb is Sihtric (Sigtryggr Silk Beard), the son of Amlaíb Cuarán. After being soundly beaten by Brian Bóruma at the Battle of Glen Máma in 999, he was given Brian's daughter Sláine in marriage as a way of forging peace between Munster and Dublin. It didn't work.

Brian's daughter is likening the fleeing vikings to cattle under heat-stress and needing to cool down.

The vikings are frequently referred to as wearing mail coats. The byrnie (from Norse brynja*) was generally ring mail armour covering the wearer from the upper arms to the upper thighs. Though mail armour was invented by the Continental Celts, Irish warriors usually fought without any such protection at this time. However, references in the legendary epic* Táin Bó Cúailnge *make mention of leather armour composed of layers of bullhide tough enough to repel missiles that may have been used by the Gaelic leadership.*

Geraldus Cambrensis, a Cambro-Norman historian and archdeacon writing in the 1180s, refers to the expertise of the Irish warriors with the tuagh catha or battle axe. Shorter-hafted than the viking axe, but just as deadly, it was wielded in one hand with such lethal power that the keen-edged heavy blade could cleave a helmeted head and hack through mail armour at a stroke.

The Dál gCais had become particularly famed for the use of such axes, wielded to devastating effect at Clontarf.

Death of the King

King Brian is in conversation with his attendant when the latter notices the approach of a party of outlanders. Brian asks what manner of people they are, and the attendant answers: 'A blue, stark naked people.' But Brian identifies them as 'the foreigners of the armour.' It turns out to be Jarl Bróðir, with two companions. It is possible that the blue, stark naked people the attendant refers to are Bróðir's companions – Irish warriors of the fiann type, raiders blue with woad. Bróðir would have worn mail coat armour. Brian rises from the cushion where he has been praying and draws his sword. Bróðir passes without noticing him. One of his companions, who has previously served Brian, identifies him as the king. But Bróðir takes him for a noble priest instead.

'By no means,' insisted the warrior, 'that is the great king, Brian.'

Bróðir turned around and brought up his bright, gleaming battle axe. Brian gazed at him and then swung at him with his sword, severing his left leg at the knee and carrying on down to cut off his right foot. Bróðir's axe then split Brian's head open, and Brian killed the second man that accompanied Bróðir, and they both fell by one another's hand.

Brian's death here in the Irish text differs from the account in Brennu-Njáls saga, *in which Bróðir breaks through the thinning shield wall around the king by surprise to decapitate him with a blow of his sword, and is later captured by*

Ulfr Hreða and Kerthjalfad to suffer the grisly death by disembowelment round the tree. Here Bróðir uses an axe and Brian confronts him with a sword, hewing off Bróðir's left leg and right foot, while the viking's axe cleaves the king's head as he falls.

The Slaughter of the Outlanders' Cattle

To both Gael and Norse an abundance of cattle equalled wealth and prestige and it was ever a coveted part of the plunder and spoils of war.

Donnchad had seized a prey of twenty-eight oxen, and they were taken to be slaughtered there on the green of Áth Cliath, and the sight of having their cattle killed in front of them so tormented the outlanders in Áth Cliath that they threatened to attack Donnchad and those of the Dál gCais who were with him. And a message was sent out from the son of Amlaíb, telling the Irish that they should take one ox out of every twenty, and to leave the bulk of the oxen behind.

Then Donnchad said: 'We were not in the pay of the son of Ímar before, nor shall we be from this day forward, for it seems to us that our enmity toward each other is now greater than ever.'

After that, any of the cattle still alive were killed there in front of the outlanders of Áth Cliath, but the outlanders left off any attack from fear of Donnchad and the Dál gCais.

Donnchad calls Sihtric the son of Ímar here, citing the King of Dublin's ancestor and founder of the Uí Ímair dynasty.

The twenty-eight oxen are clearly only a part of what the Dál gCais are taking for plunder, as Sihtric, who is in no position to bargain, is clearly referring to the Dublin cattle herds in general when he says that the Irish should take one out of every twenty and leave the rest.

The slaughtered oxen may be intended for a feast but seem to be meant more as a humiliation for Sihtric and those others watching. The Irish are slaying their livestock right in front of their eyes and contemptful of them doing anything about it. Not only have the Dublin vikings been beaten in arms, but they are being made to watch their wealth and the prestige that goes with it being ruthlessly diminished, in the same way that they have done to others countless times.

PART THREE

GORE GATHERED ON GLEAMING SWORD EDGE, TONGUES OF EAGLES OFTEN BLOODED…

ORKNEYINGA SAGA

(Saga of the Orkney Jarls)

ÞÓRFINNR THE MIGHTY

Þórfinnr Sigurðarson was Jarl of Orkney from c.1016 – c.1065. He was known as Þórfinnr inn riki (Þórfinnr the Mighty), the most powerful of the Orkney jarls, according to the famous Icelandic historian Snorri Sturluson. Þórfinnr's father was Sigurðr Digri and his mother Olith, daughter of Mael Coluim Forranach (The Destroyer), Ard Rí Albann *or High King of Alba. When Sigurðr fell, carrying his raven banner at the Battle of Clontarf in 1014, Þórfinnr was being raised by his grandfather Máel Coluim, who made him jarl or mormaer of Caithness and Sutherland. Þórfinnr thus spent his earliest years in the wardship of the House of Ailpín, no doubt strongly influenced by that powerful Pictish Gaelic dynasty. He was later fostered by Þórkel Amundason, who would prove to be both a loyal retainer and formidable enforcer.*

We take up the saga here after the fall of Þórfinnr's father in battle. A precocious, belligerent and acquisitive child, he loses no time in making demands…

Division of the Jarldom

With the fall of their father Jarl Sigurðr in battle, his three eldest sons Sumarliði, Einar Wry Mouth and Brúsi, divided the jarldom between them. Þórfinnr, the youngest, was just five winters old at the time, being raised by his grandfather, Máel Coluim King of Scots. The king made Þórfinnr jarl of Katanes and Suðrland, with picked men to guide him.

It so happened that Sumarliði, the oldest of the brothers, died in his bed. Þórfinnr, who was growing into a bold and ambitious child, then claimed Sumarliði's share of Orkneyjar. Einar was having none of this, pointing out that his little brother already had Katanes and Suðrland, which were included in the jarldom, and indeed made up a third of it.

Brúsi, the most easy-going of the brothers, was happy with the share he already had and didn't mind if Þórfinnr got what he wanted. Einar was less accommodating and took his dead brother's share for himself. He proved to be a hard and unpopular ruler, levying taxes on the farmers to such an extent that it led to great hardship and famine.

Those living on the islands where Brúsi ruled were far better off.

Katanes and Suðrland (*Caithness* and *Sutherland*).

Þórkel Amundason

There was a man called Amundi, who had a farm at Sandvík in that part of the jarldom ruled by Einar. Amundi was a wise man, wealthy, influential and well-liked, so it was no great surprise when the disgruntled farmers asked him to talk to the jarl about all the dues and duties he was imposing on them.

Amundi was far from convinced that this was a good idea, as Jarl Einar was so hard to deal with. He advised them not to get on the wrong side of the jarl, who was only likely to make their lives even more miserable.

The farmers then had a word with Þórkel, Amundi's son, who eventually gave in to their pleas after a lot of persuasion. Amundi didn't think this too sensible. Nevertheless, Þórkel went with the farmers to meet Jarl Einar, who was getting ready for one of the viking expeditions their taxes were paying for. He explained to the jarl how much the farmers were suffering and asked him to be a bit more lenient with them.

Jarl Einar seemed to take this well enough and replied that although he had originally meant to have six ships for the expedition, he would now take only three. He then warned Þórkel not to ask him for anything else.

The farmers were well pleased with what Þórkel had done for them, but the next spring following his viking trip, Jarl Einar laid another heavy tax on his subjects and Þórkel spoke once again on their behalf. This time the jarl flew into a rage and told Þórkel that he had only made matters worse, and that only one of them would be around for the next assembly.

When Amundi learned how things had turned out, he thought it would be a good idea for Þórkel to put some distance between himself and the jarl. The upshot was that Þórkel crossed over to Katanes and joined Jarl Einar's little brother Þórfinnr. Þórkel raised the boy and that's how he came to get the nickname Fóstri, the Fosterer.

Sandvík *is Sandwick on Mainland, Orkney.*

Einar's father Sigurðr grew popular for restoring the land rights to all the farmers on Orkney. Einar, on the other hand, lays heavy taxes on them to finance his regular viking expeditions. Þórkel's good nature and sense of justice in standing up for the farmers puts him on a collision course with Einar.

Þórfinnr and Einar at Odds

Þórfinnr celebrated his coming of age by repeating his claim for one *þriðjungr*, or third, of the islands, something his elder brother Einar took a rather dim view of. So Þórfinnr started raising an army. When Jarl Einar got word of this, he mustered his own forces and set out to confront his little brother, but Jarl Brúsi came between them and persuaded them to come to peaceful terms. The result was that Þórfinnr got his third of Orkneyjar while his elder brothers put their own thirds together to rule in common. If either Brúsi or Einar died, the two thirds would fall to whoever survived the other. Þórfinnr picked stewards to govern his third of Orkneyjar and continued to spend most of his time in Katanes.

It was a custom among the Gael for a chieftain or king that came of age to prey upon the territory and possessions of an enemy. Þórfinnr's grandfather Máel Coluim may have carried out such a creach rígh *or royal prey when he invaded Bernicia in 1006. Þórfinnr, possibly influenced by the advisors his grandfather has chosen for him, or indeed by his grandfather himself, coincides this important rite of passage with a renewed demand for the late Sumarliði's share of Orkney, and is clearly able to draw on the powerful military resources of Máel Coluim to threaten his big brother. Probably facing a greater force and persuaded by the peace-making efforts of Brúsi, Einar backs down and Þórfinnr gets Sumarliði's share.*

Jarl Einar would often go on viking trips, but the meagre spoils he accumulated on his raids hardly seemed worth the effort. During one of these expeditions, a raid in Ireland, he was beaten by King Konofogor at Ulfreksfjorðr and lost a lot of men.

The following summer a man called Eyvindr Úrar Horn was leaving Ireland for Norway when his ship was hit by bad weather near Orkneyjar. Eyvindr and his crew put in at Ásmundarvagr on Meginland while the storm raged. Eyvindr was a retainer of King Óláfr Haraldsson and held in high esteem. Jarl Einar received the news, gathered his men and ordered Eyvindr seized and killed. Most of the crew were allowed to live, however, and in the autumn, they continued on to Norway, bringing the news of

Eyvindr's murder to King Óláfr. The king didn't say much, but it was clear that he considered Eyvindr's killing a personal loss and a grave crime.

Ulfreksfjorðr *is Lough Larne,* Ásmundarvagr *is Osmundwall and* Meginland *is Mainland, Orkney.*

*Eyvind Úrar Horn had previously supported King Konofogor (*Gaelic *Conchobor) against the Orkneymen. According to* Óláfr Haraldsson's saga, *Jarl Einar was angry at the Norse who had sided with Konofogor before and smarting from his recent defeat by the Irish king, jumped at the opportunity for revenge.*

Þórkel Fostri went north to the islands to collect Þórfinnr's tributes but returned sharp to Katanes when he was warned that Jarl Einar planned to kill him. Einar blamed Þórkel for stirring things up against him when his little brother Þórfinnr claimed his share of Orkneyjar.

'Only two ways are open to me,' Þórkel told his foster son back in Katanes. 'Either I have it out with Jarl Einar and settle things, or I get as far away from him as I can.'

Þórfinnr could tell that it was only a matter of time before things came to a head between his foster father and Jarl Einar, his brother. So he advised Þórkel to leave for Norway, where he would be held in high esteem, and that he should speak with King Óláfr. Þórkel accepted the advice and set off for Norway, where he stayed with King Óláfr all winter. The king thought very highly of Þórkel and often followed his counsel. On the subject of the jarls it was plain for King Óláfr to see that Þórkel favoured Þórfinnr over Einar, and not without good reason.

Removing a Rival

King Óláfr sent a message of goodwill to Þórfinnr in the spring with a request for him to come to Norway. Þórfinnr accepted the invitation and set sail and on his arrival received a friendly welcome from King Óláfr. Þórfinnr was an honoured guest for most of the summer and King Óláfr gave him a present of a big well-equipped longship. Þórfinnr then gave his foster father Þórkel the ship he had come over to Norway in, and they sailed back home in fine style, having established good relations with King Óláfr.

Óláfr Haraldsson was King of Norway from 1015 until 1028. He was killed at the Battle of Stiklestad in 1030 and was later made a saint.

That autumn Þórfinnr sailed to Orkneyjar with his foster father, provoking Jarl Einar, who started mustering forces. Jarl Brúsi once again made peace between his two brothers, upon which they took oaths. In the spirit of reconciliation, it was agreed that Þórkel Fóstri and Jarl Einar should patch up their differences by each providing a feast for the other.

Þórkel arranged the first one, a bounteous affair at Sandvík, yet even though he had provided the best of everything, Jarl Einar wasn't in the mood to appreciate it, and when the feast came to an end he seemed impatient to be off. The plan now was for Þórkel to accompany the jarl to the banquet he was supposed to be organising, but he was suspicious of Jarl Einar and had some of his men check the route they were to take. They returned to tell Þórkel that there were men waiting in ambush along the route at not one, but three separate places. It was obvious that the jarl was not to be trusted, and so Þórkel gathered his men. There was a door at either end of the feasting hall and he had them wait outside one of them while he kept going in and out of the other, appearing very busy.

Jarl Einar told him it was time to go, but Þórkel replied that he had a few things to take care of before he was ready to leave. Finally, he came back in and he had an Icelander with him called Hallvarðr from the East Fjords. Hallvarðr shut the door while Þórkel strode up to where Jarl Einar was sitting by the long fire.

The jarl asked him if he was ready yet. Þórkel said that he was and gave the jarl a hard strike to the head, knocking him to the floor.

Hallvarðr pretended to upbraid Jarl Einar's men for not pulling him out of the fire, then slipped the curved blade of his Irish axe under the jarl's neck and hoisted him back on the bench. He then followed Þórkel out the other door, where his men were waiting ready.

Jarl Einar's followers could see that he was dead but made no move against his killer. For one thing they were taken by surprise at what had just happened, and for another most had laid aside their weapons for the feast, while Þórkel had strong support from his comrades and better luck.

With no respect for the hospitality shown and his heavies waiting to ambush Þórkel after the feast he has laid on, Einar is clearly not to be trusted, and honour demands that things can only end one way.

Hallvarðr carries an Irish axe. With its curved blade and shorter haft, it was every bit as effective as a viking one and could be wielded in one hand.

King Óláfr Lays Claim

After this, Þórkel sailed off to Norway and stayed the winter with King Óláfr. As has already been told, Jarl Einar had executed Eyvindr Úrar Horn, a man the king thought very highly of, so he was not the least bit put out by the news that the jarl had himself been killed.

Back in Orkneyjar, Jarl Brúsi took over his dead brother Einar's share of the islands, in accordance with their previous agreement. But Þórfinnr was of the opinion that he and Brúsi should split the jarldom between them, and so he claimed half the islands. Brúsi was having none of it and stated that he was only keeping to what had been agreed. Þórfinnr said that a third of the jarldom should be sufficient for Brúsi, alluding to his peace-loving temperament. However, with neither one prepared to budge on the matter, all attempts by others to reconcile the two fell by the wayside.

Einar is barely below ground before Þórfinnr claims an even greater share of the jarldom, alienating his surviving brother Brúsi, of whom he clearly does not have a high opinion.

Brúsi sailed off to see King Óláfr, as he knew that he couldn't successfully stand up to his little brother, given Þórfinnr's superior resources as well as the armed support of his grandfather, the King of Scots. He took his son Rögnvaldr with him, then ten winters old.

When he reached Norway, Brúsi explained to King Óláfr that his jarldom was under threat and appealed for his help in maintaining it. King Óláfr replied that King Haraldr Hárfagri had originally taken Orkneyjar, Hjaltland and the Suðreyjar and appointed the first jarl in the islands, which were held in fief. And that, for example, the jarls paid homage to Eiríkr Blood Axe when he visited Orkney with his sons.

'Your own father, Jarl Sigurðr submitted to my kinsman Óláfr Tryggvason,' he told Brúsi. 'So, as long as you become my man and pay me homage in turn, you can have the islands in fee.'

It would then be decided which had the more weight, he said, his backing of Jarl Brúsi or King Máel Coluim's support for Þórfinnr. If Brúsi refused to comply, added Óláfr, he would take control of all the *uðal* rights for himself.

Jarl Brúsi now realised what a difficult position he had placed himself in by seeking King Óláfr's support. He discussed the matter with his followers but had to concede that the king had the upper hand. The upshot was that he swore fealty to King Óláfr and lost direct control of his jarldom thereby.

Hjaltland *is Shetland and* Suðreyjar *is the Hebrides.*

Uðal *rights were allodial rights, free of bonds or liabilities or written title deeds, originating from a first settler's land claim.*

Unable to realistically defy his little brother, Brúsi seeks the backing of the King of Norway and unwittingly imperils his fragile hold over the jarldom even more when the latter asserts his royal claim over it.

King Óláfr's Ultimatum

When Þórfinnr heard that Brúsi had gone to Norway seeking King Óláfr's help, he was not overly put out by the news. He had faith in the good relations he had enjoyed earlier with the king and was confident about receiving the support of other important people. With this in mind he set sail hard at his elder brother's back, intending to give Brúsi as little time as possible with King Óláfr before he himself turned up seeking an audience.

He was of course too late, as the king had already settled the affair in a manner neither one of them had quite suspected. King Óláfr now had complete control of Brúsi's jarldom and wanted Þórfinnr's share as well on the same grounds – that his forebears had always held royal authority over the islands, with the jarls ruling them in trust. He expected Þórfinnr to pay him homage as his elder brother had done, and again cited the instance of Þórfinnr's father Jarl Sigurðr having paid homage to his predecessor Óláfr Tryggvason.

Þórfinnr knew that his father hadn't had much choice in the matter, as he was being threatened with death at the time. Jarl Sigurðr and his people had also been forced into Christian baptism by Óláfr Tryggvason and his young son Hvelp taken hostage. The boy had died shortly after he was taken to Norway, and Jarl Sigurðr had refused to pay homage from then on.

Þórfinnr realised what a tricky situation he was in and decided to try a ploy. He told the king that he would be pleased to give him support when needed, but that he couldn't pay him homage.

'I'm already subject to the King of Scots,' he explained, on the grounds that he was unable to serve two rulers, being a jarl of King Máel Coluim.

King Óláfr wasn't satisfied with Þórfinnr's answer. He warned him what would happen If he did not comply with the demands as his brother had. 'I'll appoint a jarl of my choosing to govern the islands, in which case I'll want you to relinquish all claim to Orkneyjar and cause no further trouble.' He would expect him to swear oaths to that effect.

Þórfinnr asked the king for time to think over the matter, as he had to seek the advice of his friends, and the king granted that. Then Þórfinnr pushed it a little further by asking the king to grant him till next summer, as he wished to go back home.

'All those who counsel me are there,' he said, 'and I'm only a young lad.'

But the king was having none of it and told him to decide there and then.

Þórkel Fóstri, who was still a guest of the king, sent men discreetly to the boy jarl, advising him not to think of parting from King Óláfr without settling things in the manner demanded of him, as he was in the king's hands.

Þórfinnr could see that there was no other option but to go along with what King Óláfr wanted, though it struck him as a poor choice to give up his heritage and swear an oath that those without a natural right to the jarldom should enjoy it without contention. Yet since he was in doubt as to whether he would be allowed to leave otherwise, he gave himself over to the king's hand and agreed to be his vassal, just as his elder brother Brúsi had done.

However, King Óláfr could tell that Þórfinnr had a much bolder spirit than Brúsi, and so had less trust in the boy jarl's promises, given the backing Þórfinnr could expect from the King of Scots if he broke the agreement. Brúsi had bowed to Óláfr's terms all unwillingly and promised no more than he was forced to. For his part, Þórfinnr seemed glad enough about every condition now that his mind was made up, and no longer wriggled like a fish on a hook over what King Óláfr expected. But the king doubted whether he would keep his word.

This episode serves to illustrate the difference with which Þórfinnr and his father Sigurðr before him view their position in the islands compared with the royal claims of the Norwegian king. The latter argues that his ancestors originally took possession of the islands and appointed jarls to govern them in the name of the crown. But Sigurðr, half Irish, a heathen, and with closer connections to a Norse-Gaelic world where his authority was strong rather than to a distant Norwegian king demanding his obeisance, had (rightly or wrongly) come to see the islands as his own, and had passed this understanding on to his sons, of whom Þórfinnr, the youngest, embraced it the most. He has initially been willing to enjoy dealings with the King of Norway for what he might get out of it, just as he enjoys the benefits of being the grandson of the King of Scots, whose army he can frequently threaten people with, but now all that he holds dear is in jeopardy while he is in Óláfr's hands.

King Óláfr's Ruling

Once King Óláfr had mulled the matter over, he had them blow the trumpets and summoned both jarls to a great gathering.

Then he said: 'I will now declare the settlement between the jarls of Orkneyjar and myself. They have acknowledged my absolute right over Orkneyjar and Hjaltland and have become my vassals, binding their allegiance with oaths. I will now give to Brúsi in fief one *priðjungr* of the islands and one to Þórfinnr, as they have already held. That *priðjungr* that belonged to Jarl Einar I take for myself, since he killed my retainer and comrade-in-arms Eyvindr Úrar Horn. And that lot of the land I will do with as I please. The next thing I lay on both you brothers, my jarls, is that you accept an atonement from Þórkel Amundason for the slaying of your brother Einar, and I wish to lay down the terms of the atonement, if you are agreeable.'

The brothers said yes to this, as to every other condition already laid before them by the king.

Then Þórkel stepped forward and accepted the king's judgement, and at that point the meeting came to a close.

King Óláfr awarded an atonement for Jarl Einar equal to that for three king's thanes, but on account of the jarl's own offences, a *priðjungr* of this account was to be disregarded.

Þórfinnr then asked leave of the king to go, and as soon as it was granted, lost no time in getting himself ready for the trip back home. On the day he was about to set sail, the boy jarl was drinking aboard ship when Þórkel

Amundason approached stealthily, laid his head on Þórfinnr's knee and put himself at the mercy of his foster son.

Þórfinnr asked him what he was about. 'The king's judgement has already settled things between us,' he said. 'So, get on your feet.'

Þórkel rose and said that he would accept the settlement King Óláfr made in respect to Brúsi, but that he was ready if Þórfinnr should choose to have his own way in the matter.

'Though the king has granted me my estates in the islands and the right to bide there, I ken your mettle well enough that I could never fare to Orkneyjar without your goodwill.'

He then bound himself to promising that he would not go to the islands, whatever King Óláfr had said on the subject.

The boy jarl was quiet at this and slow to speak. Finally, he said: 'If you wish my judgement on the matter rather than the king's, then you should indeed accompany me to Orkneyjar, bide with me there, and never part from me without my leave, and that you should guard my lands and do all those things that duty demands as long as we both live.'

'You shall have that, my lord,' Þórkel said, 'as well as anything else in which I have a say.'

Þórkel then bound himself to this with formal oaths, and Þórfinnr said that he would make his judgement in regard to the death fine for his brother Einar later. Þórkel then accompanied the boy jarl, who set sail as soon as he was ready. Þórfinnr never saw King Óláfr again.

In this brief episode Þórkel Fóstri's loyalty and dedication to the young jarl could not be any clearer. He is confirmed in his role of guardian, protector and enforcer by solemn oath.

Brúsi was slow to leave and took more time in his preparations. Before he fared away, the king met with him and said: 'It looks to me, jarl, that you are like to be my faithful vassal west-over-sea. So, I want you to have the two thirds of the islands that you had before, and that you should be a man of no less standing, nor less powerful than you were before, now that you have given yourself into my hand. But to ensure your loyalty, I want you to leave your son Rögnvaldr here. I would see then, that with two thirds of Orkneyjar and my trust, you should hold your own against your brother Þórfinnr.'

Brúsi accepted the two thirds with thanks. He stayed on a little longer and then sailed out, reaching Orkneyjar about autumn.

Rögnvaldr Brúsason was left behind with the king. He grew to be one of the fairest of men, with a fine head of silken blonde hair. Not only was he tall and strong but came to be renowned also for his wit and courtly ways. He bided with King Óláfr a long while.

Óttar the Black composed this ode to the king:

Kent well among thy thanes,
brave boys of Hjalti's land,
secured ye a handy realm
of folk lords;
No ruler before you on this earth,
warrior king,
bowed beneath his yoke
the isles of the west.

Óláfr's skáld positively crows over his king's acquisition here, and for good reason. With Brúsi effectively putting himself at the king's mercy, Óláfr seizes the opportunity by laying claim to all of the islands, clips Þórfinnr's wings, gets restitution for the killing of his man Eyvindr, confirms Brúsi's wardship over the two thirds of the islands along with his backing, and takes Brúsi's son as hostage to ensure loyalty.

On returning to the west and Orkneyjar, the brothers took up once again the rule of their lands, Brúsi having his two thirds and Þórfinnr one. Þórfinnr was always in Katanes and Scotland, but had men appointed to take charge of the islands on his behalf. Brúsi kept guard over the isles. At that time they were always being warred on, for Norsemen and Danes, raiding in the west, often came there to take this or that ness. Brúsi was not happy that his younger brother Þórfinnr contributed nought to the defence of Orkneyjar and Hjaltland yet kept his share of the tributes and dues. Then Þórfinnr made an offer, that Brúsi should take one *priðjungr* of the islands while Þórfinnr took two and the overall duty of warding the jarldom. This didn't come about right away, but gradually came into being, that Brúsi ended up with one third, while Þórfinnr got two. This happened at the time Knútr ruled Norway and King Óláfr had been forced to quit the land.

Óláfr was driven into exile in Kievan Rus by King Knútr inn ríki of Denmark and the Norwegian nobility in 1029. With Óláfr no longer in a position to enforce his authority over the islands and Brúsi vulnerable in his inability to stem the piracy in his territory, Þórfinnr takes advantage and secures the two thirds of the islands in return for protecting them from the Norwegians and Danes.

After the death of Máel Coluim the Destroyer, High King of Alba, Þórfinnr's grandfather, the saga tells us that a certain Karl Hundason takes the throne. There has been some speculation as to the identity of Karl Hundason, and indeed if he was even king of Alba as is suggested rather than a mormaer or king of Moray. Nowhere else is his name mentioned. The name itself is Norse. Karl is derived from Háriolus or Army, which carries some irony, since the man in question was a repeated failure in battle. Hundason means Hound Son, which might be construed as an insult by some, though personal names of a canine nature in early tradition often suggested positive attributes such as faithfulness, hunting ability or tenacity.

Both Eben William Robertson and William Forbes Skene considered Karl Hundason one and the same as Donnchad mac Crínán (Duncan I, King of Scots). There is good reason for this. Donnchad's father was Crínán of Dunkeld, known as The Hound Earl, which would naturally make Donnchad Hundason in Norse terms. He was Þórfinnr's cousin, as was Macbeth, Donnchad's enemy.

Karl Hundason (or Donnchad) demands tribute from Þórfinnr for Caithness and Þórfinnr refuses on the grounds that he has been given the territory by his grandfather, Máel Coluim, the late High King of Alba. The conflict that ensues between them takes up a good part of the saga concerning Þórfinnr and is characterised by Karl's stubborn but futile invasions and the repeated defeats he suffers going against his cousin, the Orkney jarl.

According to a theory of Skene, the cousins Þórfinnr and Macbeth defeated Donnchad together and split the kingdom between them – Þórfinnr taking the north and Macbeth the title of king and the old heart of the Picto-Scottish realm based at Scone, to which Gruoch, his queen, had a natural claim through her family line. The Scottish scholar Donald A. Mackenzie supported this theory, as did Professor Gordon Donaldson.

The control of Caithness and adjoining territories had been an issue between the Orkney Norse and the rulers of Moray for generations. Máel Coluim, whose power appears to have extended much further north than previous High Kings of Alba, had appointed his grandson Þórfinnr mormaer of these territories because it made good sense. Because of his blood, Þórfinnr could represent both Orkney and the House of Ailpín against its long term rival the House of Loairn, and Máel Coluim could maintain control of the north through him. Máel Coluim had no surviving sons of his own and had chosen Donnchad, the son of Crínán and his daughter Bethóc, to succeed him. Not the best of choices.

We take up the saga here after Máel Coluim dies. Donnchad (Karl Hundason) takes the throne and demands tribute from Þórfinnr for Caithness, provoking a fight and knowing that this will give him a pretext to invade and install his nephew Muddan (Gaelic Máel Dúin) as mormaer. The immunity from raids by the Orkney Norse that Alba had enjoyed during Máel Coluim's reign is now well and truly over.

Karl Hundason

Jarl Þórfinnr made himself an outstanding chief. He grew to be among the tallest and strongest of men, ugly, black-haired, sharp-featured, with a big nose and rather scowling brows. He was mighty in the fray, grasping for gold and honour, having both luck and skill in battle. He was five winters old when his mother's father, Máel Coluim King of Scots made him jarl and lord of Katanes, as was said before, and at fourteen winters he was raiding the realms of other chieftains. In the words of Arnórr Jarlaskáld:

The lord amid helmet crash
reddened broadsword edge,
ere fifteen full winters,
reddened ravens' talons;
brave lord, brother kin to Einar,
wins and wards worthy land,
no man better
below sky.

Jarl Þórfinnr got strong backing from his grandfather, the King of Scots, and his power in Orkneyjar was significantly bolstered by having that backing so near at hand. King Máel Coluim breathed his last at the time Þórfinnr and his brother Brúsi were reconciled. Karl Hundason then took over the rule of Scotland and, in the manner of previous Scots kings, laid claim to Katanes as well, from which he expected to receive tribute just like the money he was paid from other parts of his realm.

Þórfinnr refused to pay any tribute for Katanes, which he saw as his by right from his mother's father, who had given it to him. So, a great feud arose from this, with each of them harrying the other's realm. King Karl had it in mind to set up Mumtan or Muddan, his sister's son, in Katanes, with the title of jarl. Then Muddan rode on Katanes and mustered forces in Suðrland.

Þórfinnr got word of this and gathered forces from all over Katanes. He was joined by Þórkel Fóstri with a strong host from the islands. Þórfinnr then advanced on Muddan with a far bigger army. On seeing this, the Scots would not stand and, deciding to retreat, rode back to Scotland. Þórfinnr pursued them, took Suðrland and Ross into his power, and raided Scotland far and wide. He then returned to Katanes and Þórkel went back to Orkneyjar. The levies of the folk likewise fared home.

Though Þórfinnr is said to have been made jarl or mormaer over Katanes *and* Suðrland *(Caithness and Sutherland) by his grandfather Máel Coluim, Muddan is able to draw on forces from Sutherland at this time, which would suggest it had come under the control of Karl Hundason (Donnchad). It does not remain in his grasp for long however, as Þórfinnr promptly takes it back.*

Dungalsbær *(Duncansby),* Beruvík *(Berwick),* Péttlandsfjörðr *(Pentland Firth),* Dyrnes *(Deerness).*

Jarl Þórfinnr bided at Dungalsbær in Katanes, with five longships and just enough of a warband to man them.

Muddan visited King Karl at Beruvík and explained that his path to the north had been far from smooth. King Karl grew right wrathful when he found out that his realm had been harried, and without wasting any time, sailed north with eleven ships and a great host. Muddan was sent back to Katanes with a large following, to ride the high way through Scotland with the aim of trapping Þórfinnr between two forces. Karl, as it is told, never slackened sail until he reached Katanes, and there was not much space between him and Þórfinnr.

The jarl went aboard ship and sailed out into the Péttlandsfjörðr for Orkneyjar. Karl and his men could see Þórfinnr's sails as he headed east across the firth, so near were they, and immediately they set off in pursuit. Þórfinnr and his men had not noticed them and kept on sailing east for Sandvík. The jarl reached Dyrnes and sent word straight away for Þórkel to muster forces. Brúsi was in the northern half of the isles. Þórfinnr lay under Dyrnes, having arrived there late. But at first light the jarl and his men saw Karl's eleven ships advancing toward them. There were but two choices to hand – jump ashore and abandon his ships and goods to the foe or head out to confront them and let destiny decree the outcome. Þórfinnr told his men to get their weapons ready. He had no intention of fleeing and ordered them to row against the enemy. Then both sides lashed their ships together. Þórfinnr encouraged his men to mount a stout attack, as he believed that few of the Scots would stand up to them. The struggle was long and hard, and it was difficult to tell how the day would end.

Þórfinnr's confidence against greater numbers is justified in that his forces are in their home waters, with swifter, more manoeverable ships, and his faith in his own courage and in his men's superiority as sea battlers is strong and unwavering.

Arnórr tells of the battle in his ode to Þórfinnr:

I trust our lord has taught at last
a lesson to mail-clad Karl,
east off Dyrnes,
prospered the prince's rule.
Full of wrath the chieftain, with five snakes of war
turned on the king's eleven,
spurning flight, he held his course with
stout heart.
The sea-goers laid their ships abroad,
foes fell along the thwarts,
blood bathed sharpened steel,
Scots' gore blackened.
The courage of the hero did not waver,
blades bit and bowstrings sang,
shafts shot, sweat in streams,
gleaming bright the spear points quaked.

Now Þórfinnr urged his men fiercely to keep up the fight, and his ship moved closer to Karl's. The Scots' resistance wavered before the mast of the king's ship as Þórfinnr leapt aboard, advancing from the fore deck to the stern and striking out ferociously so that the enemy ranks grew thin before him and he shouted for his crew to follow him on board. When King Karl saw what was happening, he gave orders for his men to cut the ropes, take to the oars and pull away. But the jarl's men threw more grappling hooks onto the king's ship and piled aboard in substantial numbers, carrying Þórfinnr's banner. King Karl managed to scramble aboard another vessel with those of his crew that survived the onslaught, though most of them had already been killed. He gave orders for it to pull away fast, with Þórfinnr in pursuit.

As Arnórr put it:

Short the fray
for that lord of renown,
spear points swift
drove foes to flight.
Over the army, badly battered,
the sea mew screamed, bird of battle.
Red swords sheathed in kings' men,
south of Sandvík fought and conquered.

King Karl retreated south to Breidafjörðr, went ashore there and began to muster forces.

Þórfinnr turned back home after the battle and Þórkel his foster father joined him, so they soon had a great army. They sailed down to Breidafjörðr after King Karl and started harrying the country there as soon as they landed. They then received word that Muddan was in the north at Þórsá in Katanes with a large force. He had sent for help from Ireland, where he had many allies and kinsmen, and now was waiting for them to join him. It was then decided that Þórkel Fóstri should take some of the host north to Katanes while Þórfinnr lay off Scotland with his ships and plundered there.

Þórkel advanced stealthily, as all the land folk in Katanes were loyal and true to him, and no word of his approach was given out. He reached Þórsá at dead of night, surrounded the house Muddan and his men were in and set it on fire. Muddan had been sleeping in the loft at the time, and when he jumped down off the balcony, Þórkel hewed at his neck, taking his head off. Muddan's men gave up the fight after that, though some fled. There had been a fair amount slain, but also many granted quarter.

Þórkel tarried a little while there before heading back to Breidafjörðr, his army reinforced with men from Katanes, Suðrland and Ros. He rejoined Þórfinnr south of Mýræfi and told him about his trip. The jarl thanked him for his efforts and they both lay off the country there, harrying inland.

Now to tell of King Karl, he went to Scotland after the battle with Jarl Þórfinnr and mustered fresh forces. He gathered an army from far and wide all over the south of Scotland and from Sátíri. He was joined by a host from Ireland that Muddan had sent for, a great force of chieftains to go up against the jarl, and he met Þórfinnr at Torfness south of Breidafjorðr.

Breidafjörðr *is the Moray Firth,* Þórsá *is Thurso in Caithness,* Mýræfi *is Moray,* Sátíri *is Kintyre and* Torfness *is probably Tarbat Ness.*

A mighty battle then took place, with the Scottish forces far greater in number. Þórfinnr advanced before his warband, wearing a gilded helmet, girt with a sword and wielding a great spear right and left. It is said that he was to the fore of all his men. He attacked the Irish first, and was so fierce in his onslaught that they gave way before him and failed to rally themselves after. Karl then had his banner borne aloft to confront Þórfinnr and a hard battle ensued, but the upshot was that the king fled, though some said that he fell there.

In the words of Arnórr:

Gore gathered on gleaming sword edge,
Torfness the place of battle,
waged by the chieftain, young in years.
Sang the thin blades to battle south
near Ekkjal,
the sea lord sharp and sure
fared against the Scots king.
Hjaltland's ruler bore high the helm
'mid spear crash,
in Irish blood his red blade dabbled.

The free-handed chief under British shield,
Kinsman of Hloðvér,
pitted his strength 'gainst the host,
set fire to their farms.

Þórfinnr attacks the Irish first, a great force led by powerful chieftains, as they have been specifically sent for by Muddan with the intent of swinging fortune in the Scots' favour. He knows that by overcoming the Irish forces, the morale of the enemy will collapse.

Arnórr makes mention of Þórfinnr using a British shield during the battle. This is likely to have been made by a Brythonic craftsman in one of the Cymric-speaking territories, such as Strathclyde or Lothian.

The line Kinsman of Hloðvér *refers to Þórfinnr, who was the paternal grandson of Hloðvér, father of Sigurðr Digri.*

As the maternal grandson and ally of Máel Coluim, Þórfinnr would have kept Alba's northern border secure. Now, with Máel Coluim gone and Karl (Donnchad) in his place, and with a hostile population making war on him and not to be trusted to keep their word in surrender, Þórfinnr goes on the rampage throughout his grandfather's former kingdom, burning, killing and taking prisoners as far south as Fífi or Fife.

Þórfinnr pursued the enemy deep into Scotland, and far and wide laid the country under his power, going as far south as Fífi. Wherever he went, he prevailed, and the folk surrendered. So, he sent Þórkel Fóstri away with some of his forces, and when the Scots got word of this, those who had given themselves up turned against the jarl. On hearing of their guile, Þórfinnr mustered his forces and advanced on the enemy. The Scots were half-hearted in their onslaught when they saw the jarl was ready for them. Þórfinnr moved to attack, but they would not stand and fled away into the woods and wastelands. Þórfinnr chased after the fleeing foe, and afterward told his men they could burn the land all around where they were as payment to the Scots for their enmity and guile. The jarl's men went among the hamlets and farms and set fire to them all so that not a cottage stood after. Any fighting men they found were killed, but the women and old folk fled into the woods and wastelands, weeping and wailing. Many of the people were taken captive and bound, then driven before them.

In the words of Arnórr:

Homesteads in blazes that day,
danger did not miss them,
flame flared over reeking roofs
throughout that land
warriors paid dearly.
Three times in one summer
the lord left them lacking.

After this Jarl Þórfinnr made his way back north through Scotland to his ships and laid the country under his power wherever he went. He fared to Katanes and bided the winter there. From then on, he had his levies out to raid the western lands every summer but would little bestir himself during the winter. The jarl became renowned for providing his retainers and many other notable men with meat and drink the winter through, so that no one needed to look for either inn or boarding house, just as lords and chieftains in other lands provided for their followers during Yule.

As Arnórr put it:

Through serpent scourge (winter),
Rögnvaldr's noble offspring
sipped at the lake of barleycorn,
shone with glory.

Rögnvaldr and King Magnús

It was at this time Jarl Brúsi passed away and Þórfinnr took over all of the Norðreyjar. But now we must say of Rögnvaldr, Brúsi's son, that he was at the battle of Stiklarstaðir when king Óláfr the Saint fell, and escaped with the rest of those that fled. He brought the king's brother Haraldr Sigurðarson sorely wounded out of the fight. Rögnvaldr left him in the small house of a freeman to be looked after while he fared off east over the Kjolen Mountains to Jemtland, and from there on to Sweden to see King Önundr. Haraldr bided with the freeman till he was recovered enough to follow after Rögnvaldr, and the freeman's son accompanied him as a guide. Haraldr wore a hood a lot of the time to conceal his identity as they travelled east to Jemtland and on to Sweden. While they were riding through some thickets Haraldr composed a stave:

From one wood to another
worthless I wander;
who knows if one day
I'll be widely known.

On arrival in Sweden Haraldr was reunited with Rögnvaldr Brúsason. They then went off to Garðaríki and they were accompanied by many folk who had been loyal to King Óláfr. For the sake of the hallowed king's memory they were made welcome in Holmgarðr by King Jarisleifr. He made all of them guardians of the land under Jarl Eilifr, son of Jarl Rögnvaldr Ulfsson.

Norðreyjar *is the Northern Isles,* Stiklarstaðir *is Stiklestad in Norway,* Garðaríki *is the Kingdom of Cities – Kievan Russia.* Holmgarðr *is Veliki Novgorod,* Miklagarðr *is Constantinople and* Aldeigjuborg *is Old Ladoga. King Jarisleifr is Yaroslav the Wise, Grand Prince of Rus (1019-1054).*

Rögnvaldr Brúsason bided in Russia while Haraldr Sigurðarson fared to Miklagarðr, and he had the wardship of the land in summer but stayed in Holmgarðr over winter. He was held in high regard by King Jarisleifr and the rest of the folk. Rögnvaldr was taller and stronger than most other men, very fair of face, a man gifted in many ways and none to match him. According to Arnórr Jarlaskáld, Rögnvaldr won ten pitched battles in Russia:

Like a fruitful tree in flourish,
and for battle as a war god,
ten times in Russia he prevailed,
shield-tested by sword storm.

Einar Thambarskelfir and Kálfr Árnason fared east to Russia, looking for Magnús, the son of the late King Óláfr. In Aldeigjuborg they encountered Rögnvaldr. It was Kálfr who had given King Óláfr his death blow, and Rögnvaldr was just about to go for him when Einar let him know why they were there. He explained that Kálfr greatly regretted killing the sainted king and wanted to make it up to his son Magnús by helping him become King of Norway, and that he would help him against the reigning Knútlings. On hearing this, Rögnvaldr settled down. Einar then asked him to accompany them to Holmgarðr to win the support of King Jarisleifr, and Rögnvaldr consented. They made their way to Holmgarðr and laid their case before King Jarisleifr, that the rule of the Knútlings in Norway had become unbearable, especially that of the queen, Alfífa, and that they could no longer serve them. They entreated King Jarisleifr to allow Magnús Ólafsson to rule them instead. Rögnvaldr backed them in this, as did Queen Ingigerðr and a good many other chieftains, but the king was in no hurry to hand Magnús over to the Norsemen, given their treatment of his father, the sainted King Óláfr. So, the upshot was that twelve of the noblest among the Norse swore an oath to King Jarisleifr that all was right and proper, that he could trust them in their intent. The king would not have Rögnvaldr take the oath, as he already trusted his word. Then Kálfr swore the oath to Magnús, vowing to follow him within the realm and without, and do everything Magnús considered best for his power. The Norsemen accepted Magnús as their ruler and bound themselves to him. Kálfr and his company bided in Holmgarðr till after Yule, then travelled to Aldeigjuborg, sailing out when the ice broke up in the spring. Rögnvaldr Brúsason went with Magnús. They travelled first to Sweden, as is told in King Magnús' saga, and afterward to Jemtland, then across the Kjolen Mountains to Veradalr. On arrival in Niðaróss all the people there swore their lealty to him. At Niðaróss during the *Eyraþing* he was recognised as ruler over the whole land. After that came about the dealings he had with King Sveinn, as is recounted in the *Lives of the Kings of Norway*.

Rögnvaldr has grown to adulthood at the court of King Óláfr and was there at the Battle of Stiklestad where the king was given his death blows by Kálfr and at least two others during the fight. Loyal to the king's memory, his first instinct is to attack Kálfr until Einar manages to restrain him.

The Knútlings referred to here are King Knút's son Svein and his English mother Ælfgifu (Norse Alfífa*) who ruled Norway badly from 1030 to 1035. Heavy handedness, oppressive taxes, and scarcity drove the Norse to rebel, and the hated pair were driven out, Svein dying of wounds in Denmark in 1036.*

Kálfr Árnason c.990-1051, was a prominent chieftain in Norway and later the Hebrides. Reputed as having landed a death blow to King Óláfr Haraldsson at the Battle of Stiklestad in 1030, he helped bring his son Magnús to the throne in 1035, as is referred to here.

On arrival in Norway, Rögnvaldr heard about the death of Brúsi his father, and that Jarl Þórfinnr now ruled the Norðreyjar. Rögnvaldr was keen to visit his homeland and asked leave of King Magnús to go. King Magnús could see he was right eager and stood by him in his intention. Bestowing on Rögnvaldr the title of jarl, he gave him three well-manned longships and also that third of Orkneyjar King Óláfr had owned and given to Rögnvaldr's father Brúsi. King Magnús promised to give Rögnvaldr his friendship and support whenever he required it, and that he was to consider the power of the king as his own to draw on at need.

The Meeting of the Jarls

Rögnvaldr Brúsason took ship out to Orkneyjar, fared first to the steadings which had been owned by his father, and sent Jarl Þórfinnr a message petitioning for that *priðjungr* of the islands which had been ruled by his father. In addition to this, he made it plain that he was also claiming that third of Orkneyjar that had been owned by King Óláfr, and he sought his kinsman Þórfinnr's acknowledgement of this. At that time Þórfinnr was very much at odds with foes from the Suðreyjar and the Irish and needed all the help he could get. He told the messengers that Rögnvaldr should take the third of the islands which he owned by right, 'but the *priðjungr* claimed by Magnús, that was given over then to King Óláfr when we were in his power, and not because we thought he had a right to it. So, we and our kinsman Rögnvaldr will agree more readily if we don't discuss that *priðjungr*, as it has been the cause of discord for a long time. But if Rögnvaldr will be a trusty kinsman to me and lend his strength, I deem my realm will be well served if he has that *priðjungr* for his enjoyment and for the greater strength of us both. His support is more value to me than any tax I get from it.'

The messenger returned to Rögnvaldr and said that Þórfinnr had given over to him the two thirds of the islands he had claimed in return for his support, as kinship demanded. In Rögnvaldr's opinion he had only laid claim to what he believed he had a right to. But since Þórfinnr had readily given over the lands, he agreed to be his ally and lend him his support as was proper for kinship's sake. So Rögnvaldr took the two thirds of the islands allotted to him, and that's how things stood that winter. But as soon as spring came around, Jarl Þórfinnr sent a message to his kinsman Rögnvaldr, asking him to go pillaging with him and to bring as many men as he could. On receiving this word, Rögnvaldr did not tarry, but mustered a host and a good many ships and went to meet Jarl Þórfinnr. Þórfinnr, who also had a strong force ready, welcomed him warmly and they undertook an alliance.

Raiding

That summer Þórfinnr and Rögnvaldr harried the Suðreyjar and Ireland and all about Scotland's western firths. Þórfinnr laid the land under his power wherever they went. They had a hard fight at a place called Vatnsfjörðr and a lot of men lost their lives there. They took the battle smartly to the enemy and won an outstanding victory.

In the words of Arnórr Jarlaskáld, who was present at the battle:

At Vatnsfjörðr was I

with my lord in muckle danger.

I ken his mettle well;

the warriors from the ships bore quickly the shield wall.

O'er the corpses of many a man

I saw the grey wolf gaping.

The hard battle here is fought at Loch Vatten (Vatnsfjörðr) on the Isle of Skye.

After that conflict, they returned to Orkneyjar and bided there in peace after winter. So, eight winters passed, with Rögnvaldr having his two thirds of the islands and no complaints from Jarl Þórfinnr. But when summer came round, they would go off raiding, sometimes together, sometimes on their own.

As Arnórr says:

The warrior was often busy,

Ireland's kindred dropped before him.

On British people he pounced,

fire blazed over the Scottish land.

The kinsmen were always on good terms when they met, and whenever tale bearers tried to cause trouble between them, they settled things amicably. Jarl Þórfinnr would bide most of the time in Katanes, while Rögnvaldr stayed in the isles.

It so happened one summer that Jarl Þórfinnr plundered in the Suðreyjar and the west of Scotland. He lay off Gaddgeðlar, where it borders on England. He sent a part of his force south into English land to procure and slaughter some cattle, as the Gaddgeðlar folk had fled, driving their livestock with them.

When the English got word the vikings were taking their cattle, they gathered together and attacked them, took back their livestock and killed all the best men, sparing a few runagates to tell Jarl Þórfinnr that this was how they put the vikings off their plundering. They added to the message some very scornful terms.

When Jarl Þórfinnr was told how badly things had turned out, he was far from pleased at the loss of his men, who were beyond his help now. But he stated his intention to pay the English back for their gibes and mockery over the matter. He added that they would part for now, but that if he was alive and kicking next summer, he would be paying them a visit.

Gaddgeðlar *is Galloway in what is now Southwest Scotland.*

The English, who come to regret provoking Þórfinnr here, are ruled by Hardeknútr (Hard Knot), son of Knútr inn ríki, who was King of Denmark from 1035 to 1042 and King of England from 1040 to 1042.

Þórfinnr Defeats the English

At that time Hardeknútr was ruler of England and Denmark. After the failed raid, Þórfinnr returned to Orkneyjar and wintered there. In the spring he mustered forces from all over his realm and asked Jarl Rögnvaldr to join him. Rögnvaldr agreed and also gathered forces. Jarl Þórfinnr raised a host from Orkneyjar and Katanes and a strong host from Scotland and Ireland. Many Hebrideans from the Suðreyjar also flocked to his banner. Leading this mighty force, he fared off down to England as he had vowed. Hardeknútr was in Denmark at this time. As soon as the jarls landed in England they harried and pillaged. The chiefs who were set to guard the land went against them with a force, and there was a hard and muckle battle, but the jarls prevailed. After this, they ranged far and wide throughout England, plundering, killing and burning farms wherever they pleased.

In the words of Arnórr:

That was one spear storm
the English would ever remember –
the ring-giving lord bore the greater
force to battle,

thin-ground blades bit stalwart warriors.
Rögnvaldr's men fared hard and undaunted under shield boss,
south of Mön, across the main,
on English land
the jarl his banner bore.
Tongues of eagles often blooded,
Men-at-arms carrying ensigns forward.
Fires flared up, the halls in blazes,
flame licked sky high, enemies fleeing
the forest foeman's dread glare.
Hard blew the war horns –
battle bold through burgs
advanced the ruler,
his banner billowing bravely
that rainy Friday,
dawn of battle,
warriors fierce he routed;
weapons flashing –
wolves were fattened.

Forest foeman *is a kenning for fire.*

Jarl Þórfinnr had two pitched battles against the English and gave them many a defeat forbye. He stayed for most of the summer, but returned to Orkneyjar in the autumn, and that's where he wintered.

Þórfinnr is not only fighting Scots and Irish but having to defend himself against other vikings in the Hebrides or Ireland. He is also sometimes in alliance with groups of Hebrideans, Irish and Scots, as in his campaign against the English here. Again, this is not simply a matter of Norse against Gael or Saxon. Many vikings in the west were either partly or mostly Gaelic by this time. In Þórfinnr's case, he has Gaelic blood through his mother Olith, who was a daughter of Máel Coluim, High King of Alba and from his father Sigurðr, who also had Gaelic blood from his Irish mother Eithne, a daughter of King Cerball.

New Developments

We take up the saga again with the arrival of Kálfr Árnason from Norway, fleeing King Magnús, who now wants him dead for landing one of the killing blows on his father, the sainted Óláfr, at the Battle of Stiklestad in 1030. Kálfr is the uncle of Þórfinnr's wife Ingibjörg, and his arrival with a big following puts an immediate strain on Þórfinnr's resources, setting up a collision course with Rögnvaldr over his larger share of the islands...

Around about this time Kálfr Árnason fled Norway to escape from King Magnús. He sailed west-over-sea to Jarl Þórfinnr, his nephew-in-law. Þórfinnr had to wife Ingibjörg Jarl's Mother, Kálfr's niece and the daughter of Jarl Finn Árnason. Kálfr held Jarl Þórfinnr very highly. Kálfr had a considerable following with him, and for the jarl to maintain them, it wasn't cheap. Many people gave their opinion that in the light of this extra expense, Þórfinnr shouldn't let Rögnvaldr keep the two thirds of the islands he then enjoyed. After that, Jarl Þórfinnr sent messengers to the isles to claim from Rögnvaldr that *þriðjungr t*hat had belonged to his elder brother Jarl Einar Wry Mouth. Rögnvaldr took counsel with his friends and advisors over this claim and then spoke to Þórfinnr's messengers. He said that the *þriðjungr* in question had been bestowed on him by King Magnús, who considered it his own father's heritage. He added that it was up to King Magnús which of the jarls should have it, but that as long as the king wanted him to hold on to that third, he had no intention of letting it go.

The messengers returned to Jarl Þórfinnr and told him how things had turned out. After what Jarl Rögnvaldr said, they couldn't see his claim being trouble free. Jarl Þórfinnr grew right wrathful at this and poured scorn on the idea that King Magnús should have a right to his late brother Einar's third. He added that he and Jarl Brúsi had only agreed to giving up the third to King Óláfr because they were in his power at the time and didn't have much choice in the matter, not because they believed he had any right to it.

He said that this was a fine way for Rögnvaldr to pay him back, considering Þórfinnr had let him enjoy that *þriðjungr* of the land for a while, forcing his kinsman to fight for his late brother Einar's rightful heritage.

Not long after this, Jarl Þórfinnr sent men to muster forces from the Suðreyjar and Scotland. He let it be known that he intended to steadfastly pursue his claim and to take from Rögnvaldr by force what had been denied him by peaceful means.

When Jarl Rögnvaldr got word of this, he gathered his friends and advisors around him, declaring that his kinsman Jarl Þórfinnr had mustered an army and was looking for trouble. He asked them what support they could give him, as he was loth to lose that *priðjungr* gifted him by King Magnús without a struggle. Opinions were mixed on the matter. Some were for Rögnvaldr, that he shouldn't give up the land, while others argued that it was only fair that Þórfinnr should have it for a while, the heritage of his late brother Einar, since Rögnvaldr had already enjoyed it. It was added that Rögnvaldr would be badly advised going against Þórfinnr, as he could only raise a fighting force from two thirds of Orkneyjar, whereas Þórfinnr could muster forces not only from his own *priðjungr*, but also from Katanes, Scotland and the Suðreyjar. Others advised that in the interests of kinship and with a view to a peaceful settlement of the dispute, Rögnvaldr should offer Þórfinnr half of the isles. When Rögnvaldr found that his views were at odds with most of his advisors, who in general counselled him not to fight over this, he made it plain that he had no intention of giving up his possessions by any means, but that he would leave them only long enough to go and see King Magnús, his foster brother, and find out how much backing he could get to hold onto them. He then made preparations and sailed straight for Norway, explaining matters to King Magnús. The king gave Jarl Rögnvaldr a warm welcome and said he could stay as long as he pleased, and to receive from him as much land as was adequate for the maintenance of himself and his following. However, Jarl Rögnvaldr replied that he would prefer to have help in keeping his possessions. King Magnús said that he would give him whatever assistance he required. Rögnvaldr only lingered briefly in Norway before setting off back to Orkneyjar with a large well-armed host provided by King Magnús. The king also sent a message to Kalfr Árnason to the effect that he could have his estates back and be free to live unharmed in Norway if he took Jarl Rögnvaldr's side against Jarl Þórfinnr.

Rögnvaldr is adamant that he will not give up the priðjungr Þórfinnr has allowed him to enjoy all this time, again arguing that he has it with the blessing and support of King Magnús, whereas Þórfinnr sees the land as his heritage, to which he has a natural right. Rögnvaldr knows that Þórfinnr can draw on superior forces there in the west, not only from his lands on Orkney, but also from the Hebrides, Caithness and Scotland. Rögnvaldr's only recourse, as he sees it, is to sail to Norway and come back with a royal army. King Magnús conveys the message to Kálfr Árnason that he can have his Norwegian estates restored and live unharmed if he backs Rögnvaldr over Þórfinnr, knowing that this could tip the scale against the latter and improve Rögnvaldr's chances.

The Sea Battle off Rauðabjorg

Jarl Rögnvaldr sailed west-over-sea for Orkneyjar. He put in at Hjaltland, mustered forces there and then sailed on to Orkneyjar, where he gathered his friends and rallied more men to his banner. Jarl Þórfinnr was in Katanes at the time, but on hearing that Rögnvaldr was back, he raised an army from Scotland and the Suðreyjar. When Kálfr Árnason received King Magnús' message from Rögnvaldr, he seemed content with the proposition offered to him by the king.

Jarl Rögnvaldr mustered his forces in Orkneyjar, aiming to head for Katanes. He had thirty sizeable ships when he sailed into the Pettlandsfjörðr to confront Þórfinnr, who had sixty ships, many of them smaller by comparison. They clashed off Rauðabjorg and commenced battle right away. Kálfr Arnason appeared with six big ships, but did not commit himself to the fight.

The battle was ferocious, with both jarls urging on their men. When the fight had gone on for some time, Þórfinnr's side began suffering heavy losses, largely due to the difference in ship sizes.

Rauðabjorg, *the headland near where the battle takes place, can be translated as* Red Fortress.

In a close sea battle it was easier to attack smaller ships from a greater height and harder for smaller ships to put up a defence or attack bigger ships with their higher decks and greater ramming power during an engagement.

Þórfinnr had a big well-equipped vessel in which he bravely advanced against the enemy but was attacked from both sides when his smaller ships were being put out of the fight, and found himself in dire straits. Many of his men were slain or badly wounded. Jarl Rögnvaldr issued the command for his men to jump aboard, but Þórfinnr had the grappling ropes cut that fixed the ships together when he realised what was about to happen and headed for land. Seventy corpses were removed from his vessel as well as the badly wounded and taken on shore. Þórfinnr then told Arnórr Jarlaskáld, whom he held in high esteem, also to go ashore.

Once he was on dry land, Arnórr spoke these verses:

From my friends I will not conceal this,
though 'tis right to follow one's chief,
yet I am reluctant
to meet the son of Brúsi so.
When these battle-fierce jarls
clash in the fray, then our portion will be
hard beyond that of most
in this – the test of our comradeship.

Jarl Þórfinnr chose those most able to man his ship and went over to ask Kálfr Árnason for help. He told Kálfr that since he was already banished, he could not expect to enjoy the goodwill of King Magnús, even if promised.

'To be sure,' he added, 'if Rögnvaldr beats me and King Magnús lords it over here in the west, you will not be welcome, but if I gain the upper hand you will lack for nothing that it is in my power to give you. If we fight together, we can match anybody here in the west, and I doubt if you will be happy crouching like a cat among rocks while I fight for the both of us. Furthermore, our bonds of kinship are so close, it would be unseemly for us not to help each other, since you share no blood ties with our foes.'

When Kálfr considered Þórfinnr's argument, he called on his men to back the jarl, his kinsman. Þórfinnr and Kálfr then had their ships rowed back into the battle just as those men of Þórfinnr's who had still been fighting Rögnvaldr's forces were on the brink of flight, many of them having already fallen. Þórfinnr had his ship driven up against that of Jarl Rögnvaldr, and the fight was renewed with as much ferocity as before.

In the words of Arnórr:

I saw then the two gold-scatterers
hacking down each other's warriors.
Fierce the fray in Pettland's rising sea
as red rain blooded the bending timbers,
while shield-rims sheened with hot blood
dripping, reddened warriors' gear.

Kálfr's big ships went up against Rögnvaldr's smaller vessels and cleared them in no time. The hired warriors from Norway cut the grappling cables and took to flight when they saw this, leaving Jarl Rögnvaldr with only a few vessels and victory going Þórfinnr's way.

In the words of Arnórr:

Then the battle-fierce lord,
of brave viking kin,
all the old land might have taken
with Islemen's aid.
Fewer were his fallen heroes,
but the mighty men of the chief, in hard helmets,
all up to northern Hjaltland
pursued the faltered foe.

When the main body of the enemy was in flight, Kálfr and Jarl Þórfinnr made for Jarl Rögnvaldr's vessel together and killed a great number of his men. When he realised the extent of the danger, and that he could not hope to withstand Þórfinnr and Kálfr, he ordered the grappling ropes cut and took to flight.

It was late in the day by this time, with darkness descending. Jarl Rögnvaldr headed out for the open sea, making straight for Norway. King Magnús gave him a warm welcome as before and invited him to stay. Rögnvaldr accepted the invitation and stayed for some time.

When Þórfinnr makes Kálfr realise that King Magnús will not honour his promise to him, and that he has better prospects there in the west, he sees the sense in fully committing himself in going against Rögnvaldr. It has clearly been a hard fight, but when victory seems to be within Rögnvaldr's grasp, Kálfr unleashes his war ships. The greater size of the royal vessels has given Rögnvaldr the advantage, but Kálfr's ships are even bigger yet and his forces are fresh. Rögnvaldr is left facing Þórfinnr and Kálfr when the royal forces disengage and flee the battle, and it is not long before Rögnvaldr follows suit.

Jarl Þórfinnr Takes Over the Islands

On the morning after the battle, Jarl Þórfinnr sent out boats with men to search the islands for any fugitives. Many were slain, though some were given quarter and pardoned. Jarl Þórfinnr took over all the islands and made everyone swear their allegiance to him, even those who had sworn their oath to Rögnvaldr. Þórfinnr then based his residence in Orkneyjar, accompanied by a powerful following. Provisions were imported from Katanes. Kálfr Árnason he sent to the Suðreyjar, with orders to remain and exert his authority there.

When Jarl Rögnvaldr had remained with King Magnús for some time, he let the king know that he wished to return to the islands. The king saw little wisdom in this and advised him to stay until winter was over and the sea was free of ice. He added, however, that he would give him as many men and ships as he needed. Rögnvaldr answered that this time he would go without the king's men, adding that he could not lead a force against Þórfinnr without heavy losses, as he had such wide dominions to draw upon in the west.

'This time,' he said, 'I aim to go west in a single ship, as well manned as possible. In this way I expect no news of our coming will precede us. And if I get to the islands, I shall take them by surprise, and then we may gain such a swift victory as would be less likely with a larger following. But if they become aware of our presence, we can trust our care to the sea.'

King Magnús replied that he could go as he pleased and return to him when he liked.

After this, Rögnvaldr made ready his ship and shrewdly picked men to man it. Several of the king's henchmen accompanied him, so that he had a choice crew. They sailed out to sea when they were ready, with a fair wind. This was in winter.

The Burning

Rögnvaldr first arrived off the coast of Hjaltland and got word that Jarl Þórfinnr was on Orkneyjar with only a few retainers, as he did not expect to be attacked in winter. So Rögnvaldr went straight to Orkneyjar. Jarl Þórfinnr was in Hrossey, suspecting nothing, when Rögnvaldr landed and took him by surprise, making fast all the doors in which Jarl Þórfinnr and his men were. It was dead of night, with most inside asleep, but the jarl was still awake over his drink. Rögnvaldr and his men then set fire to the house. When Jarl Þórfinnr realised he was being beset by enemies, he sent men to the main door to see if they could find out who it was. They were informed from outside that it was Jarl Rögnvaldr. They all then took to arms, but there wasn't a lot they could do in the way of fighting, as they couldn't get out of the doors. The house was on fire, and Jarl Þórfinnr told them that those who would be granted quarter should ask for it now. Jarl Rögnvaldr, when asked, replied that he would let all the women and thralls get out, but that Þórfinnr's men would be no more use to him alive than dead. Those given quarter were then hauled out while the house was burning down. Jarl Þórfinnr came up with a plan, knocking down the timbers in a part of the house and breaking out, carrying Ingibjörg, his wife, in his arms. As it was pitch dark, he managed to get away shielded by the smoke and unnoticed by Jarl Rögnvaldr's men. During the night, he rowed a boat across to Katanes. Jarl Rögnvaldr burnt the house to the ground with everybody in it, and it was generally believed that Þórfinnr had perished along with them.

Hrossey *(Horse Island) is another name for Mainland, Orkney.*

Having had no luck in confronting Þórfinnr in battle, Rögnvaldr resorts to stealth in winter when an attack is least expected and attempts to burn his uncle alive in the house, one of the favoured ways of getting rid of your enemy in the northlands.

After this, Jarl Rögnvaldr took over all the islands. He also sent word to the Suðreyjar and Katanes that he intended on having those dominions of Þórfinnr as well, and no one spoke to the contrary. Jarl Þórfinnr was in hiding in Katanes at the time with his supporters, and no word got out of his escape from the burning.

The Slaying of Rögnvaldr

Jarl Rögnvaldr stayed in Kirkjuvág and arranged provisions and all other things needed to see through the winter. He had a great following and entertained them generously. Just before Yule, the jarl went with a great many men into Papey Minni to collect malt for the Christmas brewing. They were a long time sitting round the fires that evening, keeping themselves warm, and the man whose task it was to keep the fires going told them they were running out of wood. The jarl then made a slip of the tongue when he said: 'We shall be old enough when those fires are burned out'. What he meant to say was that they'd be warm enough. 'I made a slip of the tongue just then,' he said. 'I don't remember ever doing that before, but now I remember what my foster father King Óláfr said at Stiklarstaðir, when I noticed a slip of the tongue he himself made – that if I ever made a slip of the tongue, I shouldn't expect to live long after it. It could be that Þórfinnr, my kinsman is still alive.'

Suddenly they heard men surrounding the house where they were and soon realised that it was indeed Jarl Þórfinnr and his followers. The house was then set on fire and a great heap of wood piled before the door. Þórfinnr let everybody go apart from Jarl Rögnvaldr's men, and when most of those who were granted quarter were out, a man garbed only in linen clothes asked Þórfinnr to lend the deacon a hand. The man took a grip on the woodpile and vaulted over it and the ring of gathered men as well, landing a good way off and vanishing swiftly into the dark.

Jarl Þórfinnr ordered his men to set off in pursuit, explaining that it must have been Jarl Rögnvaldr. 'That was his feat and no other's,' he said.

The men split into groups to hunt him down. Þórkel Fóstri and a few others searched the beach and heard a dog barking among the rocks. It turned out to be Jarl Rögnvaldr's lapdog that he had been carrying with him when he escaped, and it gave away his hiding place. Þórkel had his men grab the jarl and offered them money as an inducement to kill him, but they refused to do it. So Þórkel killed him instead, as he well knew that one of the jarls had to die. Þórfinnr then arrived and had no issue with Þórkel Fóstri's deed. They spent the night on the island and all of Jarl Rögnvaldr's followers were hunted down and slain.

In the morning they filled a barge with malt, fixed the shields of Jarl Rögnvaldr and his men along the bulwarks, and rowed out for Kirkjuvág. Those men of Rögnvaldr's who were there came out unarmed to welcome the jarl, who they believed was in the boat. Þórfinnr had thirty of them seized and killed, most of them henchmen and retainers of King Magnús. The jarl spared one of the men and told him to back to Norway and tell King Magnús everything that happened.

Kirkjuvág *is Kirkwall and* Papey Minni *is Papa Stronsay.*

Rögnvaldr vaults over the woodpile and the ring of men, disguised as a deacon, but his athleticism gives him away, as does the lapdog he escapes with, barking to reveal his hiding place. Þórkel can be relied upon to kill Rögnvaldr if no one else will do it, as the latter will not cease being a deadly threat to Þórfinnr unless he is stopped permanently. Rögnvaldr's men are also wiped out, including all but one of the king's retainers, who is sent off with the message for Magnús.

Jarl Þórfinnr Visits King Magnús

The remains of Jarl Rögnvaldr were taken to Papey Meiri and there interred. It was generally said that he was one of the most gifted and well-loved of the Orkney jarls, and the folk lamented his passing.

Jarl Þórfinnr then took possession of all of the islands and no one opposed him.

In early spring, word of these events got to King Magnús in Norway. He considered the death of his foster brother Rögnvaldr a great loss and stated his intention to avenge him at some point, as at that time he was at war with Svein Ulfsson, King of Denmark.

It came about that King Haraldr Sigurðarson, uncle to King Magnús, arrived in Norway and Magnús gave him half of the kingdom. After a year of joint rule, they mustered forces from all over Norway with the aim of attacking Denmark. While they lay at anchor off Seley, two war galleys skimmed across the water into the harbour and up to King Magnús' ship. A man in a white cloak made his way from one of the strange ships to the quarterdeck of the king's vessel.

King Magnús was sitting at table when the man greeted him, tore off a chunk of bread and started eating. The king acknowledged his greeting and handed him the cup when he saw him eat the bread. The king then asked who the man was.

'I am Þórfinnr,' the man said.

'Are you Jarl Þórfinnr?' asked the king.

'That is how I am known in the west,' Þórfinnr replied, 'and I have come here with two ships of twenty benches apiece, well-manned and equipped to the best I can afford, and I would like to join you in this expedition, if you will accept my assistance. My men and myself are in God's hands and yours, my lord, on account of the offences I have committed.'

By this time others had gathered and were listening in on the conversation.

'The truth of the matter is, Jarl Þórfinnr,' responded the king, 'that it was my intention, if ever we met, to ensure that you would never tell how we parted. But as things stand now, it would not become my dignity to have you killed, and so you shall accompany me. Whatever the terms of our reconciliation, I will let be known to you when I am less preoccupied.'

Jarl Þórfinnr left the king then and returned to his ship.

King Magnús and his forces lay at anchor off Seley for quite some time and more men rallied to his banner from Vík. It was his aim to sail for Jutland when he got a good wind. Þórfinnr spent many a time talking with the king, who was friendly with him and would have him in attendance whenever he held a council.

One day the jarl boarded the king's ship and went up to the poop deck. The king invited him to sit down and have a drink and soon they were having a merry time of it. A tall stalwart man in a red tunic then approached and greeted King Magnús, who gave him a courteous welcome. He was one of the king's retainers.

'I've come to see you, Jarl Þórfinnr,' the man said.

'What is it you want?' asked the jarl.

'I would like to know what man-geld you aim to give me for my brother, who was slain at your command out west at Kirkjuvág, together with other retainers of King Magnús.'

'Have you not heard,' replied the jarl, 'that I'm not in the habit of forking out money for the men I get killed?'

'I have little interest in how you've dealt with other people, if you pay the man-geld it is my duty to seek. I lost money there myself and was treated shabbily to boot. It is more pressing on me than any other to look for compensation for my brother and myself, and I demand it now. The king may forgive any offences made against himself, even if he deems it of no account if his retainers are taken out like sheep to the slaughter.'

'It is clear to me the advantage I have in not being in your power,' said the jarl. 'Are you not the man I gave quarter to?'

'I am indeed,' came the reply. 'It was in your power to have me slain like all the others.'

The jarl replied: 'So there is truth in the saying – *That often happens to many which they least expect.* I never thought I would be put in such a position that it would be baleful for me to show mercy to my enemies. But now I'm expected to pay for having let you go? You wouldn't have vilified me in front of these chieftains today if I'd had you killed along with your friends.'

The king grew blood red and addressed the jarl: 'Here it comes out again, Jarl Þórfinnr, that you deem you have not slain enough of my retainers without paying man-geld.'

The jarl got up then and strode off back to his own ship, and it was quiet the rest of the night. In the morning, when everyone awoke, there was a fair wind and they all set off. King Magnús headed for Jutland with his fleet, but Jarl Þórfinnr's ship sailed some distance from the rest during the early part of the day, and then took a westerly course to Orkneyjar, where he resumed control of his dominions.

King Magnús and Haraldr sailed to Denmark, where they spent the summer. King Svein was in no hurry to engage them and remained in Skáney with his forces. That summer King Magnús took ill and died. The whole kingdom of Norway then went to his uncle Haraldr, in accordance with his wishes.

Papey Meiri *is Papa Westray.*

The man who demands man-geld from Þórfinnr for his slain brother is the one who was spared to carry the message to King Magnús after Rögnvaldr's killing. Þórfinnr is not in the habit of paying out compensation, and his attempt to smooth things over with the king is clearly ruined here when Magnús gets a stark reminder of the men he has sent against the Orkney jarl, who have died as a result.

Jarl Þórfinnr meets King Haraldr Harðráði and goes to Rome

Jarl Þórfinnr now ruled the Norðreyjar as well as all his other territories. Kálfr Arnason was often in his company. He occasionally made viking raids in the west, pillaging particularly in Scotland and Ireland. He spent time in England as well, where he was chief of the *Þingalið*.

When Jarl Þórfinnr got word that King Magnús was dead, he sent men with a message of goodwill to King Haraldr, who received it well and sent the men back with a message of friendship to the jarl. Þórfinnr then prepared two ships with twenty benches apiece, and more than a hundred able men, and sailed east for Norway. He met King Haraldr in Hörðaland and got a warm welcome, and when he left, the king gave him rich gifts. The jarl then sailed south along the coast to Denmark, where he met King Svein in Alaborg. The king invited him to stay and had a lavish banquet prepared for him. Jarl Þórfinnr declared that he was heading for Rome. He next travelled to Saxland and visited the Emperor Heinrek, who gave him an enthusiastic welcome and many fine gifts. He also supplied him with numerous horses, and the jarl rode south to Rome, where he had an audience with the Pope, who absolved him of all his sins.

Then the jarl set off on his return journey and had a safe trip back to his own lands. He left off setting out on viking expeditions and devoted himself to the administration of his dominions and of his people, and to the making of laws. He stayed often in Birgishérad, and built the grand church of Christ's Kirk there, the first bishop's see on Orkneyjar.

Þórfinnr's wife was Ingibjörg, the mother of the jarls. They had two sons – Páll and Erlendr. They were big built men, of fine appearance, wise and gentle, and taking more after their mother's kin. The jarl and his people held them in the warmest affection.

The Þingalið *was an assembly retinue or standing army in England.*

Saxland *is Saxony and* Birgishérad *is Birsay.*

There has been some speculation that Þórfinnr may have visited Rome around the year 1050 in the company of his cousin Macbeth at this time, who is said to have scattered silver like seed to the poor *there, according to Marianus Scotus, an Irish monk and chronicler.*

Death of Jarl Þórfinnr

Jarl Þórfinnr ruled all his territories until his passing, and he was truly considered the mightiest of the Orkney jarls. He gained possession of eleven jarldoms in Scotland, all of the Suðreyjar and a good part of Ireland.

In the words of Arnórr Jarlaskáld:

Before Þ*órfinnr the raven feeder*
armies were forced to yield.
From Thussasker to Dyflinn
the truth is told.

Jarl Þórfinnr was five winters old when his mother's father, Máel Coluim, King of Scots made him a jarl. He was a jarl for seventy winters, after which he passed away toward the end of Haraldr Sigurðarson's reign, and was buried at Christ's Kirk, Birgishérad, which he had built. His passing was considered a great loss by the folk throughout his hereditary territories, but in those lands he had subdued through force of arms, the people held a quite different view, having had a hard time of it under his rule. So many of those provinces that he had conquered went back to their native chiefs.

The following verses were composed about the conflict between Jarl Rögnvaldr Brúsason and Jarl Þórfinnr:

Since the friendship of the jarls was sundered
I can find no peace.
Raven feast of corpses
has each in turn provided.
Off the isles the mighty lord
rent the sea's blue tent in twain.
Foul birds' feathers in red blood dabbled
'neath high boughs.

Did you hear how Kálfr followed
Finn's son-in-law to battle?
Swiftly you unleashed your ships
'gainst those of the jarl.
To bring down Brúsi's son,
brave commander of ships,
reluctant, ventured,
but mindful of bale,
ye did help Þór*finnr.*

When the jarls strove in onslaught
'mid the blood fray,
men fell thick and fast.
Hard beneath Rauðabjorg
Many a worthy man gained wounds
in the spear storm.

Gloom shall gather over gleaming sun,
Earth sink beneath black billows,
Austri's burden burst asunder.
wild sea rear above the mountains,
'ere among the isles
a fairer chief be born –
true lord of thanes,
may God guard Þórfinnr*.*

If Skene's theory was true, that Þórfinnr and Macbeth split the Picto-Scottish realms between them after the defeat of Donnchad mac Crínán, Þórfinnr would have ruled territories in Moray – most certainly Caithness and Sutherland, which he already considered his, but also Ross and probably more. After his death the native chiefs, long-time enemies of the Orkney Norse and probably particularly so of Þórfinnr, who represented their age-old rival, the Mac Ailpín dynasty, recovered their lands.

The poet clearly loved both jarls, and it must have pained him badly to see them at odds.

Austri's burden *in the final lines of the poet's verse refers to the sky. Austri (East) is one of the four dwarves that support the dome of heaven in Norse mythology. This part of the poem, in tribute to Þórfinnr, bears a remarkable similarity to the ancient Celtic oath formula, that unless a series of cataclysmic things occur, such as the sky falling, or the waves overwhelming the earth, or the earth itself gaping open, something that is promised or intended will be honoured. Or in this case, that unless the sun is blacked out, or the earth is flooded, or the sky bursts, a better chief than Þórfinnr will not arise. It is perfectly possible that this Celtic element, among others, made its way into the Nordic* skáld's *stock-in-trade of poetic references, especially in the Norse Gaelic west.*

For examples of this Celtic oath, see the author's book The Celtic Heroic Tradition in Myth & Legend.

THE VOYAGE OF JARL RÖGNVALDR

The Jarl Rögnvaldr of the title began life as Kali Kolsson at Agder in Norway in the year 1103. At the age of fifteen he was on a trading voyage to Grimsby when he befriended Gillikristr or Haraldr Gilli, the half Irish son of King Magnús Bare Legs, and later supported Haraldr's rise to power as King of Norway.

In 1129 he was made jarl of Orkney and Shetland by King Sigurðr Jórsalafari, who also gave him the name Rögnvaldr after Jarl Rögnvaldr Brúsason, and people considered this a good luck sign.

After opposition from Jarl Páll Hákonarson, who refused to give him his share of Orkney, Rögnvaldr was advised by his father Kollr to vow that he would build a church in memory of his martyred uncle Magnús Erlendsson if he was successful in getting a foothold on the islands. The notorious viking Svein Ásleifarson later kidnapped Jarl Páll and handed him over to Maddad, Mormaer of Atholl, paving the way for Rögnvaldr to take over Orkney in 1136.

In Orkneyinga saga *Rögnvaldr is something of a cultured, debonair gent proud of his talents, as well as being a warrior. He is a wise, fair and popular jarl, generous and good-natured, multi-skilled and literate, but he can also be rash and naïve and charmingly eccentric.*

In the following verse he lists his skills:

I'm accomplished at the gaming board
and at nine arts skilled;
Rune lore I ken and of books am fond -
able with tools and steady on snowshoes.
I'm deft with the bow and can pull an oar -
I'm good with the harp, and at verse-making.

The ability to read and write is often taken for granted these days, but in Rögnvaldr's time most people were illiterate. As well as reading books and composing verses, Rögnvaldr lists rune lore as one of his skills. This refers to knowledge of an old alphabet used by the Norse and known as the fuþark *after the first six characters. It was normally carved on wood or stone for memorials, love messages and traders' slogans, and also used in spells. For more information see the author's book,* The Viking Runes.

Rögnvaldr is noted in Orkneyinga saga *for his good deeds. In one instance, disguised under a white cowl, he helps an old man get the fishing in and afterwards distributes his own share of the catch among the poor.*

At the encouragement of his guardian Jarl Erlingr, King Ingi, the son of Haraldr Gilli, sends an invitation for Rögnvaldr to come to Bjørgvin *(Bergen) in Norway. Rögnvaldr eagerly accepts and sets sail with the young Haraldr Maddaðarson, then joint jarl of Orkney, and they are given a warm reception there. During his stay, a well-travelled chieftain called Eindriði Ungi, lately arrived from* Miklagarðr *(Constantinople) encourages Rögnvaldr to go on a voyage to the Holy Land.*

Though this is meant to be a pilgrimage to Jerusalem, Rögnvaldr and his followers manage to fit in an assault on a Galician castle and an attack on a Moorish ship. These are viking pilgrims after all…

When the jarls were ready, they sailed from the west with some merchants, having an eminent following, and landed in Norway in early spring. They joined King Ingi in Bjørgvin and he gave them a good welcome. Jarl Rögnvaldr met many of his friends and blood kin and passed a good part of the summer there.

Eindriði Ungi came from Miklagarðr, where he had long served, and told many an entertaining tale of his time there. The jarl talked with him often, and on one occasion, Eindriði said: 'It appears strange to me that you yourself have not considered faring to the Holy Land, and that you should think it enough just to be told of all the things there. It would be only right for men like yourself, with your attainments, to go there, and you will be esteemed above all others whenever you come among well born men.'

When Eindriði said this, there were many who supported the idea and urged the jarl to lead any proposed expedition. Erlingr delivered a long speech backing the venture and said he would join the party himself if the jarl agreed to be their leader, and many other important men said they would go too. And when the jarl and Erlingr were discussing the matter, these men came forward. Among these were Eindriði Ungi, who was to guide them, Jon Pétrsson, Áslákr Erlendsson, and Guðþormr Mjolukollr from Hálogaland.

It was decided that none there should have a vessel larger than thirty benches apart from the jarl, and no ornamentation on it either. The idea was to prevent anybody getting jealous if someone among them had better men or a grander ship than the jarl. Jon Foot was to construct the ship for the jarl and have it fitted out to the best of his ability.

Jarl Rögnvaldr returned home in the autumn and had it in mind to stay two winters. King Ingi gave him two long-ships, both small but very grand and specially built for rowing, and the swiftest of ships. Jarl Rögnvaldr gave one of them, called *Fifa,* to Jarl Haraldr. The other was called *Hjalp.* The jarls put to sea in these ships, bearing westward. Jarl Rögnvaldr had many fine gifts from his friends. It was a Tuesday evening when they set out and had a fair wind, but on the Wednesday a fierce storm sprang up, and in the evening they sighted land. It was very dark, with breakers on all sides. Up to this time they had kept together. They had no alternative but to run the ships ashore, which they did. The beach was rocky and narrow, bounded by cliffs. All the men survived, but a great deal of their goods were lost, though the sea cast some of these things forth during the night.

Typically, Jarl Rögnvaldr bore himself better than any man there. He was in such good spirits that he twiddled his fingers and proceeded to speak in rhyme. Taking a gold ring from his hand, he composed this verse:

Thus, I hang the hammer-beaten
hand ring from my rounded fingers.
So, the nymph of the raging sea
cast me, blithesome, into a rocky cleft,
there to twiddle my thumbs.

When they had borne their stuff from the sea, they ventured inland to find any houses, as they believed they had landed in Hjaltland. They soon discovered some farms and distributed themselves between these. The folk gave the jarl a warm reception, and when they questioned him with regard to his trip, he answered with this verse:

Both my ships on beach were wrecked -
when waves carried off my men,
stricken sudden by the breakers
were the hulls of Hjalp *and* Fifa.
Surely this disaster
of the peril-prone sea rovers

will not soon slip the minds

of the soaking wet.

The mistress of the house brought a fur cloak to the jarl, who reached for it with a laugh, and composed this verse:

Here I shake in a grizzled fur cloak –

to be sure, it's far from showy.

All our gear lies in the field of ships,

too wide to search for.

Only just then, all the little sea horses

draped us in their grand gear,

as we drove the masthead steeds

over the breakers

and into the cliffs.

The above verse is an example of the use of kennings – compound expressions of a metaphorical nature used in Old Norse poetry. Here field of ships *is the sea,* the sea horses' grand gear *is seaweed, and* masthead steeds *are ships.*

Large fires were made, around which they gathered to get warm. A servant girl then entered, shaking with the cold, and she mumbled something to herself, but most of them couldn't grasp what she said because of her violent shivering obscuring the words. But the jarl understood her and interpreted what she said in a verse:

Ása, you are bone-weary,

at-a-ta-ta-

'tis the water,

hoo-too-too-too-

where shall I sit by the fire?

It's freezing.

The jarl sent a dozen men to Einar at Gulberuvík, but he said he would not have them unless the jarl came himself. When Jarl Rögnvaldr was told this, he composed a verse:

Einar declared he would feed none of Rögnvaldr's lads

unless the jarl came himself.

Empty words, I think,

for I ken the amiable one would never

break his vow.

Count us in where the fires blaze brightly

through the night.

The jarl stayed a good while in Hjaltland, then in the autumn sailed south to Orkneyjar, returning there to his domain. That autumn two Hjaltlanders came to visit him. One was called Armóðr, a skáld, and the other Oddi Glúmsson the Little, who also knew a thing or two about verse. The jarl gave them a fine welcome and they joined his company. The jarl arranged a grand Yule feast, to which many were invited, and he distributed gifts. He handed a gold-inlaid spear to the poet Armóðr, shook it at him and asked him to recite a poem on the spot.

Grand gifts the battle rouser

with no penny-pinching hand doles out.

Skáldic greatness is not appraised

by the presents given to others.

The protector of his bounds

and the leader among chieftains,

*from his own hand passes Armó*ðr

the gold-tipped blood candle. (kenning for spear)

One day during Yule the guests were looking at a wall hanging and the jarl challenged Oddi the Little to compose a verse about the scene depicted on it, to have it done by the time he had completed his own stanza, and to use none of the same words as the jarl, who composed this verse:

The aged one on the hanging

has a scabbard-stave on his shoulder, (scabbard-stave - kenning for *sword*)

though he won't advance another step.

regardless of his fury.

Oddi the Little responded:

The warrior bends to deliver a strike
from the tapestry –
pay heed to where the danger's greatest –
high time for ships' captains
to make peace ere ought happens.

It is quite common in the sagas for poets to compose verses spontaneously. Here Rögnvaldr challenges Armóðr to do just that, but goes one step further with Oddi, by confidently expecting him not only to have his verse ready by the time the jarl has finished his, but to use completely different words also.

That Yule the jarl welcomed Bishop William and a good many of his chiefs. Then he said that he intended going to the Holy Land and asked the bishop to accompany him, as he had been educated in Paris, and the jarl wanted him as an interpreter. The bishop agreed to this and said he would go. These are also the chiefs that accompanied Jarl Rögnvaldr – Magnús, son of Hávarðr Gunnisson, Svein Hróaldsson, ship commanders, and these other men, though of less standing – Þórgeir Skotakollr, Oddi the Little, Þórbjörn Svarti, Armóðr the skáld, Þórkel Krokauga, Grímkell of Flyðrunes and Bjarni his son.

When the two winters set aside for their planning were over, Jarl Rögnvaldr sailed out of Orkneyjar in the spring eastward to Norway to see how well the landholders there were progressing with their own preparations for the journey, and when he reached Bjørgvin, Erlingr Skakkr, Jon Foot the jarl's brother-in-law, and Áslákr were there, with Guðþormr arriving shortly after.

Also at Bjørgvin was the ship Jon Foot built for the jarl. It was an outstanding work of craftsmanship, magnificently ornamented. All of the carvings on the prow and stern were gilded as well as the vanes. It was a truly grand vessel.

Eindriði visited town often through the summer and claimed he would be ready in a week. The jarl's men grumbled about having to hang about so long, pointing out that voyages such as this did not depend on Eindriði turning up. But a short time after, Eindriði arrived in town and told them he was ready. So the jarl said that they should put out to sea whenever there was a favourable wind, and when that day came, they sailed out, though the breeze was not strong at first, and the jarl's ship moved slowly, as it needed a strong wind. Accordingly, the other chiefs lowered their sails, as it was not proper to leave the jarl lagging behind.

When they were out past the islands, the wind grew to such strength that the smaller ships had to take in sail, while the jarl's ship now sped through the waves. Then they spotted two big ships coming after them fast and racing to pass them. One of these, a dragon, was very finely turned out, richly gilded at prow and stern, white at the bows and splendidly painted above the sea to get the maximum attention.

The jarl's men guessed that it had to be Eindriði's and said to the jarl: 'He has not kept to the deal that nobody but you should have an ornamented ship, sir.'

The jarl replied: 'Eindriði is so puffed up with pride that he should perhaps be excused for not fancying being on the same level as the rest of us, as we are so low-grade by comparison. But it is difficult to tell whether his luck runs ahead of him or at the same pace, though we should not let our actions be affected by his excitability.'

Eindriði passed the lot of them in his big ship, but the jarl kept all his ships together and had a fine voyage. They landed safely in Orkneyjar in the autumn. It was decided that they should winter there, some living at their own expense and others quartered with the farmers, while many more stayed with the jarl.

Viking long ships were famous for their gracefully curved clinker-built hulls, speed and flexibility at sea, with shallow draughts that allowed them to be beached during a raid. Here the shipbuilder Jon foot adorns the jarl's ship with gilded carving, while the dragon ship of the vain Eindriði is also richly gilded and painted for maximum attention.

The viking longship design probably influenced that of the birlinn, a vessel used in the Hebrides and West Highlands. The Norse Gaelic term may come from the Norse byrðingr. *Twelve to eighteen-oared birlinns and eighteen to twenty-oared galleys were used by Somerled, King of the Isles and the later Clann Domnaill, among others.*

The second largest viking longship discovered in modern times, the Skuldelev 2 *as it is called, was built near Dublin in approximately 1042, constructed of oak timber from Glendalough in what is now County Wicklow. A reconstruction of this ship, the Havhingsten fra Glendalough or* Sea Stallion from Glendalough *was built in Denmark at the Ship Museum in Roskilde and launched in 2004. It later embarked on a voyage to Dublin in 2007.*

We take up the saga again in the islands, where the Orkneymen and the Norwegians start brawling...

There was then trouble in the islands, with the Orkneymen and the Austmen (Norwegians) at loggerheads over trade and women, among other things. The jarl had his hands full trying to keep the peace, for both parties felt obligated to him, while at the same time seeking his approval and esteem in everything.

It is said that when Eindriði got to Hjaltland, his fancy ship was wrecked, and he lost a lot of goods to the sea, though his other ship was saved. He spent the winter there but sent men back to Norway to have a new ship built for the voyage to the East.

One of Eindriði's men was called Arni Stick Leg. He went to Orkneyjar in the winter, accompanied by nine men. He was very vicious, bold and an out and out troublemaker. He and his companions lived at their own expense during the winter, but then Arni got malt and meat from a tenant of Svein Ásleifarson and when the man asked for the money, Arni was slow in paying. The man then asked for it a second time and got loaded with abuse as well as a blow from the back of Arni's axe.

'Go and tell that champion of yours, Svein, who you're never done praising, to get the payment for you,' said Arni.

So, the man went to see Svein and asked him to obtain what was owed to him, but Svein's response was less than satisfactory and he replied that he would give no promises.

One day in spring Svein set out to collect his rents. He took three men with him in a ten-oared boat. As they had to pass by the island where Arni was staying, Svein said he would put in there. It was an ebb tide. Svein went ashore unaccompanied, armed only with a short-hafted axe. He instructed his men not to ground the boat.

Arni Stick Leg and his comrades were staying in a house not far from the sea. Svein strode up and found them all indoors. They exchanged greetings, and Svein told Arni that he should pay the farmer, but Arni said there was plenty of time for that. Svein asked him to do it as a personal favour to himself, but Arni was having none of it. Svein said he wouldn't ask again and buried the axe in Arni's skull up right to the haft, and then ran out.

Arni's companions started chasing him down to the beach, and as Svein reached the muddy shore, the swiftest of his pursuers came up with him. There were large clumps of seaweed lying in the mud. Svein snatched up one of these and smashed it into the man's face, and as the fellow stood there, clawing the mud out of his eyes, Svein cleared off in his boat back to Gáreksey.

A little while after that he went over to Katanes on some business and sent word to the jarl to settle the matter of Arni Stick Leg's killing. When the jarl received word, he gathered everybody about him who would seek compensation for Arni and settled things himself, paying the money out of his own pocket. In addition to this, the jarl also paid out for many other incidents of violence between the Orkneymen and the Austmen that winter.

In all fairness to Svein, who may have been feeling a little lenient that day, he does give Arni two chances to make good before he puts the axe in his head. Svein now clearly expects Rögnvaldr to pay for the trail of dead men he leaves behind him, having helped the latter to secure the jarldom by kidnapping his rival, Jarl Páll. In addition, the injuries and damages from the ongoing knockabout between the Orkneymen and the Norwegians has Rögnvaldr forking out money right, left and centre.

In early spring he arranged a *þing* (assembly) in Hrossey, to which came all the chieftains of his realm. He then declared his intention to set out from Orkneyjar to the Holy Land and said that he was leaving his dominions in the care of his kinsman Haraldr, and that he expected his friends to obey him and give him their support while he himself was gone. Haraldr was nearly twenty then, tall and robust, but ugly. Yet he was a wise man withal, and the folk thought he had the makings of a good leader.

In the summer, Jarl Rögnvaldr got ready to set out from Orkneyjar, but it was well into summer before he could sail, as he was again delayed by Eindriði, this time waiting for his new ship to arrive from Norway. But when they were finally ready, they sailed out in fifteen ships. The commanders were Jarl Rögnvaldr, Erlingr Skakkr, Bishop William, Áslákr Erlendsson, Guðþormr, Magnús Hávarðarsson, Svein Hróaldsson, Eindriði Ungi, and those others that accompanied him are not named.

From Orkneyjar they sailed over to Scotland, then to England, and when they arrived at Norðimbraland, off the mouth of the Hvera, Armóðr composed this verse:

High the wave crests
as we passed Hvera's mouth.
Masts were bending,
and the low land met the waves
in long stretches of sand.
Salt spray blinded our eyes
while at home the lads from the Þing-field
were a-horseback.

Norðimbraland *is Northumberland and* Hvera *is the River Wear.*

Armóðr dramatizes the details of hanging about a river mouth in his verse to the level of adventure and compares it to what the lads from the assembly field are probably doing back home.

The ships continue south to Valland *(Gaul) and put in at a port called* Verbon *(possibly Narbonne in Southern France).*

They sailed on south of England and then on to Valland. There is nothing to say of their voyage until they reached a seaport called Verbon. There they discovered that Geirbjörn, the jarl that had ruled the city, had recently passed away, and left a young and lovely daughter called Ermingerda. She had control of her legacy, with the guidance of noble kinsmen. Their advice to the queen was to invite Jarl Rögnvaldr to a grand feast, telling her that she would enjoy wide renown if she gave a fitting welcome to such well-bred gentlemen from distant parts. The queen trusted the arrangements to her advisors, and as it had now been decided, men were sent to the jarl with the word that the queen invited him to the feast, along with as many of his companions as he wished to accompany him. The jarl was well pleased with the invitation and picked the best of his men to go with him. They went cheerfully to the feast, and there was no sparing the honour accorded the jarl.

On a certain day, when the jarl sat dining, the queen entered the feasting hall, attended by her many ladies. In her hand was a cup of gold and she was draped in luxurious robes. Her hair was loose, as was customary with maidens, and she had a gold diadem about her forehead.

She served the jarl his wine, and the ladies played for them. The jarl took her hand along with the cup and sat her beside him, and they conversed through the day.

Then he composed this verse:

Fair lady, your form exceeds
all maidens' beauty -
though I've reddened the avid eagle's claws -
draped in costly raiment,
and bedecked in precious gems,
silken tresses in lustrous splendour
tumble o'er the shoulders
of this gold-ring goddess.

Obviously smitten, the jarl pulls out all the stops here with his silver-tongued verse- praise of Ermingerda.

The jarl stayed on a good while and was lavishly entertained. The natives of the city were keen for him to establish his residence there, along with the offer of the queen's hand in marriage. The jarl answered that he wished to complete his journey, but that he would come back there on his return, upon which they might do as they saw fit.

After that, the jarl set off with his company and sailed round Þrasnes. They got a fair wind, and sat and drank, and were of good cheer. Then the jarl composed this verse:

Long in the prince's memory
shall linger Ermingerda's gentle words.
It is her wish that we
ride the waves to Jordan,
but these riders of the sea-stallion
faring back from southern parts,
shall plough their way o'er whale pond
to Verbon in the autumn.

Sea stallion *is a kenning for a ship, and* whale pond *is a kenning for the sea.*

Then Armóðr recited:

Ne'er again shall I see Ermingerda,
if my fate be unlucky –
many are now missing her.
To be with her just one day
would be a joy,
a blessing once again
to see her face.

Then Oddi recited:

If truth be kenned, hardly worthy are we
of Ermingerda.
The smart and sonsie princess -
queen of maidens -
best describes the glory of her looks.
May her lot be ever joyful
long as she bides beneath sun-ray.

The jarl's poets wax lyrical over the memory of Ermingerda, as if they too have been wooing her.

They sailed on until they reached Galicia, five nights before Yule-tide, and had it in mind to spend it there. They asked the people there if they would sell them provisions, but as food supplies were scarce, the folk considered it a trial to feed such a large company. The way things were, the country was then under the rule of an outlander, who stayed in the castle, and rode roughshod over the people. He would attack them if they refused to carry out his wishes and threatened them constantly with cruelty and oppression.

When the jarl asked the folk to sell him provisions, they agreed to do so until Lent, but offered certain conditions – that Jarl Rögnvaldr should attack their oppressors and have all the money he might get from them. The jarl put this to his men and asked them their opinion on the matter. Most of them were for attacking the castle, as they considered it a likely target for plunder. So, Jarl Rögnvaldr and his following agreed to the people's terms.

When Yule-tide was approaching, the jarl gathered his men about him and said: 'We have been tarrying here a while and have not bothered the men in the castle, and the folk are getting fed up supplying us. It may be that they don't consider our promise to amount to much, but it is not the manly thing for us to put off trying to do what we said we would. Now, I would like your ideas on how best to take the castle, as I deem you men of great discernment, and I ask everybody here to state what plan is most likely to succeed.'

Erlingr answered the jarl: 'I will not stay silent, as you command us to speak, though I am not a man given to wise counsels, and it seems to me that those with more experience in such tasks should be asked in particular, such as Eindriði Ungi. But, as the saying goes, *shoot at the bird before we catch it.* I will give my advice, for what it's worth. If you and the other ship masters do not think it a bad idea, we shall all go today to the woods, and each carry three bundles of faggots to the castle, as it is doubtful whether the lime would stand for much heat being applied to it. Let's do this for the next three days and see what happens.'

They did as Erlingr advised, and by the time they had completed their task, Yule was near, and the bishop refused to let the men in the castle be attacked during that time. The chief commanding the castle was called Godfrey, a crafty man and getting on in years. He was a fine scholar, had fared widely, and knew many tongues. He was also avaricious and high-handed.

When he saw what the strangers were up to, he gathered his men around him and said: 'This plan of the Northmen appears to me a prudent one, and in all likelihood will bring great danger to us. We will see that the wall round the castle is not strong enough to withstand a fire. Furthermore, the Northmen are brave and of great strength, and we can only expect a fierce onslaught from them if they get the chance.'

He then asked for their advice with regard to the perilous position they were in, but they said that they trusted in him to do the best thing under the circumstances.

'My plan is that we should tie ropes together and lower me down the castle wall. I will garb myself in beggar's rags, visit the Northmen's camp, and see what I can discover.'

They followed his orders, and he went to Jarl Rögnvaldr's camp in the guise of a beggar and spoke Valska (French), as they understood a little of that. So, he wandered about, begging for food. He noticed that the Northmen were divided by jealousy into two factions, one led by Eindriði Ungi and the other by Jarl Rögnvaldr.

Godfrey approached Eindriði and conversed with him, saying that the lord of the castle had sent him to the camp to make an alliance.

'He asks that you grant him quarter if the castle is taken,' he told Eindriði, 'and he would rather that you have his treasure, if you will protect him, than those who want him dead.'

They spoke in such wise for a while, making sure that all was kept secret from the jarl, and then Godfrey returned to the castle. No property was removed from the building, as it was by no means certain that the attack would succeed, and the ordinary folk could not be trusted.

The tenth day of Yule-tide was a grand one, and Jarl Rögnvaldr arose and gave the order for his men to take up their weapons and for the trumpets to signal the assault. They dragged the bundles of wood up to the castle walls and piled them high. The jarl then issued orders with regard to where each should make his attack. He himself would lead the men of Orkneyjar from the south, Erlingr and Áslákr from the west, Jon and Guðþorm from the east, and Eindriði Ungi from the north. When all were ready to mount the assault, they set the wood ablaze and the jarl recited a verse:

Maidens decked in snow-white linen and lace
served us sparkling wine.
Ermingerda was fair to see
when we met her on our journey.
Now we venture 'gainst the castle
with blazing oak firebrands.
Swift-leaping from the scabbard
the keen-edged striker glitters.

Rögnvaldr, in typical eccentric form, pauses during the assault to recite a verse about Ermingerda before drawing his sword. This combination of romance and bloodshed will continue as a poetic theme throughout the jarl's voyage.

Now they began a fierce attack on the castle, with both weapons and fire. They assailed it with a shower of missiles, for this was the only means of attack open to them. The defenders would not stand steady at the ramparts, as they were wary of the missiles. They dropped burning pitch and brimstone, though this did little damage to the jarl's men. What Erlingr thought might happen did - the lime could not withstand the heat of the fire and the wall collapsed, leaving large gaps.

The jarl's stepson, Sigmundr Öngull, was one of the foremost in the assault, and was often ahead of the jarl, though then barely full grown. When the attack had gone on for some time, the defenders were driven back. The south wind blew all the smoke toward Eindriði, and as the flames swiftly started to spread, the jarl ordered that water be poured over the charred stones to cool them down, and there was a lull in the assault.

The jarl composed a verse:

Now I mind the Yule-tide
spent with friends and bold men,
east of Agðir's mountains,
with the brave warrior Sólmundr.
Here now, at another Yule,
I busy myself in the same way,
adding to the weapon clamour
south at the castle walls.

Then he made another:

Glad was I when the grand lady
listened to the words of my love tale.
Led a helpless hostage
by a Valland maid in autumn,
I love that fair lady still.
Here I lay out the eagles' feast –
stone and lime, once bound together,
now collapse asunder.

To lay out the eagles' feast *is to kill foes and leave them as carrion.*

Sigmundr Öngull then composed a verse:

When ye fare over seas
to Orkneyjar in spring,
tell that lady I most love –
the lady of the lovely raiment –
that none advanced more bravely
beneath the castle ramparts
than this young lad.

The jarl and Sigmundr then got ready to force their way into the castle, and with little resistance being offered, made their way in, and many were slain, though those that gave up were spared. They took a large amount of plunder in the way of property, but could not find the lord of the castle, and hardly any treasure.

Godfrey's escape was greatly discussed, and how he could have arranged it. Suspicion soon arose that Eindriði Ungi had assisted him, and that he must have slipped away under the screen of the smoke into the woods.

Throughout the saga, Eindriði Ungi proves himself untrustworthy and something of a liability, from holding up the expedition twice because his ships were being built, to causing division in the ranks and making a secret pact with Godfrey.

After that, Jarl Rögnvaldr and his men stayed on a little longer in Galicia, then set their course along the west of Spain. They raided widely throughout the heathen areas, accumulating a large amount of booty.

They went against a certain village, where the people gathered and put up a hard fight, but finally broke and scattered, after many were slain.

Then the jarl composed this verse:

When I went for a fight in Spainland,
swiftly we beat the foe.
Weary of our stout hacking,
they fled to their sweethearts at home.
Corpses were stretched out all across that country –
worthy of Ermingerda -
our fame in song shall be sung.

Rögnvaldr's idea of a romantic tribute – a bloodbath of strewn corpses – would probably not be appreciated by the elegant golden-haired young queen in her sumptuous court back in Verbon.

They sailed along the west coast of Spain and were caught in a gale. They lay at anchor for three days, with high waves crashing over, so that the ships were nearly foundered.

Then the jarl made a verse:

I'm storm-tossed here, but undeterred,
while the cables hold fast,
and the ship's tackle holds,
as she breasts the billows.
I am sworn to the fair one
left behind in the northland.
Now a fair wind returns –
speed us to the channel.

They set sail and ran into Njorfasund with a fair wind.

Oddi made a verse:

When the leal friend of heroes,
drinking sweet mead in the guest hall,
sat beside the grand ring-scatterer –
that was a week to remember.
Now the fine wave steeds
carry the gracious Rögnvaldr and his warriors
swiftly through Njorfasund,
bearing bucklers.

Njorfasund *(Straits of Gibraltar).*

A ring-scatterer *was someone who gave out rings, a generous lord.* Wave steeds *is yet another kenning for ships.*

As they were tacking into the Sound, the jarl recited:

By an east wind, gently breathing,

as from the Valland lady's lips,
our ships are borne onward,
as we push the yards out further.
Though we lashed the canvas tighter
than expected to midmast,
south off Spain we speed away.

They sailed on through Njorfasund and the strong wind began to ebb. When they were clear of the Sound, Eindriði Ungi with his six ships parted ways with the jarl and made for Marselia. It was then said that Eindriði Ungi now settled the question of whether he had assisted Godfrey in his escape.

Marselia *is Marseilles.*

A slippery customer to the end, Eindriði parts the ways from Jarl Rögnvaldr without warning. Unfortunately, it was not the last they would see of him.

They continue south to Serkland *(Land of the Saracens).*

The jarl and his men sailed out to sea and stood south to Serkland. Then Jarl Rögnvaldr composed a verse:

Now our grand ship. spurning land,
steeps her breast in bright waters.
Long before this verse-singer
sets eye once again on northern lands,
far off Spain, heading southward,
the keen prow cleaves the billowing waves.

There is nothing to be said of the jarl's voyage until they arrived south of Serkland, and lay near Sardinia, though they were not aware of the land, as it was calm, with dense fog across the water. So, they sailed slowly, hardly able to see anything.

One morning the fog dissipated, and they arose and spotted two islets. But when they looked for them a second time, there was only one.

They told the jarl, and he said: 'Those could not have been islets you saw, but ships of a kind they have in this part of the world, which they call *dromondar*. From a distance they look as big as holms (islets). But where the other dromond lay, a blast of wind has likely swept over the water, and she has sailed off. They are probably some rovers.'

After that, he called over the bishop and all the ship commanders, and said: 'I ask of you, my lord Bishop, and Erlingr, my kinsman, if you can see a way by which we can overcome the crew of the dromond.'

The bishop answered: 'I believe you will find it difficult to attack the dromond in your long-ships, for it will be hard to reach their bulwarks with a boarding-pike, and in all likelihood, they have boiling pitch and brimstone to pour beneath your feet and over your heads. You must see, Jarl Rögnvaldr, wise as you are, that it would be foolhardy in the extreme to place yourself and your followers in such peril.'

'My lord Bishop,' said Erlingr, 'it may be that you are right in thinking that we shall not prevail by rowing at them. Yet, it seems to me that if we push close to the dromond, their missiles will land beyond our ships pressed close alongside. But if things fall otherwise, we can clear off swiftly, and they will not be able to pursue us in the dromond.'

'That is bravely spoken,' remarked the jarl, 'and suits my own mind on the matter. I will now let it be known to the ship commanders and all the men for everyone to take up arms, each in his own place, as best he can. Then let us mount the attack, and if they are Christian traders, we can come to terms with them. But if they are heathen, which I suspect they are, by the grace of the Almighty God we shall prevail over them. Whatever plunder we win, we shall give every fiftieth penny to the poor.'

Then they took up their arms and readied the bulwarks of their ships for the fray, preparing themselves as best they could. The jarl directed how each ship should take part in the attack, and then they all rowed hard toward the dromond.

*Rögnvaldr and his men are Nordic Christians, probably to varying degrees, but at the time heiðinn (*heathen*) customs were still observed by many. The latter involved honouring the Norse deities Óðinn, Þórr, Freyja and others, as well as the alfar or land spirits. Rögnvaldr clearly views Saracens as heathen who should be overcome by force, though he boasts in his poetry of knowing runes* (an originally heathen script often used for esoteric inscriptions and magical working). *However Christian he is, like any viking, he will not pass up an opportunity for plunder.*

When the crew of the dromond saw the strange ships advancing to attack them, they draped fine clothing and other valuable stuff out on the bulwarks, bawling and shouting, which the jarl's men took as a taunt.

Jarl Rögnvaldr had his ship drawn up close beneath the stem of the dromond, on the starboard side. Erlingr brought his vessel close on the larboard side, while Jon and Áslákr brought theirs under her bows, and the rest amidships on either side, all of them staying as close against her as they could. But when they closed with the dromond in this way, her sides were so lofty that the Northmen were unable to use their weapons to any effect. The dromond's crew poured blazing brimstone and boiling pitch down at them, though most of it fell beyond their ships, as Erlingr had guessed, and they did not need to shield themselves. But when the attack failed to bear fruit, the bishop had his ship and two others break away from the dromond and gathered their bowmen in these. When they had distanced themselves enough for a good range, they shot their arrows into the dromond, and this proved more effective. The dromond's crew had to defend themselves with their shields and paid little attention to what was going on in the ships below them.

Jarl Rögnvaldr then told his men to take up their axes and to start hewing at the dromond's planking where there was less iron cladding. The men in the other ships started following suit when they saw what the jarl's men were doing.

At the spot where Erlingr was, a large anchor hung from the dromond, with its fluke hooked over the gunwale and its shank hanging down towards Erlingr's ship. One of his forecastlemen was called Auðun Rauði. He was heaved up onto the anchor-stock, where he pulled others up after him. Standing as close as possible to the dromond, they hewed at the planks with all their might, much higher than the others could reach, and when they had hacked out an opening big enough, they got ready to enter the dromond. The jarl and his men boarded the lower deck while Erlingr and his men boarded the upper, and soon there was fierce fighting. The crew of the dromond were Saracens, or infidels of Mahomet. There were also a good many black men, who bravely withstood them.

Erlingr received a grave wound in the neck, near the shoulder, when he leapt aboard. It healed so badly that he carried it bent to one side thereafter and got the name of Skakkr (Skew Neck).

When Jarl Rögnvaldr and Erlingr joined one another, they drove the Saracens to the forepart of the ship, and the jarl's men boarded one after the other until their numbers were greater, and they pressed the enemy hard. Then they spotted a man greater than the others in bearing and stature, and they guessed that this must be their leader. Jarl Rögnvaldr gave orders that he was not to be wounded, if he could be captured by any other means. Then they surrounded him with their shields and seized him this way. He was sent with a few others to the bishop's ship, but they killed everybody else, winning a large amount of plunder and many valuable things. When the hardest part of the fight was over, they sat and rested.

Then the jarl composed a verse:

At the spreading of the banner,
Erlingr the mighty battle tree,
in the forefront of this dromond fight
gained victory and glory.
We slew the black-skinned warriors,
with their blood running everywhere.
When we hewed among the heathen,
sharp-edged swords were reddened.

Of slaughter we've had our fill –
piles of corpses surround us.
Our swords painting red
all morning on the dromond.
News of this sword-storm –
dealing of death blows -
will spread north to Verbon.

They talked over what had been done, every one of them bearing witness to what he had seen. Then it was debated who was the first to board the dromond, and there was no general agreement about this, a state of affairs that some said was hard to believe if they could not all tell of this great feat in the same way. They then agreed that Jarl Rögnvaldr should decide on the matter, and that everybody should tell the story as he did.

The jarl composed a verse:

The first was Auðun Rauði -
with courage and vigour –
to climb the dromond's dark sides
and bravely bear away booty.
God's good favour helped us
vanquish the heathen –
our swords in red blood steeped –
around us sprawl the dusky dead men.

After they cleared the dromond, they set it ablaze. On witnessing this, the big man whom they had captured became agitated and the blood drained from his face, but when they encouraged him to speak, he would say nothing, nor would he make any kind of sign. He was indifferent alike to both fine promises or threats. Then, as the fire on the dromond blazed up, they saw what looked like a glowing stream running into the sea, and their prisoner was greatly distressed at the sight. It dawned on them at that point that their search for the money on board had not been as thorough as it should have been, and a great deal of gold and silver had melted in the fire.

It is to be imagined that the language would have been pretty blue at that point.

Jarl Rögnvaldr and his men sailed south under Serkland and lay off a certain town there. They had a truce of seven nights with the inhabitants, selling them silver and other valuables, but nobody would buy the big man, and so the jarl let him go along with four other men.

The morning after, the big man returned to see the jarl with a large following. He said that he was a nobleman of Serkland and that the dromond and its contents had been given to him as a parting gift.

'It dismayed me most that you burned it,' he went on, 'and destroyed so much treasure, without anyone being allowed to enjoy it. Now it happens that you are in my power, but as you spared my life and accorded me such honour as you could, I in turn shall spare you. But I would be glad never to set eyes on you again, and now may you live hale and well.'

After that, he rode off into the country.

As this is Rögnvaldr's first voyage to that part of the world, his knowledge of the dromond is likely to have been gained second-hand, and his repeated reference to the skin colour of the ship's fighting crew suggests that he may never have seen black men in the flesh before, and that it may have been some kind of novelty to him, which, with the exception of far-travelled individuals such as Bishop William and Eindriði, would have been the case with many others in his company. The saga writer pays tribute to their stout resistance and apparent determination to fight to the death.

However far removed the Christian Rögnvaldr was from his heathen heritage, this episode with the Saracen nobleman would surely have served to show him that the honour and integrity preached by Christians was also to be found among non-Christians.

The jarl sails on to Crete, then Jorsalir *or* Jorsalaland *(Jerusalem) and arrives at* Akursborg *(Acre).*

Jarl Rögnvaldr then sailed to Crete and put down anchor in a strong gale. As Armóðr kept watch that night, he composed a verse:

Lie we now where squally swells
break over our sturdy ship breast.
My task is to keep watch
on this wave-treading sea stallion.
As the lads sleep sound,
I look over my shoulder to Crete.

They lay off Crete, and when they got a fair wind, they sailed on to Jorsalir, arriving at Akursborg early on a Friday morning. They then went ashore with such grand style as had seldom been seen there.

Þórbjörn Svarti composed this verse:

Often have I with comrades stout
battled in Orkneyjar,
when the feeder of crows
led his forces to the fray.
Now this Friday morning
we follow our steadfast jarl,

bearing our bucklers

gladly to Akursborg's gates.

Feeder of crows *was a kenning for warlord, whose enemies were often left on the battlefield for the birds of carrion.*

They remained in Akursborg for a while, and a disease broke out among them and many perished of it, including Þórbjörn Svarti.

Oddi the Little composed this verse:

Þó*rbjörn Svarti, skáld and comrade,*

bravely steered the chiefs' ships

'cross the sea king's highway.

Round by Þ*rasnes, and south to Akursborg,*

there I watched them pile the grave-mould

of the high church over the king's friend.

In that sunny southern land

he lies under rocky ground.

Sea king's highway *is yet another kenning for the sea.*

Jarl Rögnvaldr and his company left Akursborg and visited the sacred places of Jorsalaland. They all bathed in the River Jordan. Jarl Rögnvaldr and Sigmundr Öngull swam across and tied large knots to some shrubs.

The jarl composed a verse:

Long the way of my travels

to this desert-bound plain.

My crossing over the Jordan

will be remembered by the wise maiden.

Those who hang about their steadings

would think this too far from home.

Warm blood washes the wide heath.

Then Sigmundr made a verse:

This day I tie a stout knot
for the clodhopper sitting by the home hearth –
'tis true we play a fine trick on him.

The jarl then composed another:

Tired I came to this thicket of shrubs
where we tie knots for the fine fellow,
on Saint Lawrence's day.

The tying of knots was originally a heathen practice. Knots were tied in acts of remembrance, to bind someone magically from a distance, or free someone by a ritual untying. By tying knots, they were perhaps attempting magical constraint on the stay-at-home laggard to travel far afield as they did. The reference to spilled blood suggests the ritual practice of cutting one's palm as sacrificial payment for a spell-working. If true, they were in effect using a heathen practice to force a man to carry out a Christian pilgrimage. This brief episode serves to show that heathen ways still survived even among Christians long after the arrival of the new religion.

On the way back to Jorsalir, the jarl recited:

From the skáld's neck hangs a cross,
and in his hand he holds a palm –
let there be no hard feelings.
My men run down from the slopes.

That summer Jarl Rögnvaldr and his followers left Jorsalaland with the intention of heading to Miklagarðr. In the autumn they arrived in a town called Imbolum, where they stayed a good while. It was the custom there whenever two people approached one another in a busy street, and one of them thought it necessary to step to one side, he would call out to the other: *'Midway! Midway!'*

One night the jarl's men, among whom was Erlingr Skakkr, had walked from the town and were just crossing the bridge leading to their ships when a number of the townsfolk approached them, calling out: 'Midway! Midway!'

Erlingr was extremely drunk and didn't pay any attention, and as they came up to him, he tumbled from the bridge straight into the mud. His men rushed to help him, dragged him clear, and had to strip him of his clothing, he was so covered in muck.

In the morning, the jarl saw him and was told what happened. The jarl smiled as he delivered this verse:

A mucky misfortune befell my friend Erlingr,
he tumbled with a splash for not calling 'Midway!'
loudly like the locals.
The prince's kinsman was left looking dismal,
caked with mud at Imbolum.

Some time after this, they were all coming from town very drunk, and realised that Jon Foot was missing from their company. They sent word to the ships to search for him, but he could not be found. They could not search for him on shore during the night, but in the morning they found him dead against the city wall, and it was never discovered who had killed him. They buried him with honour at a holy church and then departed.

They went north to Engilsness and waited a few nights for a good wind that would take them to Miklagarðr. They gave their ships a grand appearance and sailed out in fine style, as they knew Sigurðr Jorsalafari had done.

Imbolum *and* Engilsness *are unidentified locations.* Miklagarðr *is Constantinople.*

King Sigurðr Magnússon was known as Jorsalafari *from having led the Norwegian Crusade to Jerusalem. He made Rögnvaldr Jarl of Orkney in 1129.*

While they were sailing their ships northward, the jarl composed this verse:

Let us ride the horses of the sea king
and leave off ploughing the fields,
as the wet prows drive onward to Miklagarðr.
There we'll take noble rewards,
payment for weapon-wielding,
fill the wolf's red palate
and win battle honours.

Horses of the sea king *is another kenning for ships, and to* fill the wolf's red palate *is to leave dead foes behind for the hungry predator. In this verse Rögnvaldr expresses his intention to serve as a mercenary, as so many other Norsemen have done in the* Væringjar *or Varangian Guard, the elite unit of bodyguards to the Byzantine emperors.*

Rögnvaldr and his men arrived in Miklagarðr and received a good welcome from the Emperor and the Væringjar. At that time Menelaus, whom we call Manuli, was Emperor of Miklagarðr. He gave them a large amount of money and offered them paid positions as mercenaries if they would stay on. They remained a good part of the winter there.

Eindriði Ungi happened to be there when they arrived and was highly esteemed by the Emperor. He had little to do with the jarl and his men and spoke disparagingly about them to others.

Rögnvaldr set out again from Miklagarðr during the winter, going first to Dyraksborg in Bulgaraland and then sailing to Apulia. Jarl Rögnvaldr, Erlingr, Bishop William and most of the other noble men left the ships there, obtained horses and rode on to Rome and then from Rome until they reached Denmark. From there they went to Norway, where the folk were glad to see them. Their journey became very famous, and all those who made it were deemed greater men than they were before.

Ögmundr Drengr, Erlingr Skakkr's brother, had died while they were away. While both were alive, he had been considered the greater of the two. After the death of King Ingi, Magnús son of Erlingr and Kristín, daughter of Sigurðr Jorsalafari, was made king, but the governing of Norway was in Erlingr's hands alone. Valdimar, the Danish king, gave him the title of jarl, and he became an outstanding chief.

Eindriði arrived from the south some winters after Jarl Rögnvaldr, and went to King Eystein, as he didn't want anything to do with Erlingr. But after King Eystein passed away, Eindriði and Sigurðr, son of Hávarðr Hold of Ror mustered forces and made Hákon Herðabreiðr (the Broad Shouldered), son of King Sigurðr Haraldsson, their king. Then they killed Gregorius Dagsson and King Ingi.

Eindriði and Hákon fought a battle with Erlingr under Sekkr, and Hákon got killed there, but Eindriði took to his heels. A little later, Erlingr had Eindriði slain at Vík.

Dyraksborg *is Dürres and* Bulgaraland *is Bulgaria.* Apulia *is Puglia in Italy.*

Eystein Haraldsson was King of Norway (1142-1157) jointly with his brothers Ingi and Sigurðr. He was born in Scotland. A civil war arose in which Sigurðr was slain by Ingi's men in 1155, and in 1157 Eystein was executed after his army retreated before the greater forces of Ingi. Those loyal to Eystein later gave their support to his nephew Hákon Herðabreið when he moved to take the throne.

Erlingr Skakki was the guardian of King Ingi during his boyhood and one of his chief advisors in adulthood. Ingi was killed in battle in 1161, defeated by his rival Hákon Herðabreið. Gregorius Dagsson was one of King Ingi's strongest supporters. Eindriði actively took Hákon's side against Ingi. Erlingr then defeated Hákon in 1162 and put an end to Eindriði.

Jarl Rögnvaldr spent the summer in Hörðaland, in Norway, and heard much news from Orkneyjar. There was a lot of trouble there, with most of the chiefs divided into factions and only a few staying out of it. At the head of one of these factions was Jarl Haraldr, with Jarl Erlendr and Svein Ásleifarson heading the other.

When the jarl heard this, he made this verse:

Though most of my nobles

have forgotten their sworn oaths -

such is the baseness of men -

their traitorous plots shall be thwarted yet.

Slow but sure shall be my rule

as long as I bear a beard on my chin.

The jarl had no ships but asked his kinsmen and friends to build some long-ships for him during the winter. They received his request favourably, consented to everything he asked, and had the ships built.

In the summer, the jarl prepared to sail west to his dominions in Orkneyjar, but he was late getting ready, as many things delayed him. He voyaged west in a merchant ship belonging to Þórhall Asgrimsson, an Icelander of good family, who had a farm south in Biskupstimgur. The jarl was accompanied by a large retinue of noblemen on board the vessel. When they arrived in Scotland, the winter was well advanced, and they lay at Torfness. The jarl arrived in his dominions just before Yule.

Despite Rögnvaldr's romantic poetry that referred to Ermingerda throughout the voyage, he did not return to Verbon, and we are to assume that his was only an infatuation with her. Whatever the case, the trouble brewing in Orkney was of more pressing import. Erlendr Haraldsson, who was joint Jarl of Orkney, along with Rögnvaldr and Haraldr Maddaðarson, had received half of his father's lands in Caithness from Máel Coluim IV, King of Scots and had taken advantage of Rögnvaldr's absence to secure for himself his cousin Haraldr's share of Orkney from King Eystein of Norway. This led to fighting between Erlendr and Haraldr. On his return, Rögnvaldr was to join Haraldr in opposing Erlendr and the latter was killed in a raid on Damsay in Orkney in 1154.

THE OUTLAW SVEIN ÁSLEIFARSON

Svein Ásleifarson (c.1115-1171), one of the most renowned and infamous of vikings, features prominently in Orkneyinga saga. *He was one of four children born to Óláfr Hrolfsson and his wife Ásleif, who had steadings on both Gairsay on Orkney and Duncansby in Caithness. His long bloodstained career begins after his father Óláfr is burned to death in his house by a foe called Ølvir Brawl. From this point on, Svein becomes known as Ásleifarson after his mother, and kills, plunders and spreads mayhem wherever he goes, becoming an outlaw and developing a love-hate relationship with the Orkney jarls.*

In the following passage he looks to Jarl Rögnvaldr Kali Kolsson for support in seeking vengeance for the killing of his father.

The Burning of Frakokk

It came about that Svein Ásleifarson asked Jarl Rögnvaldr for men and ships to wreak vengeance on Ølvir and Frakokk for burning his father Óláfr to death.

'Forget not, Svein,' responded the jarl, 'that Ølvir and the old hag Frakokk, who is good for nothing, will hardly be able to cause us scathe now.'

'They will always be up to no good while they're still alive,' answered Svein. 'I expected more after all the favours I've done for you, than that you would turn me down now.'

The jarl asked him what he needed.

'Two ships, well manned and equipped,' replied Svein.

The jarl said he would have them.

So Svein made ready to go, and sailed southward to Borgarfjörðr, where he got a northwest wind to Difeyrar, a trading post in Scotland. From there he passed Mỳræfi to Ekkjal and from there visited Jarl Maddaðr at Atjoklar. He supplied Svein with men who could lead him through the mountains and woodlands wherever he wanted to go, and he went over the mountains and through the forests, away from all settled places, and arrived in Hjálmundalr in Suðrland.

Ølvir and Frakokk had posted men to keep watch in all those places where they could anticipate an attack from Orkneyjar, and so they did not actually expect to be taken by surprise until Svein and his men appeared on a certain hill behind the houses. Ølvir faced them with sixty men, and the fight was on, but Ølvir's followers soon broke and ran, having offered little resistance, making for the houses, as they could not reach the woods. Many were cut down and Ølvir escaped to Hjálmundalr river and from there into the mountains. He then fared on to Skotlandsfjörðr on the west coast, and from there to the Suðreyjar, and he is now out of the story.

After Ølvir fled, Svein and his men advanced on the houses and pillaged freely, taking everything they could get their hands on. Then they set fire to the buildings with everybody in them, and Frakokk died there.

Svein and his men harried and plundered widely throughout Suðrland before returning to their ships. After that, they made many a foray during the summer and wreaked havoc throughout Scotland.

In the autumn Svein arrived back in Orkneyjar. Svein went to see Jarl Rögnvaldr and received a warm welcome. After that, Svein sailed over to Dungalsbaer in Katanes to spend the winter.

Borgarfjörðr *is an unidentified firth in Scotland,* Difeyrar *is Banff,* Mýræfi *is Moray and* Ekkjal *is Oykel.* Atjoklar *is Atholl (from Gaelic* Athfhotla *or New Ireland), once an important mormaerdom, now in northern Perth and Kinross.* Skotlandsfjörðr *is the Minch, a strait dividing the northwest Highlands and the northern Inner Hebrides from Lewis and Harris in the Outer Hebrides.* Hjálmundalr *is Helmsdale in Sutherland.*

Jarl Maddaðr is Madadh, Mormaer of Atholl, the son of Máel Muire and grandson of Donnchad mac Crínáin, King of Alba, according to the saga.

The tradition of burning people alive in their houses continues unabated here with Svein Ásleifarson.

Svein and Holdbodi

Svein is the type that always remembers a good turn, so when a man who had given him strong support when he needed it in the past asks for his help, he does not hesitate, though he later comes to regret it.

Then Svein got word from Holdboði of the Suðreyjar, seeking assistance against a warlord from Bretland called Robert, of English blood, who had come to the islands, forced Holdboði off his lands and thieved a lot of money. Svein didn't hang about but sailed back to Orkneyjar and asked Jarl Rögnvaldr for men and ships. The jarl asked what he wanted them for this time, and Svein explained that he had just received a plea for help from a man who had supported him when the hand of every other man seemed to be against him, and that he was not inclined to refuse it.

'You can't trust many Suðreyarmen,' responded the jarl, 'so you'd be better off parting the ways while you're on good terms. Still, you are honour bound to do whatever you think is right. So, I'll give you two ships, fully manned.'

Svein was well pleased and sailed off to the Suðreyjar, though he did not come across Holdboði until he reached the Isle of Mön, where Holdboði was lying low. When Svein arrived there, Holdboði was happy to see him, as the Welshman had wreaked a lot of havoc on the island, killing and plundering in the way he had previously done all over the south of Europe. He had slain a man of good family called Andres, who had left a widow, Ingiriðr, and a son named Sigurðr. Ingiriðr was a lady of means, with wide estates, and Holdboði counselled Svein to ask for her hand, but when he approached her, she said she would only give her consent if he avenged her dead husband Andres. Svein replied that he could do some harm to the British.

Svein and Holdboði then sailed out with five ships on a raid. They ravaged Bretland, landing at a place called Jarlsnes and wreaking destruction. One morning they reached a settlement that put up little in the way of a fight. The farmers cleared out as Svein and his men plundered the entire hamlet and set fire to six farms before breakfast.

An Icelander called Eirikr accompanying Svein composed this verse:

Half a dozen homesteads flaming,
Half a dozen households ransacked.
This was Svein's morning work –
his settling of the score -
glowing coals shared out to farmers.

After that, they returned to their ships and passed the remainder of the summer raiding by sea and piling up a large amount of booty. The Welsh warlord fled to Lundey Island, where there was a solid stronghold. Svein and his men besieged it but left off after a while when they saw they were getting nowhere and went back to Mön in the autumn.

That winter Svein married Ingiriðr and stayed on there in high honour. In the spring he gathered some men for a raid and went to see Holdboði, asking for assistance, but the Hebridean made excuses, that many of his men were too busy, and some others away trading. So Svein departed with no help from Holdboði. The reality was, however, that Holdboði had reached an understanding with the Welsh warlord and made an alliance, strengthened with gifts.

Svein sailed out with three ships regardless but got little plunder in the early part of the summer. After, he went to southward beyond Ireland and took a barge that belonged to monks in Syllingar and pillaged it. Then he made raids into Ireland, amassing considerable spoils, and returning to Mön in the autumn.

When Svein was only a short time back, he heard rumours that he could no longer trust Holdboði's loyalty, but he brushed it off. Then one spring night the watchmen told him that there were enemies coming, so Svein and his men armed themselves and rushed out in time to see a large mob of men advancing toward the homestead with blazing torches.

Svein and his men took their stand on a hill to defend themselves and sounded a horn, so that men came rushing to him from all over the area at the sound of it, and the attackers fell back. Svein and his men harried them and cut many down as they fled, and many on both sides took wounds before they parted.

The one who had led the attackers was Holdboði, who escaped and fled to Lundey Island, where the warlord Robert welcomed him.

Svein returned home and kept many of his men around him, staying alert against the Suðreyarmen. Late in the winter he sold his lands and sailed to Ljoðahús, carrying out a lot of depradation.

The Suðreyjarmen *are Hebrideans.* Bretland *is Wales and* the British *are the Welsh.* Mön *is the Isle of Man,* Syllingar *is the Scilly Isles, and* Ljoðahús *is Lewis .*

Holdboði Hundason gave Svein shelter on Tiree when he was on the run after splitting open the head of Jarl Páll's forecastleman Svein Breast Rope with an axe. Before that, Svein Ásleifarson had been given refuge by Bishop William of Orkney, who thanked him for killing Svein Breast Rope and considered it good riddance. Svein Breast Rope, described as having an unlucky look about him and of practising sorcery, was clearly not popular with the bishop.

The warlord Robert is described as being of English blood, though referred to later as Welsh. In all probability he was an English Norman and a veteran of campaigns in southern Europe, based in Wales during the events of the saga and only called Welsh insofar as he lived there.

The term British originally applied only to the Britons or Welsh, as they later became known. The Angles and Saxons, apparently with little awareness of the irony, referred to the Brythonic inhabitants of the island, whose lands they were invading, as Welsh or foreigners.

Jarl Rögnvaldr Kali Kolsson and Svein have something of a rogues' alliance. Svein had kidnapped Rögnvaldr's rival, Jarl Páll in the past, allowing Rögnvaldr to take over Orkney. Svein's relationship with succeeding jarls has a similar nature in that he indulges in a lot of mayhem, but often gets away with it because he's done them a favour.

Svein's Way of Life

Svein's viking lifestyle allows him to accumulate enough wealth to build a massive ale hall at Gáreksey *(Gairsay) and entertain large companies of men. His raiding trips are sensibly arranged so that he can sow seed and bring in the crops in between burning, killing and plundering.*

This was how Svein used to live. He would spend the winter at home in Gáreksey, where he feasted eighty men at his own expense. His drinking hall was so large, there was no match for it in Orkneyjar. In the spring he busied himself sowing seed, and afterwards went off raiding in the Suðreyjar and Ireland on what he referred to as his spring trip. He would then go back home just after midsummer and stayed until the corn had been reaped and the grain all in. He would then go plundering again and never returned until the first month of winter was over. He called this his autumn trip.

A Viking Expedition

In this passage, Svein sets out on one of his viking trips, accompanied by Jarl Haraldr Maddaðarson's son, Hákon. They rob two English merchant ships and return in grand style. Then the jarl gives Svein some sage advice.

Once Svein set out on his spring trip and had Hákon, the son of Jarl Haraldr, with him. They had five large ships, all fitted out for rowing, and started plundering in the Suðreyjar. All the folk were so afraid of him that they hid all their valuables among the rocks or buried underground. So Svein sailed down to the Isle of Mön but found slim pickings there. Then they went to Ireland and pillaged there. They were making for Dyflin when they came on two English merchant vessels loaded with valuable cloth and other goods, and so they made straight for them. Svein asked them if they wanted to fight, but the English were not in much of a mood for contention, and Svein's men took all their money and only left them with the clothes they stood in and a peedie amount of provisions. They sailed away in their vessels, while Svein and his followers carried on to the Suðreyjar and shared out the plunder. They sailed west in grand style, and whenever they lay in harbours, they draped their ships in the English cloth, just to be fancy. When they sailed on to Orkneyjar, they had the cloth stitched to their sails, and it looked like they were all made of this fine material. They called this the Skrud-viking, or the broadcloth viking trip.

After that, Svein returned to his farm at Gáreksey with the wine and English mead he had lifted from the merchant ships. When he had been home for a while, he invited Jarl Haraldr to a grand banquet, and all the folk were not short of things to say about Svein's way of living.

'I'd like it if you stopped the raiding, Svein,' said the jarl. 'It's better to be safe at home. Your plundering has maintained yourself and your men for a long time now, but most hell-raisers are fated to die unless they themselves choose to stop.'

Svein regarded the jarl with a smile on his face.

'Grand and friendly words, my lord,' he said. 'I'll heed your excellent counsel, though there are folk who might have a thing to say about your own less than peaceful ways.'

'I'm answerable for my own deeds,' replied the jarl. 'But I must say what I think.'

'I am assured that you mean well, sir,' said Svein, 'and so this is how it shall be – I'll stop pillaging, as I'm getting on in years and cannot continue to bear the rigours of war, but I will go on one more trip in the autumn and I want it to be as grand as my spring trip. When that's done, I'll relinquish the viking life.'

'It is difficult to tell which comes first, old friend,' responded the jarl. 'Death or glory.'

That was the end of their talk. When the feast was over, Jarl Haraldr left with fine presents, and he and Svein parted the warmest of friends.

Skrud *was the term for fine cloth stolen by Svein and his men.*

Hákon Haraldsson was Svein's fosterson. Fostering a child, in this case Jarl Haraldr's son, was a common practice in both Norse and Gaelic societies to forge bonds of friendship and loyalty, often between a chieftain and his retainer.

Relations between Jarl Haraldr Maddaðarson and Svein were not always so cosy. In the 1150s, during a dispute between Haraldr, Rögnvaldr Kali Kolsson and Erlendr Haraldsson over the shared rulership of Orkney, Haraldr found out that Svein's brother Gunni had fathered a child on Haraldr's mother Margaret and Haraldr outlawed Gunni. Svein fell out with Haraldr over this, took Haraldr's rival Erlendr's side in the dispute and started robbing Haraldr's retainers, plundering his ships and at one point besieging him in a fortress at Kjarrekstaðir or Cairston in 1152. Regarding the latter, when one of Haraldr's men, Arni Hrafnsson saw Svein and Jarl Erlendr advancing from their ships, he ran all the way to Kirkwall in such a panic that he tried to get in the church and came to a sudden stop when he got stuck in the doorway with his shield still on his back. Erlendr was killed in a raid on Damsay by Haraldr and Rögnvaldr's men in 1154 and after going on the run for a while, Svein was reconciled with Jarl Haraldr.

The Death of Svein

Svein sets out on what is to be his last viking raid, again accompanied by his fosterson Hákon and invades Dyflin *(Dublin).*

Not long after this Svein readied himself to go on a viking expedition with seven big longships. He had Hákon, the son of Jarl Haraldr, with him. They sailed first for the Suðreyjar but found little spoils. Then they went to Ireland and raided many a place there, faring south to Dyflin and arriving among the townsfolk so suddenly that they had no warning. Svein took the rulers of the city prisoner and a huge amount of booty, and the upshot was that they were persuaded to hand over the town and to pay whatever sum he demanded. His men were to be quartered in the town and he was to have the command of it. They swore oaths to this effect.

Svein and his men then retired to their ships for the night, with the understanding that they would come back in the morning and receive hostages.

Now it can be told what happened in the town during the night. The rulers of the town called an assembly to discuss the fix they were in. They considered it an intolerable burden to hand their town over to the Orkneymen, and most especially to the man who had proved himself the scourge of the entire west. And so, they decided to trick him if they could, and dug big pits inside the gates of the city and numerous other places besides, exactly where Svein and his men would have to pass through, with armed men concealing themselves in the buildings hard by. They placed coverings over these pits so light that they would easily collapse beneath the weight of their enemies and concealed everything by spreading straw around. Then they waited until morning.

When morning came, Svein and his men rose, took up their weapons and made for the town. As they approached the gates, the Dubliners gathered to each side along by the pits. Svein and his men, all unsuspecting, fell right into them. Some of the townsfolk dashed for the gates, while others approached the pits and attacked Svein's men with weapons. They found it hard to put up resistance in their position and Svein was killed there with all the men that had followed him to town.

They said that Svein was the last to die, declaring just before he perished: 'Let all men know, whether I die today or not, that I am the retainer of the holy Jarl Rögnvaldr, and my trust is in him where he bides with God.'

The survivors of Svein's band retreated to the ships and put to sea, and there is nothing to say of their voyage until they landed in Orkneyjar.

Svein's dying reference is to Jarl Rögnvaldr Kali Kolsson, who was canonised in 1192 and whose relics were placed in Saint Magnus' Cathedral, Kirkwall.

NAME INDEX WITH HISTORICAL BACKGROUND AND PRONUNCIATION GUIDE

Personal Names

It was an ancient custom among both Norse and Gael to have personal names that included those of gods with a view to bestowing luck and protection on a child – for example, in Norse, *Þórgils* (Thorgils - Thor's Staff) and in Gaelic *Lughaidh* (derived from the name of the god Lugh). People were also named after animals or birds – the boar or wolf for ferocity, the bear for strength etc. After the arrival of Christianity in Ireland and Scotland, many were given personal names that included those of Gaelic saints such as Brigid or Colum Cille, again for luck and protection.

Not only were Norse names Gaelicised, but Gaelic names were also given Norse versions, for example *Kormákr* for *Cormac, Tomnal* for *Domnaill,* and *Fiak* for *Fíach.* In addition, instances in which a person's name was an amalgam of both Norse and Gaelic became common – for instance, the name *Ánnbensi mac Droann* inscribed in ogam on the Bressay Stone from Shetland.

This guide should help with the pronunciation of Old Norse and Gaelic names and terms used throughout the book, as well as providing some background on the main protagonists in our saga history.

Áed (Ee) Gaelic (Fire). Áed Findliath was *Ard Rí* or High King of Ireland from 862-879. The son of Niall Caille, he belonged to the northern Uí Neill. One of his wives was Máel Muire, a daughter of Cináed mac Ailpín, King of the Picts. During his reign the Norse settlement in Ireland would become more established, despite his vigorous opposition. Though opposed to viking expansion, he was not above making alliances with the Norse against his Irish rivals. In 856 he won a victory against the Norse Gael at the Battle of Glenn Foichle. Then in 861 and 862, allied with the Dublin Norse, he pillaged Meath in opposition to his rival Máel Sechnaill mac Máele Ruanaid. In 866 he clashed with the vikings at Lough Foyle and beat them, then pillaged and burned all their longphorts in Ulster when their leaders

Amlaíb and Auisle were away raiding the Picts. In 868 Áed was confronted by an alliance of his rivals the southern Uí Neill, the Leinstermen and the Norse Gael at the Battle of Cell ua nDaigri and was again victorious. He died in 879.

Ailella (Ah-lel-a) Gaelic (Elfin).

Ailpín (Ahl-peen) Pictish (White). The House of Ailpín was a powerful dynasty ruling Pictland and later Alba from the 840's until 1034. It was also known as Clann Chináeda after its founder, Cináed mac Ailpín.

Alfífa (Al-fee-fa) Norse for Mercian Ælfgifu (Elf Gift).

Amlaíb (Aw-lay) Gaelic for Norse Óláfr. Amlaíb Conung (Norse *konungr* or *king*) was a viking leader and brother of Ímar, who founded the Uí Ímair dynasty. He raided widely in Ireland and in Pictland, where he fell in battle against King Causantín mac Cináeda in 874.

Amlaíb mac Gofraid (Óláfr Guðrøðarson) of the Uí Ímair was King of Dublin from 934-939 and King of Northumbria from 939-941. In 937 he was beaten by Æþelstan King of the Saxons at the Battle of Brunanburh. Nevertheless, he took Northumbria after Æthelstan's death in 939 and later the Five Boroughs (Norse *Fimm Borginn*) of the Danelaw – Lincoln, Derby, Nottingham, Leicester and Stamford. He died in 941 after sacking the monastery at Tyninghame in East Lothian.

Amlaíb Cenncairech (Guilty Head) was a ruler of Limerick and rival to Dublin, who campaigned in Ulster and Connacht in the 930s.

Amlaíb mac Illuilb was King of Alba from 971 or 976 to 977. He was a son of Illuilb or Indulfr, King of Alba. Amlaíb was a member of the Mac Ailpín dynasty, but also possibly descended from the Norse Gaelic Uí Ímair through his mother. He was killed by Cináed mac Máel Coluim in 977.

Amundi (Am-oon-di) Norse (Awe-Inspiring Protector).

Ánnbensi (Own-ben-si) Norse (possibly derived from Finnish *Onni* or *luck* and Norse *Bensi,* a short form of *Benedikt.*

Andres (And-ress) Norse for Greek *Andreas* (Manly).

Aodhán (Aid-awn) Gaelic (another version of *Aed* or Fire). Aodhán or Áedán mac Gabráin was King of Dál Riada from around 574 to 609. He had Colum Cille or Columba as his spiritual advisor. He might possibly have had blood links with the Britons, as he is mentioned in the*Triads* and the *Bonedd Gwŷr y Gogledd,* the latter having him as a descendant of

Dyfnwal Hen, King of Strathclyde. He also named one of his sons Ártúr, presumably after the semi-legendary Brythonic warlord. During his reign he raided Orkney and campaigned on the Isle of Man. Around 590 he won a victory in the Battle of Leithrid or Leithrig against the Miathi (Maeatae), a branch of the southern Picts, in which his sons Ártúr and Eochaid Find fell. In 599 he fought the Picts again and was defeated. He is said to have been a rival of Rhydderch Hael, King of Strathclyde, and the *Triads* mention him plundering Alt Clut or Dumbarton, the Fortress of the Britons. Around 603 Aedan and his forces met the army of Æþelfrið, King of the Bernicians at the the Battle of Degsastan in Northumbria. Although Aedan lost the battle, it may have been something of a Pyrrhic victory for Æþelfrið, as his brother Theobald fell with all his men. Aedan died in 609 at the age of 74, according to the *Annals of Tigernach.*

Armóðr (Ar-moth-ur) Norse (Eagle Courage or Wrath).

Arnfinnr (Arn-finn-ur) Norse (Finnish Eagle)

Arni (Ahr-nee) Norse (Eagle).

Arnórr (Ar-nawr) Norse (Eagle of Thor). Arnórr Þórðarson, known as Jarlaskáld (Earl's Poet) served as the personal bard of Þórfinnr the Mighty, Jarl of Orkney.

Artgal (Art-gul) Gaelic and ***Arthgal*** (Arth-gal) Brythonic (Fierce as a Bear). From Old Celtic *Artogalnos.* Arthgal ap Dyfnwal was King of Strathclyde when its main stronghold Alt Clud or Dumbarton fell to the forces of Ímar and Amlaíb Conung in 870. He was one of the many captives taken at the time and was later assassinated in 872 at the instigation of Causantín mac Áeda, King of the Picts.

Ártúr (Ahr-toor) Gaelic for Brythonic *Arthur.* Áedán mac Gabráin, King of Dál Riada named a son Ártúr, probably after the famous semi-legendary warlord of the Britons.

Ása (Ows-ah) Norse (Godly).

Ásgrímr (Ows-greem-ur) Norse (God Mask or God Grim).

Áslákr (Ow-slak-ur) Norse (God Game).

Ásleifr (Ows-layf-ur) Norse (God Descendant).

Ástriðr (Ow-strith-ur) Norse (God Beloved).

Augaire or ***Ugaire*** (Ow-ry) Gaelic (Shepherd). Augaire mac Ailella was a King of Leinster who fell at Cath Cenn Fuait or the Battle of Confey in 917.

Auisle (Aws-lay) Gaelic for Norse Auðgísl. Viking leader and brother of Ímar, founder of the Uí Ímair dynasty.

Auðgísl (Owth-gees-ul) Norse (Fortune Pledge). Gaelic *Auisle.* Viking leader and brother of Ímar, founder of the Uí Ímair dynasty.

Auðun (Owth-un) Norse (Rich Friend).

Ælfred (Ahl-fred) Saxon (Elf Counsel). Ælfred or Alfred the Great was King of Wessex from 871–886 and King of the Anglo-Saxons from 886-889. After numerous defeats, he triumphed over the vikings at the Battle of Edington in 878 and drew up an agreement whereby they retained control of the north of England. It became known as the Danelaw.

Ælla (Ah-la) Anglian, uncertain meaning. Ælla was a King of Northumbria killed in 867 by the sons of Ragnarr in revenge for their father's death.

Æþelfrið (Ah-th-ul-frith) Anglian (Noble Peace).

Æþelræd (Ahth-ul-rahd) Saxon (Noble Counsel). Æþelræd Unræd was King of the English from 978 to 1013 and from 1014 to 1016. His nickname *Unræd* or *badly advised* proved justified when he followed the advice of his leading men and magnates to order a massacre of the Danes in England on Saint Brice's Day in 1002. Svein Fork Beard, King of Denmark mounted a serious of punishing raids in reprisal, culminating in the Danish conquest of England in 1013.

Æþelstan (Ahth-ul-stan) Saxon (Noble Stone). Æthelstan was King of the Angles and Saxons from 924-927 and King of the English from 927-939. He exercised an aggressive policy toward the neighbouring nations, invading Alba in 934 with a large army and fleet of ships. According to *The Annals of Clonmacnoise,* Æþelstan was *compelled by the Scots to return* (home) *without any great victory,* which suggests the use of guerrilla tactics such as harrying and scorched earth employed so often by the Picts during past invasions. In 937 Causantín mac Áeda, King of Alba and Amlaíb mac Gofraid (Óláfr Guðrøðarson), King of Dublin invaded England and were defeated at Brunanburh by Æþelstan, though his power went into decline afterward and on his death in 939, Amlaíb took the Kingdom of Northumbria and the Five Boroughs of the Danelaw.

Bán (Bahn) Gaelic (White).

Bárðr (Bahrth-ur) Norse (a strange combination of Battle and Peace). Gaelic *Bárid.*

Bergþóra (Berg-thor-ah) Norse (Þórr's Fort or Thunder Fort). Bergþóra is the trouble-making wife of Njál in *Njáls saga.*

Bethóc (Bay-awk) Gaelic (derived from *beatha* or *life*). Bethóc was the eldest daughter of Máel Coluim the Destroyer, King of Alba. She was the wife of Crínán the Hound Earl, Abbot of Dunkeld and their son was Donnchad I King of Alba.

Bjarni (Byarn-ee) Norse (Bear).

Bjólan (Byo-lahn) Norse. From the Gaelic *Beollán* (Little Fire).

Björn (Byurn) Norse (Bear).

Blácaire (Blah-kah-ree) Gaelic for Norse *Blákári* (Blue Squall). Blácaire mac Gofraid or Blákári Guðrøðarson was King of Dublin from 939 to 945 and from 947 to 948 when he died in battle against the Southern Uí Néill.

Bóruma (Boh-roo) Gaelic (of the Cattle Tribute).

Bran (Brahn) Gaelic, Pictish and Brythonic (Raven).

Brandr (Brand-ur) Norse (Fire, Swordblade).

Brian or Briain (Bree-an) Gaelic (Noble) Norse *Brjánn.* Brian Bóruma reigned as *Ard Rí* or High King of Ireland from 1002 – 1014. He mounted a successful campaign against the Norse Gaelic Kingdom of Dublin, culminating in the Battle of Clontarf in 1014.

Bridei (Brid-ah) Pictish/Brythonic *Bruide* Gaelic (Level Spot of Land). Bridei was a popular name for Pictish leaders.

Bridei mac Maelchon was a King of the Picts from 554 to 584, with his chief stronghold thought to be at Craig Phadrig near what is today Inverness. In his *Life of Saint Columba* Adomnán recounts the saint's meeting with Bridei.

Bridei mac Bili was King of the Picts from 672 to 693. His reign is famous for his victory over the Angles of Northumbria at the Battle of Dún Nechtain in 685. He is also said to have destroyed the Orcadian sub kingdom with its pirate bases in 682.

Bróðir (Bro-th-eer) Norse (Brother). Bróðir was an 11th century Manx viking leader who fought at the Battle of Clontarf and killed Brian Bóruma, High King of Ireland, according to *Cogadh Gaedhil re Gallaibh* and *Brennu Njáls saga.*

Brúsi (Broo-si) Norse (Buck). Brúsi Sigurðarson ruled Orkney alongside his brothers from 1014 – first with Sumarliði and Einar, then with Einar and Þórfinnr after Sumarliði died in his bed, then with Þórfinnr after Einar was killed by Þórfinnr's fosterer and henchman Þórkel. Þórfinnr's desire to take as much of Orkney as he could while squeezing Brúsi out in the process drove the latter to seek the help of King Óláfr in Norway, who laid claim to the islands himself and secured oaths of fealty from Brúsi and Þórfinnr as well as Brúsi's son Rögnvaldr as surety. On Brúsi's death, Þórfinnr took full control of all the Northern Isles.

Carlus (Karl-us) Norse Irish from German *Karlus* and French *Charles* (Free Man). Carlus was the son of Amlaíb Conung. He fell in battle at Killineer in 868, opposing Amlaíb's father-in-law and former ally Áed Findliath.

Cathail (Ka-hill) Gaelic (Valorous in Battle). From early Celtic *Catualos.*

Caittil (Kat-ul) Gaelic for Norse *Ketill* (Cauldron). Caittil Find or Caittil the White was a leader of the Norse Gael defeated by Ímar and Amlaíb Conung in Munster in 857.

Causantín (Caws-an-teen) Pictish version of Latin Constantine or Constantinus.

Causantín mac Cináeda (son of Cináed mac Ailpín) was King of the Picts from 862-877. In 874 Causantín defeated the forces of Amlaíb Conung, brother of Ímar and King of Dublin, in a battle in which Amlaíb was slain. In 875 a battle occurred at Dollar between the Picts and vikings in which the Picts were heavily defeated *with great slaughter,* according to the *Annals of Ulster.* Causantín died in 877 at either Crail or Inverdovat after another battle with vikings, probably the warband of Albdann (Hálfdanr). He was buried on Iona.

Causantín mac Áeda was King of Alba from 900-943, the grandson of Cináed mac Ailpín. During the early part of his reign, Dunkeld was pillaged by vikings. In 904 viking forces suffered a heavy defeat at *Srath Erin* at the hands of the men of Fortriu, who invoked the assistance of Saint Colum Cille, and Ímar, the grandson of Ímar was killed there. In 918, answering a call for assistance from Ealdred of Bamburgh, Causantín fought a battle at Corbridge against Ragnall ua Ímair with an indecisive result. In 937 allied with Amlaíb mac Gofraid (Óláfr Guðrøðarson), King of Dublin and Owain, King of Strathclyde he invaded England and was beaten by the forces of Æþelstan, King of the Saxons at the Battle of Brunanburh. In 943 Causantín abdicated and entered a monastery at Saint Andrews, passing the kingship over to his nephew Máel Coluim mac Domnaill. According to *The*

Chronicle of the Kings of Alba, seven years later Máel Coluim plundered the English as far as the Tees, capturing *a multitude of people and many herds of cattle* at the instigation of his uncle Causantín.

Cáilte (Kweel-cha) Gaelic (Slender & Fierce). Cáilte mac Ronáin was a hero of the legendary Fíanna.

Cellachán (Kell-ah-han) Gaelic (War). Cellachán mac Buadacháin or Cellachán Caisil was King of Munster. In 939 he plundered the monastery of Clonard with Norse Irish allies from Waterford. The name Callaghan derives from *Cellachán.*

Cellaig (Kel-lay) Gaelic (Frequenter of Churches). The surname Ó Ceallaigh or Kelly derives from it. Lorcán mac Cellaig was King of Leinster in 848.

Cennétig (Kenn-etig) Gaelic (Helmeted Chief). The surname Kennedy derives from this.

Cennétig mac Gáethíne was King of the Loíches from 830-903. He defeated viking forces between 866 and 867.

Cennétig mac Lorcáin was King of the Dál gCais and the father of Brian Bóruma. He died in 951.

Cerball *(Ker-vol)* Gaelic (Fierce). Cerball mac Dúnlainge, known as Kjarvalr Írakonungr in Norse, was King of Osraige from 842 to 888. His entire reign is peppered with viking conflict. He besieged and defeated a raiding party in Osraige in 846 and trounced a warband under a certain Hákon at a place called *Carn Brammit* in 847. In 855 he wiped out the viking force of Rodolb and the same year enlisted Danish allies commanded by a leader called Horm against the Norse, beating them yet again. By 858 Cerball was allied with Ímar against the Norse Irish of Munster and in 859 with Amlaíb Conung raided Meath. In 860 he defeated a viking force in Osraige and in 862 triumphed over a Norse raiding fleet. He died in 888. He is credited in both Irish and Icelandic tradition as being the ancestor of important Icelandic families.

Cináed (Kin-ay) Gaelic (Fire Born). Cináed mac Ailpín, King of the Picts from 843-858, rose to power after the devastating battle with the vikings in 839 in which the then King of the Picts, Uuen mac Óengus, fell, along with his brother Bran and much of the Pictish elite. Cináed prevailed in the struggle for power that followed. Nicknamed *the Hardy*, he invaded Saxonia (Northumbria) six times and arranged important marriage alliances with the Irish Uí Néill dynasty, with Strathclyde and the Uí Ímair to further secure his power. *The Annals of the Four Masters* state that Guðfriðr mac Fergus, *toíseach* or chief of the Airgíalla in Ulster, supplied reinforcements to Dál Riada at Cináed's request in 836, which points to links with the Norse Irish. Cináed was the founder of the Mac Ailpín dynasty that ruled Pictland and later Alba from the 840's to 1034.

Conaing (Con-ang) Gaelic variation of *Conung* from the Norse *Konungr* (king).

Conchobar (Co-hawr *also* Con-awr) Gaelic (Hound Lover). Conchobar mac Donnchada was joint King of Meath with Lórcan mac Cathaill. He was drowned by Amlaíb Conung at Clonard Abbey in 864.

Congal (Cong-gal) Gaelic (Wolf Fierce). In 866 or 867 Congal, King of the Ciarraige defeated the forces of one Tomrar (Þórir) who had plundered Clonfert.

Congalach (Cong-gal-uch) Gaelic (derives from *Congal* or Wolf Fierce). The surname Connelly derives from it. Congalach Cnogba was *Ard Rí na hÉireann* from 944 until 956, when he was ambushed and slain by the Gall-Goídil and the Laighin.

Cormac (Cawr-mac) Gaelic (possibly Son of the Wheel, as in charioteer, or alternatively Raven Son). Norse *Kormákr.* Cormac mac Airt was a legendary High King of Ireland raised by wolves who ruled during the time of Fionn mac Cumhaill. The *Annals of Clonmacnoise* describe him as *the best king that ever ruled in Ireland.* In the tale *His Three Calls to Cormac,* the sea god Manannan mac Lir tests Cormac as a king and gives him a golden cup that breaks if three lies are uttered and is restored if three truths are spoken.

Crínán (Creen-ahn) Gaelic. Crínán was the lay Abbot of Dunkeld, known as *The Hound Earl* (Jarl Hundi in Norse sources). He was the father of Donnchad (Duncan I King of Scots), the *Karl Hundason* of *Orkneyinga saga.*

Cumhaill (Coo-al) Gaelic (Champion). Father of the famous legendary Irish hero Fionn.

Cunedda (Cee-ned-ah) Brythonic *Cunodagos* (Good Hound). Cunedda was a 5th century warlord of the Votadini or Gododdin tribe in the Clackmannan area of what is now Scotland. According to the chronicler Nennius, he overthrew the Uí Liatháin from Munster, the Déisi, and the

Laigin from Leinster who had settled in North Wales and established the Brythonic dynasty of Gwynedd.

Dagr (Dag-ur) Norse (Day).

David from Hebrew *Dawid* (Beloved). David I was ruler of the Scoto-Norman kingdom from 1124 to 1153. He appears briefly in *Orkneyinga saga* entertaining Svein Ásleifarson at his court and paying compensation to the monks Svein plundered on the Isle of May.

Diarmata (Dy-ar-mat-ah) from Gaelic *Diarmaid* (possibly Without Envy). *Diarmata* means *of Diarmaid.* Muirecán mac Diarmata was a King of Leinster who was killed by the Norse in 863.

Digri (Dig-ree) Norse (Stout). Nickname of Sigurðr Hloðvisson, Jarl of Orkney.

Djúpúdga (D-yoo-poodga) Norse (Deep Minded). Nickname of Unnr or Auðr, daughter of Ketill *Flatnefr.* She was married to Óláfr *hinn Hvíti* (Óláfr the White), who has been identified by some scholars as Amlaíb Conung, King of Dublin. She appears in the saga sources as a noble woman of wisdom, wealth and influence.

Domangairt (Doman-gart) Gaelic (Head of the World).

Domnall or ***Domnaill*** (Donn-ull *or* Dawll) Gaelic (World Ruler). Norse version *Tomnal.* Domnall Claen (the Squinting) was King of Leinster. In 983, allied with Ímar of Waterford, he was defeated by Máel Sechnaill mac Domnaill, High King of Ireland and his half brother Glúniarainn, King of Dublin.

Donada (Don-ata) Gaelic (female derivation of *Domnaill* or World Ruler). Donada was the middle daughter of Máel Coluim the Destroyer, High King of Alba. She was married to Findláech mac Ruaidri, King of Moray.

Donnchad (Don-ah-hah) Gaelic (Brown Haired Warrior). Norse version *Dungad.* Dungad or Dungal was a Mormaer of Caithness on good terms with the Norse. Duncansby (Norse *Dungalsbaer*) was named after him.

Donnchad (Duncan I King of Scots) or *Karl Hundason* of *Orkneyinga saga* opposed both Þórfinn the Mighty and Macbeth. He was repeatedly beaten by the former and slain in battle against the latter in 1040. He has the nickname *An t-Ilgarach* (Much Diseased or Sick) in *The Prophecy of Berchan.*

Donnchad mac Briain was a son of Brian Bóruma who fought at Clontarf.

He was King of Munster until he was deposed in 1063. He died on a pilgrimage to Rome in 1064.

Donngaile (Don-ah-lay) Gaelic (Brown Valour). The surname Donnelly derives from this.

Dorruðr (Daw-ru-th-ur) Norse (Spear Fighter). Dorruðr was the man who witnessed the *Valkýrjur* magically weaving the outcome of the Battle of Clontarf.

Drengr (Dreng-ur) Norse (Brave, Gallant Man).

Droann or ***Druian*** (Droo-an) Gaelic (possibly from Irish *Deoradháin,* pronounced *Doran* – Wanderer, Exile)

Dubh (Doo) Gaelic (Dark).

Dubhgall (Doo-gawl) Gaelic (Dark Haired Outlander).

Dungaðr (Dun-gath-ur) Norse for Gaelic *Donnchadh.*

Dúnflaith (Dun-a-lah) *Donflaith* Gaelic (Brown Princess).

Dúnlaing (Doon-layng) Gaelic *Dobhailen* (Defiant), from which the surnames *Dolan* and *Dowling* derive.

Dyfnwal (Duv-noo-al) Brythonic (World Ruler). Gaelic *Domhnall.*

Ealdred (Ee-al-dred) Anglian (Old Strength) Ealdred was ruler of part of Bernicia in the 10th century.

Eadwulf (Ee-ad-woolf) Anglian (Wealth or Fortune Wolf). Eadwulf Cudel (Cuttlefish) was an 11th century Earl of Bernicia beaten by Máel Coluim Forranach, King of Alba at the Battle of Carham in 1018, after which he surrendered Lothian to the triumphant Scots.

Ebric (Eh-brik) Gaelic for Norse *Eiríkr.*

Ecgfrið (Egfrith) or *Ecgbryht* (Bright Eye). Ecgfrið was King of Northumbria from 670-685. In the second year of his reign he defeated the Picts at the Battle of Two Rivers and annexed all the territory between the Firth of Forth and the Tweed. From 674 he proceeded to make war on the Mercians and in 684 he sent his general to plunder Brega in Ireland, resulting in the pillaging of churches and the taking of large numbers into slavery, which was deplored by Bede and other members of the clergy. In 685, despite warnings from Saint Cuthbert, he moved against Bridei mac Bili, King of the Picts. Invading Fortriu, he was slain at the Battle of Dún Nechtain and his army annihilated.

Echmarcach (Eh-mar-kah) Gaelic (Horse Rider). Echmarcach mac Ragnaill was King of Dublin from 1046-1052. He also had control over some or all of the Isles and parts of Galloway. He is mentioned as attending a peace meeting between Máel Coluim the Destroyer, High King of Alba and Knútr *inn ríki,* King of Denmark, Norway and England in 1031.

Edmund (Ed-mund) Anglian (Protector of Riches). Edmund was King of East Anglia from 855 to 869, when he was killed by the men of Ímar and Ubba. Later made a saint.

Edmund Ironside was King of England for a short period from 23rd April 1016. He was defeated at the Battle of Assandun on 18th October of that year by Knútr the Great and died on 30th November, after which Knútr added all of England to his dominions.

Egill (Eh-yil) Norse (from early Scandinavian *agilaR,* from which Old Icelandic *agi* – awe or terror, derives). Egill Skallagrímsson (c. 904- c. 995) was a famous Icelandic warrior bard and rune master and the larger than life hero of *Egils saga.*

Eilifr (Eye-leef-ur) Norse (One Life).

Einar (Eye-nar) Norse (One or Lone Warrior) related to *Einherjar,* warriors of the god Óðinn in Valhöll, the Hall of the Slain.

Einar Rangmunnr or Wry Mouth was a son of Sigurðr Digri and jarl (along with his brothers Sumarliði, Brúsi and Þórfinnr) of Orkney from 1014. In *Orkneyinga saga* Einar is an unreasonable bully who demands high taxes from the farmers to pay for his viking expeditions. Þórkel, the fosterer of Einar's young brother Þórfinnr, makes a deadly enemy of Einar when he speaks out on the farmers' behalf, and the enmity is only made all the worse when Þórfinnr claims more of a share of the jarldom than what Einar considers fair. After a feast that is supposed to settle their differences, Þórkel learns that Einar plans to get rid of him and ends up killing Einar first.

Eindriði (Eye-n-dreeth-ee) Norse (Self Willed). Eindriði Ungi (the Young) was the untrustworthy chieftain who accompanied Jarl Rögnvaldr Kali Kolsson on his voyage to the Holy Land in 1151. He supported Hákon Herðabreiðr (the Broad Shouldered) against King Ingi Haraldsson, who was slain in battle in 1161, but went on the run after Erlingr Skakki defeated and killed Hákon in 1162. Erlingr later had Eindriði Ungi put to death.

Eiríkr (Ay-rikk-ur) Norse (One Ruler). Eiríkr Blóðøx (Eirikr Bloodaxe) was King of Norway from 931-933 and of Northumbria from 947-948 and 952-954. He appears in *Egils saga* as the royal enemy of the warrior bard Egill Skallagrímsson, who curses him with a *niðing* pole – a wooden pole cut with runes, smeared with blood and surmounted by a horse's head.

Eithne (En-ya) Gaelic (Kernel).

Emma from Germanic *Ermen* (Whole). Emma of Normandy was Queen Consort of Knútr inn ríki, King of Denmark, Norway and England. Together with her brother Richard, Duke of Normandy she brokered a peace between her husband and Máel Coluim, High King of Alba in 1031.

Eógan (Oh-gan) or ***Éoghan*** (Oh-ann) Gaelic (Yew Born).

Erlendr (Er-lend-ur) Norse (Foreign). Erlendr Haraldsson was joint Jarl of Orkney, along with Rögnvaldr Kali Kolsson and Haraldr Maddaðarson, from 1151-1154. During Rögnvaldr's absence on his voyage to the Holy Land, Erlendr received half of his father's lands in Caithness from Máel Coluim IV, King of Scots and Haraldr's share of Orkney from King Eystein of Norway. On his return, Rögnvaldr joined Haraldr in opposing Erlendr and the latter was killed in 1154.

Erlingr (Err-ling-ur) Norse (Jarl Descendant). Erlingr Skakki Kyrpinga-Ormsson was a Norwegian jarl and guardian of King Ingi Haraldsson, who accompanied Jarl Rögnvaldr Kali Kolsson on his voyage to the Holy Land. He got the nickname *skakki* from taking a wound to the neck that set his head at a crooked angle when it healed. He returned to Norway on hearing of the passing of his brother Ogmundr. After the death of King Ingi Haraldsson in battle in 1161 against his rival Hákon Herðabreiðr (the Broad Shouldered), Erlingr defeated and killed Hákon in 1162. Eindriði Ungi, who had supported Hákon against King Ingi, was later put to death by Erlingr. Erlingr died in 1179. His son Magnús was King of Norway from 1161 until 1184.

Ermingerda (Ermin-gerda) Norse version of Germanic *Ermengarde* (Whole Enclosure or All-Protection). Ermingerda is the young noblewoman in Verbon (possibly Narbonne), with whom Jarl Rögnvaldr becomes smitten during his voyage to the Holy Land in *Orkneyinga saga.*

Eystein (Ay-stin) Norse (Island Stone). Eystein Haraldsson was King of Norway (1142-1157) jointly with his brothers Ingi and Sigurðr, all sons of Haraldr Gilli. Eystein was born in Scotland. A civil war arose in which Sigurðr was slain by Ingi's men in 1155, and Eystein himself was executed in 1157 after his army retreated before Ingi's greater forces. Those loyal to Eystein later gave their support to his nephew Hákon Herðabreið when he moved to take the throne.

Eyvindr (Ay-vind-ur) Norse (Lucky Winner).

Feilan (Fee-lan) Norse Gaelic from the Irish *Fáelán* (Wolf Cub). Nickname of Óláfr Þórsteinsson (890-940), grandson of Unnr Djúpúdga (the Deep Minded).

Fergus (Ferr-guss) Gaelic (Vigour). Pictish *Urguist.*

Fíach (Fee-uch) Gaelic (Raven). Norse version *Fiak.* Fíach was a fifth century Irish saint and bishop of Sletty.

Findláech (Find-lay) Gaelic (Fair Haired Hero). Norse version *Finnleikr* (Finn-layk-ur). The name Findlay derives from this.

Findláech mac Ruaidri, King of Moray was the father of Macbeth, who was to become High King of Alba. According to *Orkneyinga saga,* Findláech (or Finnleikr in Norse) fought a battle with Jarl Sigurðr Digri, the father of Þórfinnr, which Sigurðr won with the aid of his Irish mother's sorcerous raven banner. Findláech was murdered in 1020 by his nephews, the sons of Máel Brigte.

Fingal or ***Fionngal*** (Fin-gal) Gaelic (Fair Haired Outlander).

Finn (Fin) Norse (Finn, Lapp).

Findliath (Fin-lee-ah) Gaelic (Fair Grey Hair).

Fionn (Fin) Gaelic (White or Fair Haired). Fionn mac Cumhaill, the Irish legendary hero, was in some traditions half Norse. In the old tales, he and his followers, the Fíanna, defend Ireland from invaders, both natural and supernatural.

Flannacán (Flann-ac-an) Gaelic (Fiery Red). The surname Flannagan derives from this.

Flatnefr (Flatnef-ur) Norse (Flat Nose).

Flosi (Flossi) Norse (Cheeky). Flosi Þórdarson was an Icelandic chieftain who led the Burners in their destruction of Njál and his family in *Njáls saga.* He later atoned for his actions and was reconciled with Njál's son-in-law and avenger Kári Sólmundarson.

Forbflaith (Firra-flah) Gaelic (Sovereignty). Norse *Hvarflóð.*

Fóstri (Fawst-ri) Norse (Fosterer). Þórkel Fóstri was the fosterfather and enforcer of Þórfinnr the Mighty, Jarl of Orkney.

Frakokk (Frah-kok) Norse (Courageous) – from *frakkr,* or from *frakka,* the Norse word for *franca* or spear of the Franks.

Fróði (Fro-thee) Norse (Wise One), also a name of the fertility god Freyr.

Gabrán (Gow-rawn) Gaelic (possibly related to *garbh* or rough). Gabrán mac Domangairt was King of Dál Riada in the mid 6th century.

Geirbjörn (Gerr-byurn) Norse (Spear Bear).

Gilla Coemgáin (Gilla Cow-ghan) Gaelic (Devotee of Coemgáin). Gilla Coemgáin was Mormaer of Moray. In 1020 he was involved in the killing of his uncle Findláech, the father of Macbeth and in 1032 he was burned to death with fifty of his followers.

Gilla Pátraic (Gilla Pawdrig) Gaelic (Devotee of Patrick). Gilla Pátraic was a son of Ímar, King of Waterford.

Gillebríd (Gilly-breed) Gaelic (Devotee of Brigid). Gillibríd was Thane of Argyll c.1090-1164, the father of Somerled.

Gilledomnán (Gilly-dom-non) Gaelic (Devotee of Adomnán).

Gillemuire (Gilly-murrah) Gaelic (Devotee of Mary). Gillemuire appears as a name in early sources and tradition among the Norse Gael.

In 1013, according to *The Annals of Innisfallen,* the sons of Gillamáire were killed raiding Munster with the Dublin vikings.

Mac Gille Máire, son of Allgoirt of Waterford, referred to as *the best outlander that was in Éirinn,* was killed in 1130.

Gillemuire or Gillemoire was a natural son of Óláfr Guðrøðarson (Óláfr the Black) King of the Isles (1226-1237), according to *The Bannatyne Manuscript.* Gillemuire is said to be the progenitor of the clan Mac Giolla Mhoire or Morrisons of the Hebrides, hereditary brehon lawmen. His half brother Leod, another natural son of Óláfr, was the ancestor of the Mac Leods.

Mac Gillemuire is the name from which the surname *Morrison* of Lewis is said to derive.

Gille/Gilla (Gilly/ Gill-ah) from Gaelic *Giolla* (Devotee), usually followed by the name of a saint e.g. *Gillebríd* (Devotee of Brigid), *Gillecolum* (Devotee of Colm Cille or Columba), *Gillepádraig* (Devotee of Pádraig or Patrick), *Gillefionnán* (Devotee of Fionnán), *Gillemuire* (Devotee of Mary).

Gillikristr (Gilly-krist-ur) Norse for Gaelic *Gille Críst* (Devotee of Christ). Gaelic name of Haraldr Gilli, the half Irish King of Norway (1130 – 1136).

Giraldus (Jir-al-dus) Latin from German *Gerald* (Spear Rule). Giraldus Cambrensis or Gerald of Wales (*Gerallt Gymro*) c.1146-c.1223 was a Cambro-Norman historian and archdeacon of Brecon, famous for his works on Ireland and Wales.

Glúmr (Gloom-ur) Norse (Gloomy Faced, Bearlike).

Glúniarainn (Gloon-yern) Norse *Járnkné* (Iron Knee). Glúniarainn was the son of Amlaíb Cuarán and King of Dublin after his father was defeated at the Battle of Tara by Máel Sechnaill mac Domnaill, *Ard Rí na hÉireann* in 980. Máel Sechnaill, who was half brother to Glúniarainn, placed the latter in power as his sub king. According to the Irish annals, Glúniarainn was killed by a slave in 989 when drunk.

Gneisti (G-nay-stee) Norse (Spark).

Goddi (Godd-ee) Norse (possibly related to Goði, a heathen priest).

Godfrey (God-fray) Norse (God Peace). The name of this warlord in *Orkneyinga saga*, who is not Norse, is more likely to have been the Germanic Gottfried.

Godwin (God-win) Anglo Saxon (God Friend).

Gofraidh (Go-fray) Gaelic for Norse *Guðrøðr, Guðfriðr* or *Godfrey.* Gofraidh mac Ragnaill, ruler of Lochlann according to *The Fragmentary Annals of Ireland*, was said to be the father of Amlaíb Conung and Ímar, on behalf of whom they extorted tribute, or protection money in 849. The placename *Lochlann* or *Laithlind* has been applied to both Norway and the Norse areas of Scotland and the Isles. Professor Donnchadh Ó Corráin is of the opinion that Ímar belonged to a Norse dynasty based in Scotland. *The Fragmentary Annals of Ireland* report the *death of Gothfraid the King of Lochlann of a sudden and horrible fit* in 873.

Gormflaith (Gor-um-lah) Gaelic (Blue Sovereignty). Gormflaith ingen Murchada, the Kormlöð of Icelandic saga, was an Irish queen 960-1030. Married to Amlaíb Cuarán, King of Dublin and York until 981 and to Brian Bóruma, King of Munster and later High King of Ireland. Saga tradition gives her an implacable hatred toward the latter, who put her aside. She sends her son Sihtric (Sigtrygg Silk Beard) to promise her hand to Sigurðr the Stout, Jarl of Orkney and to Bróðir, a Manx viking warlord, to go against Brian. The Battle of Clontarf follows from this.

Guðfriðr (Gooth-frith-ur) Norse (God Peace).

Gregorius (Greg-o-ree-us) Greek (Watchful, Alert). Gregorius Dagsson was one of King Ingi Haradsson's stoutest supporters. He was killed in 1161 opposing Ingi's rival Hákon Herðabreiðr (the Broad Shouldered).

Greiloð (Gray-loth) and ***Grélaða*** (Gray-lath-a) Norse (the full meaning obscure, but *loð* translates as *invitation*).

Grímkell (Greem-kell) Norse (Grim Cauldron).

Grímr (Greem-ur) Norse (Grim).

Grjótgarðr (Gr-yot-garth-ur) Norse (Stone Enclosure).

Gróa (Gro-ah) Norse (Grow).

***Gruaidh** (Groo-ay)*

Gruoch (Groo-och). Variation *Gruaidh.* Gaelic, probably from *Gruagach* (long haired, green-clad elfin woman of the *Aes Sídhe* or People of the Mounds, originally the *Tuatha Dé Danann* – Tribe of the Goddess Danu, the Irish gods and deified heroes).

Gruoch ingen Boite (1020-1054) was Queen of Scots and wife of Macbeth. There is no historical evidence to support the idea that she was anything like the scheming psychopath of Shakespeare's lurid play.

Gunnar (Goon-ar) Norse (Battle Warrior).

Gunni (Goon-ee) Norse (Battle, Fight).

Gunnhildr (Goon-hild-ur) Norse (Battle, Fight). Gunnhildr Konungamóðir (Mother of Kings) c.910-980 was a powerful matriarch and Queen-Consort of Norway. Part legend, part fact, she appears in several Icelandic sagas, including *Njáls saga, Egils saga and Laxdaela saga.* According to *Egil saga,* she was the wife of Eiríkr Blóðøx (Eirik Bloodaxe), King of Norway 931-933 and of Northumbria 947-948 and 952-954.

Guðfriðr (Gooth-frith-ur) Norse (God Peace or Protection).

Guðmundr (Gooth-moond-ur) Norse (God Protection).

Guðrøðr (Gooth-rith-ur) Norse (God Fame). Guðrøðr Crobhán was ruler of Man from 1079 and of Dublin from 1091. He established the Norse

Gaelic Crobhán dynasty that lasted from the late 11th century to the middle of the 13th century. He died in 1095.

Guðþormr (Gooth-thorm-ur). Also ***Guþrum.*** Norse (God Merciful). Guðþormr was a commander in Jarl Rögnvaldr Kali Kolsson's expedition to the Holy Land.

Guþrum was King of the Danish vikings in northern England and ruler of the Kingdom of Guþrum in East Anglia. In 876 he led an army against Wessex and defeated Ælfred the Great in battle, who then made a truce with the vikings. In 877 Guþrum disregarded it and moved again on Wessex, repeatedly beating the Saxons. Ælfred again made peace. In 878 Guþrum drove Ælfred into hiding in the Somerset marshes, from which he mounted guerrilla attacks on the vikings. At the Battle of Ethandun Ælfred was victorious over his enemies and Guþrum received a Christian baptism. After yet another peace treaty, it was agreed that the vikings should continue to control what became known as the Danelaw, the territories in northern England under Danish rule and law. Guþrum died in East Anglia in 890.

Hallaðr (Hawk-ath-ur) Norse (Battle Rock)

Hallgerðr (Hawtch-gerth-ur) Norse (Stone Enclosure). Hallgerðr is the trouble-making wife of the hero Gunnar in *Njáls saga* who stirs up the bloody feud of the tale along with Njál's wife Bergþóra.

Haraldr (Har-ald-ur) Norse (Army Ruler). Haraldr Gilli Magnússon or Gillikristr was the half Irish King of Norway who ruled from 1130 -1136. His father was King Magnús Bare Foot. Haraldr passed the ordeal by fire that tested the truth of his claim to be Magnús' son and half-brother to the reigning king, Sigurðr Jórsalafari. Haraldr then accepted the condition that he would not have a share in the kingdom's rule until after Sigurðr and his son Magnús had died.

Though relations between Haraldr and Sigurðr appear to have been friendly, Sigurðr's son Magnús was hostile. One night during a drinking session, according to the historian Snorri Sturluson, Magnús overheard Haraldr telling someone that there were men in Ireland who were so fast on their feet that they could overtake a running horse. Magnús called Haraldr a liar and challenged him to a contest, staking his gold ring on Haraldr staking his head. Haraldr said that he had not claimed to be so swift himself, and that he was referring to those Irishmen who were, but Magnús insisted on having the race regardless, riding his fast Gautland horse. The next day

Magnús set out the length of the course, and when Haraldr complained that it was too long, Magnús made it longer. Haraldr kept pace with the running horse all the way and Magnús accused him of holding onto his saddle girth. On the second go, Haraldr led the way for the entire length of the course and Magnús then claimed he had an unfair start. On the third go, Haraldr allowed Magnús to set off at a gallop and still managed to overtake the horse with so much distance between them that he was able to rest at the finishing line, then get up and wave at Magnús as he rode in.

When King Sigurðr got to hear about this, he turned on Magnús angrily and said: *'You call Haraldr useless, but I think you are a great oaf, and understand nothing of the ways of foreign people. Do you not know that men in other countries train themselves in feats other than filling themselves with beer, and driving themselves mad, and so unfit for everything that they scarcely know each other? Give Haraldr his ring, and do not try to make a fool of him again, as long as I am above ground.'*

Haraldr honoured his promise not to pursue a share in the rule of the kingdom until Sigurðr's death in 1130. With the support of Rögnvaldr Kali Kolsson and other important men, Haraldr was accepted as king over half of Norway, and the oath he had made was judged to have been made under duress. Four years later Magnús moved against Haraldr and defeated him at the Battle of Färlev in Götaland in 1134. Haraldr fled to Denmark but returned with a fresh army after Magnús had disbanded his own, and attacked Bergen, where Magnús was spending the winter. Magnús was taken captive and maimed. Haraldr then ruled Norway until 1136, when Sigurðr Slembe, a pretender to the throne, had him murdered in his sleep.

Haraldr Harðráði was King of Norway from 1046-1066. He served as a mercenary commander for the Kievan Rus and also in the Varangian guard. In 1046 he allied himself with Svein Ástriðarson, the long-running rival of Haraldr's nephew, King Magnús. Magnús then offered him half the kingdom of Norway, which Haraldr accepted. In 1047, after Magnús died, Haraldr became sole ruler of Norway. He fought stubbornly for years to take Denmark, which had come under the rule of his previous ally, Svein, but eventually dropped his claim. In 1066 he made a move on the throne of England, beating the English at Fulford, but then being defeated in turn and slain at Stamford Bridge by the forces of King Harold Godwinson.

Haraldr is said to have been of exceeding height, according to the Icelandic historian and poet Snorri Sturluson, and may have been five ells (seven feet tall).

Haraldr Maddaðarson (Gaelic *Aralt mac Mataid*) was Jarl of Orkney and Mormaer of Caithness from 1139-1206. The son of Matad, Mormaer of Atholl, he was opposed to the Scoto-Norman royal house of William I and the settlement of Norman nobles in the north of Scotland. In 1201 Haraldr secured Caithness by force, driving out the stewards of the King of Scots and having the tongue of the Scots bishop Jon cut out and a knife shoved into his eyes, according to *Orkneyinga saga.* Shortly afterward, King William advanced against Haraldr with a large army. Haraldr avoided a fight and a settlement was agreed in which a quarter of Caithness revenues would go to William. Haraldr's son Þórfinnr was captured by the Scoto-Normans at some point. They blinded and castrated him, and he later perished. In 1194 Haraldr got the blame for sending a contingent of fighters from Orkney and Shetland to join Sigurðr Magnússon, a rival for the throne of Norway, in opposing Sverre Sigurðarson, the king at that time. Sverre defeated Sigurðr and his forces and took Shetland from Haraldr as a punishment.

Hardeknútr **(**Hardy-k-newt-ur) Norse (Tough Knot). Hardeknútr was King of Denmark from 1035-1042 and of England from 1040-1042.

Harðráði (Harth-rah-thee) Norse (Hard Ruler). Nickname of Haraldr Sigurðarson, King of Norway from 1046-1066.

Hákon (Hawk-on) Norse (Horse Kin or High Kin). Hákon the Old was King of Norway from 1217-1263.

Hálfdanr (Hahf-dan) Norse (Half Dane). Gaelic ***Albdann.*** Hálfdanr Ragnarsson was a viking leader and possible brother to Ímar, founder of the Uí Ímair dynasty. Hálfdan may have been a son of Ragnarr Loðbrók (Shaggy Breeks).

Hárekr (Hah-rek-ur) Norse (High Chieftain).

Hárfagri (Har-fagri) Norse (Fair Hair). Nickname of Haraldr, King of Norway from 872-930.

Hávarðr (How-varth-ur) Norse (Battle Guard).

Heinrek (Hine-rek) Norse for German *Heinrich.*

Helga (Hel-gah) Norse (Holy).

Helgi (Hel-gee) Norse (Holy).

Herfiðr (Herr-fi-th-ur) Norse (Fighting Finn).

Hildigunna (Hild-ee-goon-ah) Norse (Battle, Fight).

Hjalp (Hee-yalp) Norse (Help).

Hloðvér (Load-vir) Norse (Loud or Famous Fighter). Hloðvér, son of Þórfinnr Hausakljúfr (Skull Splitter), was Jarl of Orkney from c.980-991. He married Eithne, daughter of King Cerball of Ireland and their son was Sigurðr Digri, the father of Þórfinnr the Mighty.

Holdboði (Hold-both-ee) Norse. Combination of *Holti* (Woodland) and *Boðvarr* (Battle Warrior).

Horm (Hawrm) variation of Norse *Ormr* or *Gormr*. Horm was a leader of the Danes allied with Cerball mac Dúnlainge against the Norse Gael in 855. He was slain in Wales by Rhodri ap Merfyn, King of Gwynedd in 856.

Höðskuldr (Hith-skoold-ur) Norse (Battle Bound). Höðskuldr Dala-Kolsson was a prominent Icelandic chieftain c. 910 – 965. He was the father of Óláfr the Peacock by the Irish princess Melkorka. He features in *Laxdaela saga*.

Hrafn (H-raff-in) Norse (Raven).

Hreða (H-ray-th-ah) Norse (Rowdy). Nickname of Ulfr, brother of Brian Bóruma.

Hróaldr (H-roll-d-ur) Norse (Mighty Fame).

Hrútr (H-root-ur) Norse (Ram).

Hundi (Hoondi) Norse (Hound).

Hvelp (H-velp) Norse (Whelp).

Hvíti (Vee-tee) Norse (White).

Indulfr (Ind-oolf-ur) from Norse *Hildulfr* (Battle Wolf). Gaelic *Ildulb*. Indulfr or Ildulb *an Ionsaighthigh* (Indulfr the Aggressor) mac Causantín was King of Alba from 954 to 962. Edinburgh was taken under Scottish control during his reign. A sister of Indulfr was the wife of Amlaíb mac Gofraid (Óláfr Guðrøðarson), King of Dublin and Northumbria, and a son of Indulfr was also called Amlaíb, possibly after his brother in law. According to the *Chronicle of the Kings of Alba,* Indulfr was fighting Norse raiders in 962 at the Battle of Bauds in Moray. Though the Norse were beaten, Indulfr died in the encounter. He was buried on Iona.

Ingi (Ing-ee) Norse variation of *Yngvi,* a name for the god Freyr. King Ingi Haraldsson ruled Norway from 1136 -1161, the son of Haraldr Gilli. He became known as *Krókhryggr* or Hunchback after being carried as a child into a battle in 1137 by one of his guardians, with the result that he became malformed. According to the famed Icelandic historian Snorri Sturluson, Ingi was cheerful, generous and popular with the public and the chieftains he took counsel from. He died in battle against his rival Hákon Herðebreiðr (The Broad Shouldered) in 1161.

Ingibjörg (Ingi-byurg) Norse. Yngi or Yngvi is another name for the fertility god Freyr, combined here with the word for *stronghold,* so it can be read as God Stronghold or Stronghold of Yngi. Ingibjörg Finnsdóttir was the wife of Þórfinnr Sigurðarson, jarl of Orkney. She was known as the *Jarls' Mother* and died around 1069.

Ingigerðr (Ingi-gerth-ur) Norse. Yngi or Yngvi is another name for the fertility god Freyr, combined here with the word for *enclosure,* so it can be read as God Enclosure or Yngi's Enclosure.

Ingimundr (Ingi-mund-ur) Norse (Protection through the god Yngi).

Ingiriðr (Ingi-rith-ur) Norse. (God Beauty, Love).

Ingjaldr (Ing-yald-ur) Norse. Yngi or Yngvi is another name for the fertility god Freyr, combined here with the word for *ruler,* so it can be read as God Ruler or Ruler through Yngi.

Ingólfr (Ing-awlf-ur) Norse. Yngi or Yngvi is another name for the fertility god Freyr, combined here with the word for *wolf,* so it can be read as Yngi Wolf or God Wolf.

Ímar (Eem-ar) from Norse *Ívarr* (Yew Bow Warrior). Ímar was the founder of the Uí Ímair dynasty, the dominant viking power in Ireland, Scotland and the Isles as well as Britain, for centuries. King of Dublin, he reigned from 857 to 873. He may have been one and the same as Ívarr hinn Beinlausi or Ívarr the Boneless, who invaded England with the Great Heathen Army in 865. The Irish Annals mention Amlaíb Conung (possibly Óláfr the White), as his brother, as well as Auisle or Auðgísl. Hálfdanr Ragnarsson (Gaelic *Albdann*) may also have been a brother.

Ímar, King of Waterford ruled from around 969 until his death in 1000. He is likely to have been a grandson of Ragnall ua Ímair. In 983, allied with Domnall Claen, King of Leinster, he was heavily defeated in battle by Máel

Sechnaill mac Domnaill, High King of Ireland and Glúniarainn, King of Dublin. Among the slain was Gilla Pátraic, Ímar's son. In 984 Ímar joined Brian Bóruma and the Kings of the Isles, Maccus and Gofraid mac Arailt, against Leinster and Dublin. Around 989-993 he was ruling Dublin until driven out by Sihtric Silkbeard. Ímar restored his control of Dublin for a short period between the years 994 and 995 until driven out by Sihtric again.

Ímar, King of Limerick or *Ímar Luimnich*, ruled from c.960 until his death in 977. He is also referred to as *Ímar ua Ímair*, probably indicating a blood connection with the Úi Ímair. In *Cogadh Gáedhel re Gallaibh* he is the archenemy of Mathgamain mac Cennétig and his brother Brian Bóruma of the Dál gCais. According to the text, his extortion of tribute or protection money was widespread and particularly oppressive. He was heavily beaten at the Battle of Sulcoit in 968 by the Dál gCais, who plundered and burned Limerick afterwards. Ímar may have been involved in the betrayal and death of Mathgamain in 976 at the hands of Máel Muad mac Brain, King of Munster. In 977 Ímar, along with his sons Amlaíb Cuallaid (Wild Dog) and Dubcenn (Dark Head) were slain on Inis Cathaigh or Scattery Island by Brian Bóruma, Mathgamain's brother.

Jarisleifr (Yaris-layf-ur) Norse for Slavic *Yaroslav.* Yaroslav the Wise was Grand Prince of the Rus from 1019-1054.

Jarlaskáld (Yarl-ah-skaw-ld) Norse (Earl's Poet from *jarl* – earl, and *skáld* – poet). Nickname of Arnórr Þórdarsson, Þórfinnr the Mighty's bard.

Jon (Yon) Norse for *John.*

Jorsalafari (Yorsa-la-fari) Norse (Jerusalem Farer).

Jórunn (Yor-un) Norse (Horse Lover).

Kali (Kah-li) Norse (To Freeze, to be Cold).

Karl (Kah-rl) Norse (from *Háriolus* - Army). Not to be confused with *karl* or freeman. Karl Hundason is referred to as King of Scots in *Orkneyinga saga,* though it has been a matter of debate among scholars as to his identity. Eben William Robertson equated him with Donnchad mac Crínáin (Duncan I), who reigned as King of Alba from 1034-1040.

Kálfr (Kalf-ur) Norse (Calf). Kálfr Árnason (c.990-1051) was a prominent chieftain in Norway and later the Hebrides. Reputed to have landed the death blow to King Óláfr Haraldsson or Saint Óláfr at the Battle of Stiklestad in 1030 and then helped bring his son Magnús to the throne in 1035.

Kári (Kah-ri) Norse (Wind, Squall). Kári Sólmundarson is a viking adventurer from the Hebrides who features as an important character in *Njáls saga.* Befriending Helgi and Grímr Njálsson, he settles in Iceland and marries their sister Helga. His main role in the saga is as the avenger of his father-in-law, the chieftain Njál and his family, after they are burned to death by their enemies.

Ketill (Ket-il) Norse (Cauldron). Ketill Flatnefr (Flat Nose) Björnsson was a 9th century King of the Isles. He features in *Laxdaela saga, Eyrbyggja saga* and *Landnámabók.*

Kerðjalfad (Kerth-yal-fad) Norse for Brian Bóruma's adopted son and favourite.

Kjarvalr (K-yar-vull-ur) Norse for Gaelic *Cerball* (Brave, Fierce). Kjarvalr Írakonungr or Cerball mac Dúnlainge was King of Osraige from 842 to 888. He is credited in Irish and Icelandic tradition for being the ancestor of leading Icelandic families.

Knútr (K-newt-ur) Norse (Knot). Knútr inn ríki or Knútr the Great, son of Svein Fork Beard, was King of England from 1016 to 1035, King of Denmark from 1018 to 1035 and King of Norway from 1028 to 1035. Wessex, the main Saxon kingdom of Britain, submitted to Knútr in 1015, although several clashes followed between Knútr and Edmund Ironside, the then King of England. Knútr defeated Edmund at the Battle of Assandun and the West Saxons were forced to acknowledge Knútr as King of all England. In 1018 Knútr imposed a massive Danegeld on the English of £72,000 plus an extra £10,500 from London, an immense sum for the time. In 1031 Knútr was in conflict with Máel Coluim, High King of Alba, but a peace was brokered between them by Knútr's wife Emma and her brother Richard, Duke of Normandy.

Kolbein (Kol-byne) Norse (Black Bone).

Kollr (Kawl-ur) Norse (Bald Pate).

Konofogor (Kon-oh-fog-or) Norse from Gaelic *Conchobhar* (Lover of Hounds). Conchobhar was the legendary King of Ulaid in the heroic Ulster Cycle of early Gaelic tales. In *Orkneyinga saga,* an Irish king who defeated Jarl Einar Sigurðarson at Lough Larne.

Kormákr (Cawr-mowk-ur) Norse from Gaelic *Cormac* (possibly Son of the Wheel, as in *charioteer*, or alternatively Raven Son). Kormákr Ögmundarson is the hero of the Icelandic *Kormáks saga.*

Kormlöð (Korm-luth) Norse. From the Gaelic *Gormflaith* (Blue Princess or Blue Sovereignty). Gormflaith ingen Murchada, the Kormlöð of Icelandic saga, was an Irish queen 960-1030. Married to Amlaíb Cuarán, King of Dublin and York until 981 and to Brian Bóruma, king of Munster and later High King of Ireland.

Kristín (Krist-een) Norse for *Christina.*

Krokauga (Krok-owga) Norse (Crooked Eye).

Kváran (K-vah-ran) Norse from Gaelic *cuarán.* Deerhide or cowhide shoe, from which Amlaíb mac Sitriuc (Óláfr Sigtryggson) got his nickname.

Kylfi (Keelfi) Norse (Club).

Labhraidh (Low-ray) Gaelic (Speaker).

Lagmann (Lag-man) Norse (Law Man, Judge from Norwegian *lagmann* and Icelandic *lögmaðr*) Gaelic *breitheamh.* The Norse Gaelic Clan Mac Gille Mhoire (Morrison) of Lewis were the hereditary lawmen for the Lordship of the Isles.

Lambi (Lam-bee) Norse (Lamb).

Laoghaire (Lee-ry) Gaelic (Calf Herder). The name O'Leary derives from it.

Ljótr (Lyot-ur) Norse (Ugly).

Loingseach (Loon-sha-ch) Gaelic (Exile).

Lorcán (Lor-con) Gaelic (Small Fierce One). Lorcán mac Cathail was King of Uisnech and Meath who allied himself with the Dublin Norse. He was blinded by Áed Findliath, High King of Ireland in 864.

Lorcán mac Cellaig was King of Leinster in 848, when, allied with Ólchobar mac Cináeda, King of Munster, he inflicted a defeat on a viking force at Sciath Nechtain, near the present Castledermot, County Kildare.

Mac Amlaíb (Mac Aulay) Gaelic (Son of Óláfr). Irish name of Sigtryggr Silk Beard Óláfsson.

Macbeth, Mac Beath (Mac Beh-th) Gaelic (*Mac Bethad* – Son of Life). Macbeth mac Findláech, nicknamed *Rí Deircc* (Red King) ruled the Pictish-Gaelic Kingdom of Alba from 1040-1057. His reign was largely peaceful, and he is said to have distributed money to the poor during a pilgrimage to Rome. The *Prophecy of Berchán* describes him as *the generous king of Fortriu.* In 1054 Siward, Earl of Northumbria invaded Alba and clashed with Macbeth's forces, resulting in heavy losses on both sides. Siward's son was one of the fallen. In 1057 Macbeth met his death at Lumphannan in what is now Aberdeenshire, where he was defeated by Máel Coluim mac Donnchada (later Malcolm III). He was buried on Iona. There is no reliable historical evidence to support the idea that he was the bloodthirsty tyrant of Shakespeare's lurid play.

Mac Cenétig /Ceinnéidigh (Kenn-et-ay) Gaelic (Ugly Headed or Helmet Headed). Clan name of Brian Bóruma, from which the surname Kennedy derives.

Mac Domnaill (Mac Donn-ul) Gaelic (Son of Domnall) *Domhnall* means *World Ruler.* Máel Sechnaill mac Domnaill was *Ard Rí na hÉireann* 979-1002 and King of Meath 976-1022. He defeated Amlaíb Cuarán, King of Dublin at the Battle of Tara in 980. Allied with Brian Bóruma, he also trounced the forces of Sihtric (Sigtryggr Silk Beard), King of Dublin and those of Máel Mórda, King of Leinster at the Battle of Glenn Máma in 999. He also fought at the Battle of Clontarf in 1014.

Mac Mathgamain (Mac Mah-hawn) Gaelic (Son of the Bear), from which the surname Mac Mahon derives.

Mac Murchada (Mac Moor-da-hah) Gaelic (Son of the Sea Battler).

Mac Suibhne (Mac Sweeney) Gaelic (Son of Suibhne – *Pleasant*). A mercenary clan of *gallóglaigh* employed by the O'Donnell dynasty of Tyrconnell in the 14th century.

Maccus (Macc-us) Norse Gaelic of uncertain meaning. Maccus mac Arailt was a King of the Isles who was notably active in chronicle sources from the years 971 to 974. Maccus and his brother Gofraid strove to take the strategically important island of Anglesey for control of the Irish Sea trade routes.

Maccus son of Óláfr was the reputed killer of Eiríkr Bloodaxe at Stainmore, Cumbria in 954.

Maddaðr (Mad-ath-ur) Norse for Gaelic *Madadh* (Hound). Madadh son of Máel Muire was Mormaer of Atholl during the 1130s.

Magnús (Mag-noos) Norse for Latin *Magnus* (Great). Magnús Erlendsson was Jarl of Orkney from 1106 until his execution by his enemies in 1117 and became a martyr, with many miracles taking place after his death, according to *Orkneyinga saga*. In 1136 he was sainted by Bishop William of Orkney and his relics transferred from Christ Church on Birsay to Saint Magnús Cathedral, Kirkwall, built and named after him by his nephew Jarl Rögnvaldr Kali Kolsson.

Magnús Óláfsson the Good was King of Norway from 1035–1047 and of Denmark from 1042–1047.

Magnús Berfœttr (Bare Foot) was King of Norway from 1093-1103. He was noted for his belligerent nature and hell-raising campaigns around the Irish Sea. He got the nickname *Bare Foot* for going about bare-footed and wearing the Gaelic plaid. He was the father of Haraldr Gilli or Gillikristr, King of Norway from 1130-1136, whom he probably sired in Ireland. He laid claim to the entire Kintyre peninsula by having his ship dragged across the narrow isthmus at Tarbert while standing at the helm. On his final Irish campaign, he allied himself with Muirchertach ua Briain, King of Munster and the two rulers embarked on raids for plunder. In 1103 he was ambushed by warriors of the Ulaid and fought on bravely even after a spear went through both his thighs. He was then struck on the neck with an Irish axe, and that was his death wound.

Margaðr (Mar-gath-ur) Norse for Gaelic *Murchadh.*

Manuli (Man-ooli) Norse for Menelaus, Emperor of Constantinople.

Mathgamain (Mah-hawn) Gaelic (Bear). Mathgamain mac Cennétig, elder brother of Brian Bóruma, was King of Munster c.970-976.

Mathghamain ua Riagain was the King of Brega who exacted a huge ransom from Sihtric King of Dublin for the release of his son Amlaíb (Óláfr) in 1029.

Máel Brigte (Myal-brig-te) Pictish and Gaelic (Devotee of Brigit). Máel Brigte Tooth was a mormaer of Moray in the ninth century who was tricked in battle by Sigurðr Eysteinsson the Mighty and slain as a result. Sigurðr rode off in triumph with his enemy's severed head dangling by the hair from his saddle. Bizarrely, Mael Brigte's protruding tooth, for which he got his nickname, banged against Sigurðr's leg, wounding and lethally infecting it.

Máel Brigte was a noble of the House of Loairn, brother of Findláech mac

Ruaidri, King of Moray and father of Máel Coluim and Gilla Coemgáin, who were responsible for killing their uncle Findláech in a power struggle.

Máel Ciaraín (Myal-kee-arahn) Gaelic (Devotee of Ciaraín). Máel Ciaraín mac Rónáin was a chief of the Leinstermen who, allied with Cennétig mac Gáethíne burned down Amlaíb Conung's stronghold at Clondalkin in 867.

Máel Coluim (Myal-colum) Gaelic (Devotee of Colum Cille/Columba) from which the first name Malcolm derives. Máel Coluim mac Domnaill was King of Alba from 943 to 954. He was probably also overlord of Strathclyde. After Amlaíb Cuaran retook York around 950, Máel Coluim plundered the English as far as the Tees at the incitement of his uncle Causantín, the previous king. In 952, according to *The Annals of Ulster,* the men of Alba, the Strathclyde Britons and the English allied to fight the Norse Gaels. Máel Coluim died in battle in 954 and was buried on Iona.

Máel Coluim mac Cináeda was King of Scots from 1005-1034. The Irish annals referred to him as *Ard Rí Alban* or High King of Scotland. He was half Irish through his mother, a Leinster woman. *The Prophecy of Berchán* calls him *Forranach* or the Destroyer. An able king and politician, Máel Coluim proved a worthy opponent of viking raiders. He extended his power over Lothian at the expense of the Angles and arranged important dynastic marriage alliances, one of which was with Sigurðr Digri, Jarl of Orkney. He was grandfather to Sigurðr's son Þórfinnr the Mighty.

Máel Gualae (Myal-goo-lay) Gaelic (possibly Devotee of Dub Gualae *Black Shoulder,* an abbot of Glendalough). Máel Gualae mac Donngaile was a King of Munster of the Eóganachta dynasty in 856. He opposed the High King Máel Sechnaill mac Máele Ruanaid and was soundly beaten at the Battle of Cam Lugdoch in 858. He was captured and stoned to death by the Dublin Norse in 859.

Máel Mórda (Myal-mawr-ah) Gaelic (Devotee of Mórda). Máel Mórda mac Murchada was the King of Leinster who opposed Brian Bóruma. His sister was Gormflaith and he was uncle to Sihtric (Sigtryggr Silk Beard), King of Dublin. He died at the Battle of Clontarf in 1014.

Máel Muad (Myal-moo-at) Gaelic (Proud Chief). Máel Muad mac Brain was King of Munster, enemy of Mathgamain mac Cennétig and ally of Ímar, King of Limerick. Along with the petty king Donnubán mac Cathail, he was responsible for the execution of Mathgamain in 976. The next year, at the Battle of Belach Lechta, he was slain opposing Brian Bóruma, Mathgamain's younger brother.

Máel Sechnaill (Myal-shech-null) Gaelic (Devotee of Seachnall). *Máel Sechlainn* (variation). Máel Sechnaill mac Máele Ruanaid was *Ard Rí* or High King of Ireland from 846-862. A good part of his reign was spent fighting the vikings. In 845 he captured the viking leader Turgeis or Þórgest and had him drowned. In 856 he was making war on the Norse with Norse Gaelic allies.

Máel Sechnaill mac Domnaill was *Ard Rí* or High King of Ireland 979-1002 and King of Meath 976-1022. Victorious over Amlaíb Cuarán, King of Dublin at the Battle of Tara in 980. Allied with Brian Bóruma, he defeated the forces of Sihtric (Sigtryggr Silk Beard), King of Dublin and those of Máel Mórda, King of Leinster at the Battle of Glenn Máma in 999.

Máine (Mahn-ye) Gaelic (Wealthy). Máine Mór mac Eochaidh was the founder of the kingdom of Uí Máine.

Melsnati (Mel-snatti) Norse. From the Gaelic *Máel Snechtai* (Devotee of the Snows). In *Brennu-Njáls saga*, Jarl Melsnati (together with Jarl Hundi or Crínán) opposes Sigurðr Digri, Jarl of Orkney in battle and has a spear thrown into him by Kári Sólmundarson. Not to be confused with the later Máel Snechtai mac Lulach, grandson of Macbeth.

Mjolukoll (Mee-yawloo-kollr) Norse (Meal Head?).

Moldan (Mol-dan) Also *Muddan*. Norse for Gaelic *Máel Dúin* from which the surname Muldoon derives.

Muirchertach (Morr-ee-art-uch) Gaelic (Sea Farer). The name Murtough derives from this. Muircertach ua Briain was King of Munster and self-declared *Ard-Rí na hÉireann.* The propagandist epic *Cogadh Gáedhel re Gallaibh,* extolling the exploits of his great grandfather Brian Bóruma, was written for him. He died in 1119.

Muirecán (Murri-can) Gaelic (Sea Battler). The surname Murricane derives from this.

Murchad (Murr-chah) Gaelic (Sea Lord). Murchad mac Finn was King of Leinster, father of Gormflaith, the scheming femme-fatale of *Njáls saga.*

Mýrkjartan (Meer-kyars-tan) Norse for Gaelic *Muirchertach* or *Muirchertán.* In *Laxdaela saga* the King of the Irish. May be identified as Muirchertach na Cochall Craicinn (Muirchertach of the Leather Cloaks) of the Northern Uí

Néill and King of Ailech. He was the son of Niall Glúndub and grandson of Áed Findliath. He was slain in 943 fighting Blácaire mac Gofraid (Blákári Guðrøðarson) King of Dublin, and so died in battle against the Norse Gaels like his father before him. The name Moriarty (made famous with Conan Doyle's criminal mastermind Professor Moriarty) is derived from Muirchertach.

Niall (Neel) Gaelic (Champion). Norse *Njál.* Niall Noígíallach (Niall of the Nine Hostages) was an early Irish king and the tribal ancestor of the Uí Néill dynasty. He gained his nickname for taking hostages from each of the provinces or kingdoms he subdued.

Niall Caille mac Áeda was *Ard Rí* of Ireland in 833. He fought against vikings in the north of Ireland, defeating a force of raiders in Derry soon after taking the high kingship and again in 845 at Mag Nítha in what is now Donegal. He was given the nickname *Caille* from having drowned in the River Callan near Armagh.

Niall Glúndub mac Áedo, *Ard Rí* of Ireland, was slain along with five other kings at the Battle of Islandbridge when going up against the Dublin Norse under Sihtric Cáech in 919. He was the son of Áed Findliath and Máel Muire, daughter of Cináed mac Ailpin, King of the Picts.

Njál (Nyawl) Norse for Gaelic *Niall.* Njál Þórgeirsson is the wise and prescient lawyer of the thirteenth century *Njáls saga* who is burned to death in his house along with his family because of a feud. The other name for the story is *Brennu Njáls saga* or the Saga of Burnt Njál. It is as a result of this burning that Kári Sólmundarson hunts down the killers.

Oddi (Awd-ee) Norse (Spear Point).

Ogmundr (Oo-mind-ur) Norse (Awe Protection).

Oisín (O-sheen) Gaelic (Little Deer). Oisín, the son of Fionn mac Cumhaill, was the preeminent poet of Ireland and a hero of the legendary Fíanna.

Oistín (O-shteen) Gaelic for *Augustine.* Oistín was a son of Amlaíb Conung, King of Dublin killed by Albdann (Hálfdanr) in 875 in a power struggle.

Olith (O-lih) Gaelic. Probably a version of Órlaith (Gold Princess). The youngest daughter of Máel Coluim the Destroyer, High King of Alba, Olith was married to Sigurðr Digri, Jarl of Orkney.

Orn (Ir-n) Norse (Eagle).

Owain (Oh-en) Brythonic (Yew Born). Owain ap Dyfnwal was King of Strathclyde and an ally of Causantín, King of Alba and Amlaíb mac Gofraid (Óláfr Guðrøðarson), King of Dublin at the Battle of Brunanburh in 937 when Æþelstan, King of the Saxons got the victory.

Owain Foel (the Bald) was King of Strathclyde and an ally of Máel Coluim Forranach (the Destroyer), High King of Alba at the Battle of Carham 1018, in his victory over the English of Northumbria.

Ó***engus*** (Angus) Gaelic (One Strength). Pictish *Onuist.* Óengus mac Fergus – Óengus I - (Pictish *Onuist mac Urguist*) was King of the Picts from 732 until 761. This formidable warlord rose to power after defeating his Pictish rivals in four battles between 728 and 729. In the 730s he mounted two campaigns against Dál Riada and was again victorious. A campaign against the Britons of Strathclyde was less successful – Óengus's brother Talorcan fell in the Battle of Mocetauc in 750 and at this time Dál Riada also became resurgent under Áed Find. In 756, allied with Eadberht, King of the Northumbrians, Óengus went against Dumbarton, the fortress of the Strathclyde Britons, and forced them to accept terms. The Anglian army was afterward annhiliated on its way back to Northumbria, but the records do not specify who the enemy was. Though King of the Picts, Óengus had blood links with the Éoganachta of Munster, according to Irish records. He died in 761.

Óengus mac Fergusa – Óengus II - was King of the Picts from 820 to 834. He is said to have made Saint Andrew the patron saint of Scotland after seeing the saint's saltire formed by clouds against the blue sky and then defeating a larger force of Angles near Athelstaneford in East Lothian in 832.

Óláfr (Olahf-ur) Norse (Heir to the Legacy of the Ancestor). Gaelic *Amlaíb.* Óláfr hinn Hvíti (the White) was born in Ireland. He became King of Dublin around 853, ruling jointly with Ímar. Unnr the Deep-Minded, daughter of Ketill Flatnefr was his wife and their son was Þórsteinn Rauðr (the Red). He may have been one and the same as Amlaíb Conung, Gaelic for the Old Norse *konungr* or *king.* If so, he died in battle against Causantín King of the Picts in 874.

Óláfr Guðrøðarson (Amlaíb mac Gofraid) of the Uí Ímair was King of Dublin from 934-939 and King of Northumbria from 939 to 941. In 937, allied with Causantín, King of Alba, he fought Æþelstan King of the Saxons at the Battle of Brunanburh and lost. Nevertheless, he took Northumbria after Æthelstan's death in 939 and later the Five Boroughs (Norse *Fimm Borginn*) of the Danelaw – Lincoln, Derby, Nottingham, Leicester and Stamford. He died in 941 after sacking the monastery at Tyninghame in East Lothian.

Óláfr the Peacock c.938-1006 was an Icelandic trader and chieftain who features in *Laxdaela saga* and several others, including *Njáls saga, Egils saga* and *Kormáks saga.* He was the son of the Irish princess Melkorka.

Óláfr Kváran (Gaelic *Amlaib Cuarán*) was King of York from 941-944 and 949-952 and of Dublin from 945-947 and 952-980. He was buried on Iona.

Óláfr Tryggvason was king of Norway from 995-1000. Saga tradition makes him the great grandson of Haraldr Hárfagri. He was famous for converting people to Christianity, often on pain of the axe. One such instance was his visit to Orkney in 995, during which he threatened Jarl Sigurðr Digri, Þórfinnr's father with death if he refused to be baptised, along with all of his people. Óláfr took Sigurðr's young son Hvelp or Hundi as hostage to Norway, where he died after a few years. From then on Sigurðr refused to show obedience or fealty to Óláfr Tryggvason.

Óláfr Haraldsson was King of Norway from 1015-1028. He fell at the Battle of Stiklestad in 1030 and was later made a saint.

Ólchobar (Awl-hawr) Gaelic (Lover of Drink). Ólchobar mac Cináeda was King of Munster (847-851). In 848, allied with Lorcán mac Cellaig, King of Leinster, he inflicted a defeat on a viking force at Sciath Nechtain, near the present Castledermot, County Kildare.

Ólof (O-loff) Norse (Heir to the Legacy of the Ancestor) female version.

Óspakr (Oh-spak-ur) Norse (Unruly). Óspakr was a Manx viking who fought for Brian Boru, High King of Ireland at the Battle of Clontarf in 1014.

Óttar (Och-tar) Norse (Dread Warrior). Gaelic *Oitir.*

Ögmundr (Ug-mund-ur) Norse (Sharp Edge Guardian).

Öngull (Ung-ull) Norse (Fish Hook).

Önundr (In-ind-ur) Norse (Winner through his Ancestors).

Ølvir (Il-veer) Norse (Temple Priest - heathen).

Páll (Paw-ll) Norse for *Paul.* Páll Þórfinnson, son of Jarl Þórfinnr the Mighty, was Jarl of Orkney jointly with his brother Erlendr from 1065-1098, when they were deposed by King Magnús Bare Legs.

Páll Hákonarson, nicknamed The Silent, was Jarl of Orkney from 1122-1137. Not popular with his family, his own mother Helga and his aunt Frakokk planned to get rid of him by making him a poisoned shirt, which was inadvertently put on by his brother Haraldr instead, who died in agony as a result. Páll was later kidnapped by Svein Ásleifarson and then blinded and executed by order of his sister.

Pétr (Pet-ur) Norse for *Peter.*

Raferta (Rah-furt-ah) Norse. From the Gaelic *Rafertach* (Flood Tide or Abundance), from which the name Ó Raithbheartaigh (Rafferty) derives.

Ragnall or ***Raghnall*** (Rag-nawl) Gaelic for Norse *Rögnvaldr.* Ragnall ua Ímair was King of Mann from 914-921 and King of Northumbria from 918-921. He was active in both Ireland and Britain and took over York (Jorvík) after the indecisive Battle of Corbridge in 918. He died in 921. The *Annals of Ulster* give him the title *King of the Fair Foreigners and Dark Foreigners.*

Ragnarr (Rag-nur) Norse (Army Ruler). Ragnarr Loþbrók (Hairy Breeks) was a semi-legendary viking hero who led frequent raids against the Franks and Saxons. He died around 865, traditionally put to death in a snakepit after being captured by the forces of Ælla, King of Northumbria. Ragnarr's sons, Ívarr the Boneless, Halfdanr, Björn Ironside and Sigurðr Snake-in-the Eye then invaded England with the Great Heathen Army and subjected Ælla to death by the *blood eagle,* in which the lungs were pulled out from a cloven ribcage. Ívarr hinn Beinlausi or Ívarr the Boneless may have been one and the same as Ímar who founded the Norse Gaelic Uí Ímair dynasty.

Ragnhildr (Rann-nil-ur) Norse (Fighting Counsel)

Randver (Rand-ver) Norse (Shield Man).

Rangmunnr (Rang-moon-ur) Norse (Wrong Mouth, Twisted Mouth). A nickname of Jarl Einar Sigurðarson of Orkney.

Rauði (Row-thee) Norse (Red, Ruddy).

Rhodri (Raw-dree) Brythonic (Wheel King). Rhodri ap Merfyn or Rhodri Mawr (Rhodri the Great) became the ruler of most of Wales between the years 844 and 871. In 856 he inflicted a defeat on the Danes and slew their leader Gormr. He had two further victories over viking forces in 872 - one at Bangolau on Anglesey and the other at Manegid.

Rhun (Heen) Brythonic (Mighty). Rhun ap Arthgal was King of Strathclyde after his father Arthgal was taken captive by Ímar and Amlaíb in 870 and assassinated in 872.

Riagain (Ray-gan) Gaelic (Little Ruler). Mathghamhain ua Riagain was the King of Brega who captured Amlaíb (Óláfr), son of Sihtric King of Dublin and demanded a huge ransom for his release.

Richard derived from Germanic (Hardy Ruler), a name popular with the Norman French. Richard the Good, Duke of Normandy and his sister Emma brokered a peace between Máel Coluim Forranach (the Destroyer), High King of Alba and Knútr inn ríki, King of Denmark, Norway and England in 1031. Emma was Knútr's wife.

Rodolb (Rod-ulb) Gaelic for Norse Rauðúlfr (Red Wolf). Rodolb was a viking raider defeated by Cerball mac Dúnlainge, King of Osraige in 855.

Rögnvaldr (Roan-vald-ur) Norse (God Ruler, Ruler through the Gods, Decisive Ruler) Gaelic *Raghnall.* Rögnvaldr Brúsason was the nephew of Þórfinnr Sigurðarson, with whom he ruled Orkney jointly from around 1037 until they fell out. He was killed by Þórkel Fóstri in 1046.

Rögnvaldr Kali Kolsson (c.1103-1158) was a Jarl of Orkney and later a saint. Famous in *Orkneyinga saga* for his eccentricity, poetry and voyage to the Holy Land.

Ronáin (Ro-nahn) Gaelic (Little Seal).

Ruaidhrí (Roo-arry) Gaelic (Red King). Ruaidhrí mac Raghnaill, Lord of Kintyre was the eponymous ancestor of Clann Ruaidhrí, a leading Hebridean kindred and offshoot of the Clann Somhairle or Somerled dynasty.

Saxolb (Saks-awlb) Gaelic for Norse *Saxúlfr* (Sax Wolf). A sax was a knife. Saxolb was a viking leader killed by the Cianachta in 837.

Sighvatr (Sig-vat-ur) Norse (Brisk Victory).

Sigmundr (Sig-mund-ur) Norse (Victory Protector).

Sigtryggr (Sig-trigg-ur) Norse (Victory Trusty) Gaelic *Sitriuc.*

Sigurðr (Sigurth-ur) Norse (Warder of Victory) Gaelic form *Siucraid.* Sigurðr Digri (the Stout) was Jarl of Orkney from 991 to 1014, when he fell at the Battle of Clontarf. As well as Orkney and Shetland, his power also extended to the Hebrides and Caithness, the latter probably under the overlordship of Máel Coluim Forranach (the Destroyer), High King of Alba. He was the son of Hloðvér Þórfinsson and Eithne, the daughter of an Irish king, according to *Orkneyinga saga*. His grandfather was Þórfinnr Hausakljúfr (Skull Splitter). He was married to Olith, youngest daughter of Máel Coluim the High King of Alba and was the father of Þórfinnr the Mighty.

Sigurðr Magnusson, known as *Jórsalafari* from having led the Norwegian crusade in the Holy Land, was King of Norway from 1103 until 1130, along with his brother Eystein, whose improvements to the country brought greater prosperity and cultural enrichment while Sigurðr's exploits abroad increased Norway's international prestige. Sigurðr was the half brother of Haraldr Gilli or Gillikristr, King of Norway from 1130-1136. Sigurðr made Kali Kolsson Jarl of Orkney in 1129 and gave him the name *Rögnvaldr* for luck.

Sihtric (Sh-it-ric) Also *Sitriuc.* Gaelic for Norse *Sigtryggr.* Sitriuc or Sihtric Cáech was King of Dublin from 917-920 and King of Northumbria from 921-927. He was blood-kin of the Uí Ímair dynasty. The *Annals of Ulster* give him the title *King of the Fair Foreigners and Dark Foreigners.*

Sihtric mac Amlaíb (or Sigtryggr Silk Beard) was King of Dublin from 989-994 and from 995-1036. He was the son of Amlaíb Cuarán and Gormflaith ingen Murchada. He was famously defeated at the Battle of Clontarf in 1014, opposing the High King Brian Bóruma, but managed to hold on to power until Eachmarcach, King of the Isles forced him to abdicate in 1036. He died as an exile in 1042.

Siward (See-wurd) Anglian *Sigeweard* (Victory Warder). Siward was Earl of Northumbria from 1041-1055. He invaded the kingdom of Macbeth in 1054 and died the next year. Though bearing an Anglian name, he was probably of Danish blood. He features in Shakespeare's lurid play.

Skakkr (Skak-ur) Norse (Skewed).

Skallagrím (Skala-greem) Norse (Skull Mask).

Skarp-heðinn (Skarp-heth-inn) Norse (Sharp Hide). Skarp-heðinn is the sarcastic trouble-making son of Njál in *Brennu-Njáls saga.*

Skeggi (Skegg-i) Norse (Beardy).

Skotakollr (Scota-koll-ur) Norse (Scot Head).

Skrjúpr (Skree-yoop-ur) Norse (Frail).

Skúli (Skool-i) Norse from *Skýla* (to protect).

Sláine (Slaw-nya) Gaelic (Health). Sláine was the daughter of Brian Bóruma, High King of Ireland and the wife of Sihtric (Sigtryggr Silk beard), King of Dublin.

Snaekólfr (Snayk-olf-ur) Norse (Snow Wolf).

Snorri (Snaw-ri) Norse (two possible meanings – *to turn swiftly* or *tough fighting*). Snorri Sturluson (1179-1241) was a famous Icelandic historian, skáld and lawspeaker.

Sturla (Stur-lah) Norse (*to disturb*).

Sólmundr (Sol-mund-ur) Norse (Sun Protector).

Sumarliði (Soo-mar-lee-th-ee) Norse (Summer Sailor). Gaelic *Somhairle* (Somerled). Sumarliði was a son of Sigurðr Digri and jarl (along with his brothers Einar, Brúsi and Þórfinnr) of Orkney. He died in his bed, a rare occurrence for many of our saga characters.

Somerled mac Gillebríd was a powerful Norse Gaelic warlord who rose to prominence in the mid 12th century. In 1153, allied with the sons of Máel Coluim mac Alaxandair, rival claimants to the Scottish throne opposed to the then reigning King Malcolm IV, Somerled invaded southern Scotland and plundered Glasgow. In 1158 Somerled invaded Man and soundly defeated his rival in the Isles, Guðrøðr Svarti. Guðrøðr then fled to Norway and Somerled took all of the Kingdom of the Isles. In 1164, possibly in response to the Scoto-Norman kingdom's aggressive expansionism towards the Isles, Somerled invaded Scotland again with a large army, but either died in battle at Renfrew from a thrown spear or was assassinated through Scoto-Norman treachery, depending on the source. The name *Somerled* or *Somhairle* is derived from the Norse *Sumarliði*. Through Somerled's son Ranald arose the *Clann Dómnaill* or MacDonalds and the *Clann Ruaidhrí* or MacRuaidhrí.

Surtr (Suhr-toor) Norse (Black, variant of *Svartr* or Swarthy).

Svarti (Svar-tee) Norse (Swarthy).

Svanlauga (Svan-lowga) Norse (Swan Bather).

Svein (Svay-n) Norse (Young Man, Freeman). Svein Tjúguskegg (Svein Fork Beard), son of Haraldr Bluetooth, was King of Denmark, Norway and England between the years 986 to 1014. He mounted punishing invasions of England in reprisal for the massacre of Danes on Saint Brice's Day in 1002. Quashing all opposition, he added England to his dominions, but died five weeks later in 1014. He was the father of Knútr inn ríki or Knútr the Great, King of Denmark and Norway, who ruled England from 1016 to 1035.

Svein Ásleifarson (c.1115-1171) was an outlaw and viking with a tumultuous career of feuding, kidnapping, killing and plundering, though he did manage to make some influential friends, from Orkney jarls to Kings of Scots. According to *Orkneyinga saga,* he got killed in a Dublin ambush while on his last viking raid.

Taðkr (Tath-kur) Norse for Gaelic *Tadhg* (Poet or Philosopher, pronounced *tayg*). Youngest son of Brian Bóruma, High King of Ireland.

Talorcan (Tal-awr-can) Pictish from Brythonic *talarw* (Harsh or Strong Fronted).

Tigernach (Teer-nach) Gaelic (Lord). Tigernach mac Fócartai, King of Loch Gabair beat the Norse at Dísert do-Chonna in 848, and together with Máel Sechnaill mac Máele Ruanaid, plundered Dublin in 849.

Toirdelbach (Tar-dhel-bach) Gaelic (Inciter). The name forms *Tárlach* and *Turlough* derive from it.

Tomrar (Tom-rar) Gaelic for Norse Þórir.

Tryggvi (Trigg-vi) Norse (Trusty).

Turgeis (Tur-gays) probably Gaelic version of Norse Þórgísl (Thor Pledge).

Ubba (Oo-bah) Norse pet form of *Ulfr* (Wolf). Ubba was a brother of Ívarr the Boneless and a leader of the Great Heathen Army that invaded England in 865.

Uhtred (Ooch-tred) Anglian, uncertain meaning. Uhtred the Bold was Ealdorman of Northumbria from 1006 to 1016. He defeated an invasion force led by Máel Coluim Forranach (the Destroyer), High King of Alba in 1006 and had the severed heads of slain Scots spiked on the walls of Durham. In 1013 Uhtred submitted to King Svein Forkbeard of Denmark and in 1016 to Svein's son Knútr inn ríki (Knútr the Great). In 1018 Máel Coluim Forranach, in alliance with Owain the Bald, King of Strathclyde, returned and defeated the Northumbrians at the Battle of Carham. Uhtred's brother, Eadwulf Cudel was forced to give Lothian to the Scots.

Ulfr (Oolf-ur) Norse (Wolf).

Ungi (Oong-ee) Norse (Young).

Unnr (Oon-ur) Norse (Wave). Unnr, or Auðr, the Deep Minded, was the daughter of Ketill Flatnefr. She was married to Óláfr hinn Hvíti (Óláfr the White), who has been identified by some scholars as Amlaíb Conung, King of Dublin. She appears in the saga sources as a noble woman of wisdom, wealth and influence.

Úrar (Oor-ar) Norse (Aurochs – ancient breed of giant wild cattle).

Valdimar (Val-di-mar) Norse (Mighty & Famous Ruler).

William (from Norman French *Willaume* – Wilful Protection). William the Old was Bishop of Orkney, with his episcopal seat at Christ Church, Birsay for 66 years from approximately 1102. William had spent time in Paris. He accompanied Jarl Rögnvaldr Kali Kolsson on his voyage to the Holy Land as advisor and interpreter. Initially sceptical over the holiness of Jarl Magnús Erlendsson and the miracles that occurred after his passing, he is said to have been persuaded after going temporarily blind and getting his sight back after praying over Magnús' grave. Bishop William finally sainted Magnús and had his relics transferred from Christ Church, Birsay to Saint Magnús Cathedral, Kirkwall, built and named after him by his nephew Jarl Rögnvaldr Kali Kolsson.

William I was ruler of the Scoto-Norman kingdom from 1165-1214. Threatened from the north by Gaelic rivals to the throne as well as by the Jarls of Orkney, he had castles built to protect his northern borders. In 1202 he led a large army into Caithness to confront Jarl Haraldr Maddaðarson and forced the latter to come to terms.

Yngvildr (Ing-vild-ur) Norse (a combination of Yngvi or Freyr and battle - God Battle).

Þambarskelfir (Tham-bar-skelf-ur) Norse (Belly Shaker).

Þeobald (Thee-o-bawld) Anglian (Bold Race).

Þórbjörn (Thor-byurn) Norse (Thor Bear).

Þórfinnr (Thorfinn-ur or Torfinn-ur) Norse (Thor's Finn or Laplander, though in the case of those living in Ireland, Scotland and the Isles more likely related to Gaelic *Fionn* or Finn, meaning White or Fair Haired).

Þórfinnr Torf-Einarsson, also known as Þórfinnr Hausakljúfr (Skull Splitter), was a Jarl of Orkney. He married Grélaða (Gruaidh), a daughter of Jarl

Dungad (Donnchad) of Caithness and had five sons by her. After his death in 963, his son Arnfinnr became jarl and married Ragnhildr, the unstable daughter of Eiríkr Blood Axe, who plotted and brought about his death, that of his brother Hávarðr, who had also married her, and two nephews of Hávarðr, before marrying another of the brothers, Ljótr. Ljótr later died of battle wounds after a fight with the Scots.

Þórfinnr Sigurðarson, nicknamed the Mighty, was the most powerful of the Orkney jarls. He ruled as Jarl of Orkney from around 1016 to 1065 and his power extended over Caithness and Sutherland, the Hebrides and possibly territories in Ireland.

Þórgeir (Thor-gerr) Norse (Thor Spear).

Þórhallr (Thor-hal-ur) Norse (Thor Rock).

Þórkel (Thor-kul) Norse (Thor Cauldron). Þórkel Fóstri was fosterfather and enforcer for Þórfinnr the Mighty, Jarl of Orkney.

Þórðr (Thor-thur) Norse (shorter form of Þórfreðr - Thor Peace or Protection).

Þórsteinn (Thor-stin or Tor-stin) Norse (Thor Stone). Þórsteinn Rauði (the Red) was the son of Amlaíb Conung or Óláfr the White, King of Dublin and Unnr the Deep Minded. He campaigned widely throughout what is now northern Scotland and took tribute until he was killed between 880 and 890.

Þórunnr (Thorunn-ur or Torunn-ur) Norse (Thor's Wave).

Þúríðr (Thoo-reeth-ur or Too-reeth-ur) Norse (Thor Rider).

Tribal & Group Names

Ailpín (Ahl-peen) Pictish Gaelic (White). The Mac Ailpín dynasty or House of Ailpín was a powerful dynasty ruling Pictland and later Alba from the 840s until 1034. It was also known as Clann Chináeda after its founder, Cináed mac Ailpín and has been referred to by some scholars as the Alpinid dynasty.

Airgíalla (Arra-geela) Gaelic (The Hostage Givers). Confederation of nine tribal groups in the north of Ireland, subject to the Ulaid, after whom Ulster was named, and then to the Uí Neill dynasty.

Angles from early English *Engel* or *Angelfolc.* A Germanic people originally from the Anglia Peninsula in Schleswig who invaded Britain after the withdrawal of Roman forces and established the kingdoms of Northumbria, East Anglia and Mercia. They were later to become known as the English along with the Saxons.

Austmen /Ostmen (Awst-men) Norse (East Men, a name by which the Norse referred to themselves i.e from Norway) & *Vestmen* (Vest-men) Norse (West Men – a name by which the Norse referred to Irish & Scottish Gael).

Britons from Greek *Pretanoi.* Brythonic or Cymric-speaking Celtic peoples inhabiting Britain before the invasion of the Angles and Saxons. Those Brythonic tribes that were inheritors of Roman culture were referred to as Romano-Britons. The term *British* and *Britons* originally applied to these peoples only. The term *Welsh,* from a Germanic word meaning *foreigner,* was applied, seemingly with little awareness of the irony, to the Britons by the Angles and Saxons whose territories they were invading.

Brettar (Brett-ar) Norse for the Britons, the Cymric-speaking peoples of Wales, Cornwall, Cumbria, Strathclyde and Lothian.

Cenél Fiachach (Ken-ayl Fee-uch-uch) Gaelic (Descendants of Fiachu). A clan descended from Fiachu mac Néill, King of Uisnech in Meath.

Cenél nGabráin (Ken-ayl Gow-ran) Gaelic (Descendants of Gabrán mac Domangairt, king of Dál Riada, the most powerful of the three kindreds ruling over the early Gaelic kingdom until the late 7th century, the others being *Cenél Loairn* and *Cenél Comgaill).*

Cíanachta Breg (Kee-an-ach-ta Breg) Gaelic (People of Cíanan). A tribal grouping in Brega.

Ciarraige (Kee-arrag) Gaelic (Tribe of Ciar).

Dál gCais (Dahl Gash) Gaelic (descendants of Cormac Cas), a branch of the *Déisi Muman,* a vassal people to the powerful *Éoganachta* dynasty in Munster. In the 10th century the Dál *gCais* became strong enough under Mathgamain mac Cenétig and his brother Brian Bóruma to take the throne from the Eóganachta and successfully campaigned against the vikings in Ireland.

Déisi Muman (Day-see Moo-man) Gaelic (Vassals of Munster). A subject tribe of the Eóganachta dynasty, of possible Gaulish origin.

Dubgaill (Doo-gall) Gaelic (Dark Outlander). A viking group interpreted by Clare Downham as being of the Uí Ímair dynasty.

Eóganachta (Oh-gan-ach-tah) Gaelic (Kin of Éogan). A powerful dynasty that controlled southern Ireland from the 6th to the 10th centuries, of possible Gaulish origin.

Findgaill (Fin-gall) Gaelic (Fair Outlander). Viking grouping interpreted by Clare Downham as being distinct from the Uí Ímair and settled in Ireland before the middle of the 9th century.

Fíanna (Fee-anna) singular Fían. Gaelic (warrior band) The legendary followers of the folk hero Finn mac Cumaill. Also refers to early Irish roving warbands devoted to hunting and fighting.

Fir Bolg (Fer-bawlug) Gaelic (Men of the Bags, or Swollen Men). In Irish mythology, a people who inhabited Ireland before the arrival of the Tuatha Dé Danann. Scholars such as T.F. O'Rahilly and John T. Koch suggest a link with the historical Belgae tribe of Celtic Gaul, whose name comes from the Proto-Celtic *bolg* or *belg,* to swell, as in fury.

Fir Maige (Fer-moy) Gaelic. An early tribe of Ireland who claimed their descent from the mythological druid Mug Ruith.

Fortriu (Fort-ree-oo) Brythonic from *Vertera* (Fortress People) – the Verturiones mentioned by Ammianus Marcellinus, possibly from an original Pictish *Uerteru.* Fortriu was a Pictish kingdom located in what is now Moray and Easter Ross, Scotland. Macbeth is referred to as *King of Fortriu* in *The Prophecy of Berchan.* Gaelic sources frequently mention the Men of Fortriu or Fortrenn.

Gaddgeðlar (Gad-geth-lar) Norse for Gaelic *Gall-Góidil* or Outland Gael. Also, Norse name for Galloway in Southwest Scotland.

Gall Goídil (Gawl Goydil) Gaelic (Outland Gael). People of part Norse and part Gaelic blood in Ireland, Scotland and the Isles. Also referred to in the book as Norse Gael, Norse Irish and Norse Scots.

Gallóglaigh (Gawl-oglay) Gaelic (foreign warriors). Norse Gaelic Hebridean warriors of the mid 13th and late 16th centuries employed as mercenaries by Irish kings and warlords.

Gododdin (God-aw-thin) from Brythonic *Guotodin* and the original early tribe known as the Votadini, who controlled Lothian, the Borders and Northumbria, with their main stronghold at *Din Eidyn,* later to become

Edinburgh. An epic poem *Y Gododdin* celebrates the heroic attack of their warrior elíte on the Anglian occupied areas of Deira and Bernicia in what is now northern England in the year 600 CE.

Knútlings (K-newt-lings) Norse (*Knútlingar* – Kin of Knútr).

Laighin (L-aye-inn) Gaelic (Spearmen). An early people of Ireland, who gave their name to the province of Leinster, said to descend from the High King Labhraidh Loingsech. Tradition has it that they invaded Ireland from Gaul.

Loairn (Loh-rn) Gaelic. The House of Moray was a powerful Pictish Gaelic dynasty that controlled much of what is now Northern Scotland. Also known as the House of Loairn after the Dálriadic founder of the *Cenél Loairn,* Loairn mac Eirc, it was distantly related to, and a rival of the Mac Ailpín dynasty or House of Ailpín ruling Alba to the south, and often at odds with the Orkney Norse over Caithness and Sutherland.

Lochlannach (Loch-lan-ach) Gaelic (Men of Lochlann or Norway) – term for Norsemen.

Miathi (Mee-a-thi) Pictish. Descendants of an ancient confederation of tribes known as the *Maeatae* occupying what is now southern Scotland. The Roman governor of Brittania, Virius Lupus was forced to pay off the *Maeatae* for peace.

O'Donnell (Oh-Donnul) Gaelic *Uí Domnaill* (descendants or kin of Domnaill). Powerful Irish dynasty based in Tyrconnell (*Tír Chonaill*) or Donegal. Rivals of the Ulster O'Neills.

Osraige (Oss-ray) Gaelic (People of the Deer). An early Irish tribe traditionally descended from Óengus Osrithe, a legendary king, based in a territory of the same name in what is now County Kilkenny and the west of County Laois.

Papar (Pah-par) Norse from an Old Irish term for *father.* Irish hermit monks who once settled in Iceland before the arrival of the Norse, and in the Orkney islands of Papa Westray and Papa Stronsay.

Picts from Latin *Picti* (Painted, Tattooed) Norse *Pettar.* Brythonic *Peithwyr.* Anglian *Peohta.* The Gaels called the Picts *Cruithini* from *Brythonic* Pritani. A powerful tribal confederation that dominated most of what is now Scotland, possibly descended from the fierce Caledonii and Maeatae who warred with Roman forces. The Picts are said to have tattooed their skin from early times.

Reference is made to such tattoos in a poem by Claudian. The Picts were also noted for their sophisticated art styles found on metalwork and stone, particularly totemic animal forms as well as intricate knotwork and spiral designs. Generations of conflict with Roman and post-Roman invaders appears to have forged them into a formidable warrior society. To their west in Argyll and the Isles was the Gaelic Kingdom of Dál Riada. To their south was the Kingdom of Strathclyde ruled by the Britons and the Anglian Kingdom of Northumbria that had risen to pre-eminence in the 7th century by absorbing other Brythonic realms. The Angles had grown strong enough to extort tribute from their neighbours, including the Picts. But the latter were unhappy with the situation, as noted by the early English hagiographer Æddi Stephanus, who whined in his *Life of Wilfrid* that the Picts *despised subjection to the Saxons with a fierce disdain.* In 685 the ascendancy of the Kingdom of Northumbria was brought to a bloody halt at the Battle of Dún Nechtain when King Bridei mac Beli and his Pictish forces annihilated King Ecgfrith and his Anglian army. Dál Riada was subjugated by the fearsome Óengus mac Fergusa, King of the Picts in the 730s and may have continued as a client kingdom of Pictland, though intermarriage meant that rulers with both Pictish and Gaelic blood became increasingly common. In the 9th century Northumbria fell to the vikings, who also made frequent forays into Pictland from Ireland and the Isles. Pictish resistance to viking attacks was strong, but in 839 a catastrophic battle with the invaders wiped out much of the Pictish military elite. In the aftermath, Cináed mac Ailpín saw off his rivals to become King of the Picts in 843. The Picts and Scots were eventually to merge in a Pictish Gaelic society in the later Kingdom of Alba.

Rus (Russ) Old East Slavic *Роѹсь*. A group of East Slavic tribal states ruled by the Varangian Rurik dynasty (late 9th to mid 13th centuries).

Svertlings (S-vert-lings) Norse (*Svertlingar* – the black kin).

Ulaid (Oo-lay) Gaelic. Originally the Uolunti tribe mentioned by Ptolemy. The Ulaid were the ruling tribal confederation in Ulster.

Uí Colgain (Oh-Coal-gan) Gaelic (Descendants or Kin of Colgain), a branch of the Cíanachta Breg occupying the lands around Lusk in what is today County Dublin.

Uí Ímair (Oh-Eemer) Gaelic (Descendants or Kin of Ímair/Ívarr), powerful Norse Irish dynasty responsible for much of the viking activity in Ireland, Scotland and throughout Britain.

Uí Liatháin (Oh-lee-ah-hawn) Gaelic (Descendants or Kin of Liatháin). An early kingdom and tribe of Munster who occupied North Wales and Cornwall in the 4th century.

Uí Máine (Oh-Mahn-ye) Gaelic (Descendants or Kin of Máine). Early kingdom and tribes of Connacht founded by Máine Mór mac Eochaidh.

Uí Néill (Oh-Nail) Gaelic (Descendants or Kin of Niall Noigallach or Niall of the Nine Hostages), powerful dynasty in the north of Ireland from 6th to 10th centuries. Rivals of the O'Donnells.

Væringjar (Vye-ring-yar) Norse (Sworn Companions) Greek Βάραγγος (Várangos). Varangians – vikings who governed the state of the Kievan Rus (between 9th and 11th centuries) and formed the elite personal guard of the Byzantine Emperor.

Þingalið (Thing-alith) Norse (Assembly Retinue). Standing army of the English kings from 1013 – 1051.

Gods & Saints Names

The subject of the Norse and Gaelic gods is extensively covered in the author's previous book *The Viking Runes*. The Gaelic deities in particular are covered in his *The Celtic Heroic Tradition in Myth & Legend,* both available on Amazon and Kindle.

Adomnán (Adom-nahn) Gaelic (Timorous). Irish saint and abbot of Iona.

Andrew (An-droo) from Greek ἀνδρεία (manhood, bravery). A patron saint of Scotland, Greece and Russia among other places. The town of Saint Andrews in Fife, originally Cennrígmonaid, gets its name from him. His relics are said to have been brought from Constantinople and given to Óengus mac Fergusa, King of the Picts. In 832 Óengus defeated a larger force of Angles near Athelstaneford in East Lothian after seeing clouds in the shape of a white cross against the blue sky. Following the victory, Óengus made Andrew the patron saint of Scotland. The design of the Scottish national flag, the saltire, or Saint Andrew's Cross, is based on this tradition.

Aoibhinn (Ee-vin) Gaelic (Beautiful Sheen). The *bean sídhe* or fairy woman of the Dál gCais dynasty.

Æbbe (Eye-bah) Anglian. Northumbrian female saint, known as Æbbe the Younger. Abbess of Coldingham Priory in Berwickshire, Scotland. Martyred by Danish vikings in 807.

Badb (Bav) Gaelic (Crow). Also *Badb Catha* (Battle Crow). Goddess of war. Often takes form of raven or skald crow, birds of the battlefield. Probably originally the Gaulish goddess *Catubodua*.

Bealdhere (Beld-herr) Anglian (Bold Army). Also known as Baldred and nicknamed The Apostle of the Lothians. Northumbrian saint who founded the church at Tyninghame, which was raided by Amlaíb mac Gofraid (Óláfr Guðrøðarson), King of Dublin and Northumbria in 941.

Bede or ***Bæda*** Anglian saint of Northumbria famous for his *Historia ecclesiastica gentis Anglorum*.

Bóinn (Boyn) Gaelic. Goddess after whom the River Boyne is named.

Blathmac (Blah-mac) Gaelic (Flower Son). Irish saint and abbot of Iona martyred by vikings in 825.

Breacán (Breck-an) Gaelic (Freckled). Early Irish saint. His grandfather, Carthan Fionn, King of the Dál Cais, was baptised by Saint Patrick. The religious centre of Ardbraccan was established in his honour.

Brénaind (Bren-nan) Gaelic (Flaming Brand). Saint Brendan of Clonfert (484-577). Famous for his legendary voyage to the Isles of the Blessed. He is credited with giving victory to the Irish over the viking leader Tomrar (Þórir) at Clonfert in 866.

Brice (*Breece* in French & *Bryce* in English). A 5th century Frankish saint and Bishop of Tours. On his feast day on 13th November 1002 Danish settlers in England were massacred on the orders of King Æþelræd Unræd (Æthelred the Ill-Advised), including the sister and brother in law of Svein Fork Beard, King of Denmark. The English king's nickname proved justified with regard to the massacre when Svein invaded England repeatedly in reprisal and added it to his dominions in 1013.

Brigantia /Brigindo (Brigan-shee-ah/Brigin-do) Gaulish (the High One). Goddess of Continental Celtica, from whom Brigid derives.

Brigid (Breed-ta) Gaelic (Exalted One) Goddess of fire, fertility and poetry in Ireland, Scotland and continental Celtica. Known as *Brigantia* in Britain, from whom the tribe of *Brigantes* took their name, and *Brigindo* in eastern Gaul. The later Irish Saint Brigid of Kildare, after whom her devotees were named, probably arose from the original deity.

Buithe (Bawk-ya) Gaelic. Scottish saint who evangelised the Picts and founded the monastic settlement of Monasterboice in what is now County

Louth in about the year 500.

Cianán (Kee-anawn) Gaelic. Irish saint and Bishop of Damliag (Duleek).

Ciarán (Keer-ahn) Gaelic (Little Dark Haired One). (c.516-c.549) Irish saint and first abbot of Clonmacnoise, known as *Ciarán mac an tSaeir* (Son of the Carpenter).

Coemgáin (Cow-ghan) Gaelic (Co-Birth). The name of three Irish saints.

Columbanus (Colum-banus) Latin. Gaelic *Columbán* (White Dove). Irish saint and missionary (541-615) from Meath, active in Frankish Gaul and Lombardy. The monastery at Govan was put under the rule of Columbanus by Causantín ap Rhydderch, King of Strathclyde.

Colum Cille (Colum Killy) Gaelic (Church Dove). Irish saint, also known as Columba, a scion of the powerful Úi Néill dynasty in Northern Ireland. He established the monastery at Iona and was an advisor to rulers such as Aodhán mac Gabrán. Patron saint of Derry and a patron saint of Scotland. Later honoured by Norse kings of the isles, who gave their patronage and protection to the abbey many of their forebears had previously raided.

Cú Chulainn (Koo-hoolan) Gaelic (Hound of Cullan). Divine superhero of Ulaid or Ulster, son of the god Lug.

Cuthbert (Kuth-bert) Anglian (War Bright). Patron saint of Northern England.

Dagda (Day-dah) Gaelic from Proto-Celtic *Dagodeiwos* (Good God). Also known as *Eochaid Ollathair,* Horseman Allfather. Irish deity of fertility, strength, wisdom and druidry.

Danu (Dan-oo) Gaelic. Mother goddess of the *Tuatha Dé Danann,* the Irish gods and deified heroes.

Edmund the Martyr (Ed-mund) Anglian (Protector of Riches). King of East Anglia made a saint after being shot with arrows and beheaded by the men of Ívarr the Boneless and his brother Ubba.

Fionnán (Finn-ahn) Gaelic (Fair). Irish saint who trained at Iona Abbey and lived on an island named after him in Loch Shiel, Lochaber. He later became Bishop of Lindisfarne, off the Northumbrian coast, from 651 to 661.

Finnian (Finn-ee-an) Gaelic (Little Fair One). Irish patron saint of Meath, who established Clonard Abbey, an important monastic centre, in 520.

Finnbarr (Finn-bar) Gaelic (White or Fair Head). Fair haired Irish missionary, also known as Finnian, who founded Maigh Bhile Abbey (Movilla) in Ulster in 540. He was teacher to Colum Cille or Columba.

Finnbarr (Finn-bar) Gaelic (White or Fair Head). Irish bishop and patron saint of Cork, who established the monastic centre there in 606.

Fíach (Fee-uch) Gaelic (Raven). Fifth century Irish saint and bishop of Sletty.

Fíachra or ***Fiacre*** (Fee-uch-ra) Saint Fiacre 600-670 CE (probably from *Fíachra*) was an Irish saint from Connacht who went to Breuil in France and became a hermit and gardener famous for his herbal cures.

Freyja (Fray-ya) Norse. Goddess of love, sensuality and magic.

Freyr (Fray-ur) Norse. God of fertility.

Frigg (Frig) Norse. Goddess of wisdom and foreknowledge.

Gunn (Goon) Norse (Fight). A *valkýrja.*

Göndul (Gundul) Norse. (Spear Thrust?) A *valkýrja.*

Hilðr (Hil-th-ur) Norse (Battle, Fight). A *valkýrja.*

Hjorðrimul (Hee-yorth-rimul) Norse (Tumult of Swords). A *valkýrja.*

Hvíti Kristr (H-veet-ee Krist-ur) Norse (White Christ). The Norse view of Christ and the epithet of *White* may have been influenced by the god Baldr with his nickname *Hvíti Ás* (White God), deity of purity and joy.

Lir (Leer) Gaelic (Sea). Irish god of the sea, father of Mannanán, deity of the sea, magic and the Otherworld.

Lug (Loo) Gaelic. God of sun, sovereignty, warriorship and multiple arts. In Gaulish *Lugos,* the most popularly attested god in all Celtica.

Macha (Mach-ah) Gaelic. Goddess of sovereignty in Ulster.

Magnús (Mag-noos) Norse (Great). Magnús Erlendsson, also known as Magnús the Martyr, was Jarl of Orkney from 1106 until 1117, when he was executed by his enemies. He was later sainted in 1136 by Bishop William the Old and his relics transferred from Christ Church, Birsay to Saint Magnús Cathedral, Kirkwall, built and named after him by his nephew Jarl Rögnvaldr Kali Kolsson. He was renowned for his pious character and many miracles and healings are said to have occurred after his death, according to *Orkneyinga saga.*

Mannanán (Mann-an-ahn) Gaelic. God of the sea, magic and the Otherworld.

Mocheallóg (Mo-ch-el-oag) Gaelic. Irish saint who founded a church at Kilmallock in the 6th or 7th century.

Moire (Morr-y) Gaelic. Mary, referred to as Our Lady of the Isles in the Hebrides. The Norse Gaelic Morrisons of Lewis are known as Mac Gillemoire.

Morrígan (Mawr-ree-gawn) Gaelic (Great Queen). Goddess of battle, magic and prophecy. Like the Badb, she often takes the form of a raven or crow in the mythological sources.

Mug Ruith (M-weh-ruh) Gaelic (Slave of the Wheel). A blind Munster druid with amazing powers, who travelled in a flying vessel called *roth rámach* (Wheel with Oars).

Njörðr (Nyawrth-ur) Norse. God of the sea and fertility, father of Freyja and Freyr. May derive from an older female deity *Nerþuz.*

Nornír *(Norn-eer)* Norse. *Urðr* (Origin), *Verðandi* (Becoming), *Skuld* (Debt), the goddesses of Fate.

Ogma (Awg-maw) Gaelic. Also, Gaulish *Ogmios.* God of eloquence who created the ogam alphabet.

Óðinn (Oh-th-in) Norse. God of wisdom, runes, magic and spiritual ecstasy.

Óláfr (O-lahf-ur) Norse (Heir to the Legacy of the Ancestor). Óláfr Haraldsson was King of Norway from 1015-1028. He fell at the Battle of Stiklestad in 1030 and was later made a saint.

Pádraig (Paw-drig) Gaelic for Latin *Patricius,* father of the citizens. Patrick, patron saint of Ireland, along with Brigid and Colum Cille. Though famous in the early literature for opposing druidism, in *Acallam na Senórach* or Colloquy with the Ancients, he is presented as being on cordial terms with the famous heathen warriors of the Fíanna, Cáilte mac Ronáin and Oisín and keen for their stories and traditions to be recorded.

Rögnvaldr (Roan-vald-ur) Norse (God Ruler, Ruler through the Gods, Decisive Ruler). Rögnvaldr Kali Kolsson (c.1103-1158) was a Jarl of Orkney and later a saint. Famous in *Orkneyinga saga* for his eccentricity, poetry and voyage to the Holy Land.

Sanngriðr (Sann-gri-th-ur) Norse (Affirming Quarter). A *valkýrja.*

Scáthach (Ska-huh-ch) Pictish-Gaelic warrior goddess presiding over the Isle of Shadows or Scaíth (Skye), similar to the Norse goddess *Skaði.* Both of their names translate as *shadow.*

Seachnall (Shawch-null) Gaelic for Latin *Secundinus.* Irish saint related to Saint Patrick through his mother Lubaid. He established Domhnach Seachnall, the church of Seachnall in County Meath between 439 and 447. Máel Seachnaill mac Máele Ruanaid and Máel Seachnaill mac Domnaill, High Kings of Ireland, were named after him.

Senán (Sen-an) Gaelic (Little Old Wise Man). Irish saint of the province of Munster, who established a monastery on Inis Cathaigh (Scattery Island). One of the Twelve Apostles of Ireland.

Sínann (Shin-awn) Gaelic goddess after whom River Shannon is named. Granddaughter of the sea god Lir.

Skaði (Ska-th-ee) Norse-Lappish warrior and hunter goddess of the northern forests and mountains, similar to the Pictish-Gaelic *Scáthach.* Both of their names translate as *shadow.*

Svipull (Svip-ool) Norse (Unstable). A *valkýrja.*

Tuatha Dé Danann (Too-aha-day-danan) Gaelic (Tribe of the Goddess Danu, the Irish gods and deified heroes).

Valkýrjur (Val-keer-yur) Norse. *Choosers of the Slain,* divine battle maidens, daughters of Óðinn.

Wilfrid (Wil-frid) Anglian. Northumbrian bishop and saint (c.633-c.709).

Yngi/Yngvi (Ing-ee/Ing-vee) Norse. God of fertility, also known as Freyr or Yngvi Freyr.

Þórr (Thor or Tor) Norse. God of thunder, strength, oaths and fertility.

Place Names

Agðir (Ag-theer) Old Norse for Agder, a region in south Norway. It gets its name from the ancient people that inhabited it – the Egðir.

Ailech (Ay-lech) Gaelic. Refers to *Grianán Ailigh,* a royal seat of the Northern Uí Neill on Greenan Mountain, Donegal, Ireland.

Alaborg (Ah-la-borg) Norse (Stream Fort). Now Aalborg, Denmark's fourth largest city.

Alba (Alap-ah) Gaelic name for the Pictish Gaelic Kingdom of Scotland from CE 900, formerly Pictland. *Albannach* means people of Alba.

Aldeigjuborg (Al-day-gyoo-borg) Norse for Slavic *Staraya Ladoga* or Old Ladoga, an affluent Norse-Slavic trading post in the 8th and 9th centuries. Now a village in Leningrad Oblast, Russia.

Airer Góidel (Ahrer-Gyle) Gaelic (Coast of the Gael – *Argyll* – a coastal region in the west of Scotland corresponding to most of what was the earlier kingdom of *Dál Riada.* The islands off Argyll were known as the *Innse Gall* or Islands of the Outlanders when they were controlled by the Norse from the 9th to the 12th centuries).

Akursborg (Akkurs-borg) Norse for Acre, the old capital of the crusader kingdom of Jerusalem.

Anglesey (Angul-say) from Norse Öngullsey (Hook Island). Brythonic *Ynis Môn.* A large island off the north coast of Wales.

Apulia (Ah-pul-ee-a) Puglia, southern Italy.

Ardbrackan (Ard-bracc-an) Gaelic *Ard Breacain* (Hill of Braccan). Early religious centre in what is now County Meath, Ireland in honour of Saint Breacain. The Ui Néill had a victory over viking forces here.

Armagh (Ar-mah) Gaelic Árd Mhacha (Height of Macha). A county in Ulster.

Assandun (Ass-an-dun) Saxon. Possibly Ashingdon in the southeast of Essex or Ashdon in northern Essex. Site of the battle in which Knútr the Great, King of the Danes beat Edmund Ironside, King of the English in 1016, completing the Danish reconquest of England.

Athelstaneford (Ath-ul-stain-ford) Saxon (Ford of Æþelstan, where he was killed). A village in East Lothian. Tradition has it as the site of the battle between Óengus mac Fergusa, King of the Picts and a certain Æþelstan, the leader of a horde of invading Angles. On the night before the battle, Saint Andrew is said to have appeared to Óengus in a vision offering a triumphant outcome to the upcoming battle. A white cross was formed of clouds in the blue sky when morning came, which the Picts saw as an omen of victory and they proceeded to defeat the Angles. Scotland's national flag, the Saltire or Saint Andrew's Cross, is said to have arisen from this event.

Atholl (Ath-awl) from Gaelic *Athfhotla* (New Ireland). Norse *Atjoklar* (At-yok-lar). Once an important mormaerdom or Gaelic earldom, now in northern Perth and Kinross, Scotland.

Ásmundarvagar (As-moon-dar-vag-ur) Norse (God Protected Way) Osmundwall, South Walls, Orkney.

Áth Cliath (Aw Klee-ah) Gaelic (Ford of the Hurdles). Now used in modern times as the Gaelic name for Dublin.

Bádhbhghna (Baw-nah) Gaelic (from Bághna, a chief of the Fir Bolg). Slieve Baune in Roscommon.

Bamburgh (Bam-burra) Anglian *Bebbanburgh* (Bebba's burg). Originally *Din Guardi,* a stronghold of Bryneich, a kingdom of the Britons encompassing cross-border territories of what is now Scotland and England. The kingdom was later overrun by the Angles, who changed its name to Bernicia. Bamburgh is now a village in Northumberland.

Bangolau (Bann-o-yee-aye) Brythonic. A place on Anglesey where Rhodri the Great defeated the vikings.

Belach Lechta (Beh-lach-lech-ta) Gaelic *Beal Áth na Leacha* (Ford Mouth of the Flagstones). Site of a battle in which Brian Bóruma defeated Máel Muad mac Brain, King of Munster in 978. Now the parish of Killilagh in County Clare.

Bernicia (Bern-isha) Anglian kingdom that replaced the Brythonic realm of *Bryneich.*

Beruvík (Ber-oo-veek) Norse name for Berwick in Northumbria.

Birgishérad (Birgis-herad) Norse for Birsay in Mainland, Orkney.

Biskupstimgur (Bisk-up-stim-gur) Norse. Probably Biskupstungur in Iceland.

Bjørgvin (Byirg-vin) Norse (Green Mountain Meadow). Bergen, second largest city in Norway.

Bothgobhann (Both-gow-an) Gaelic (Booth of the Smith). Location of Donnchad mac Crínáin's place of death from mortal wounds after his final battle with Macbeth. Probably the modern Pitgavenny.

Boyne (Boyn) Gaelic *an Bhóinn,* a river in Leinster, Ireland.

Bordeyri (Bord-ay-ree) Norse (a hamlet in northwest Iceland).

Borgarfjörðr (Borg-ar-fyirth-ur) Norse. Not the Borgarfjörður in Iceland, but an unidentified firth in Scotland.

Brega or ***Magh Breagh*** (Moy Bray-a) Gaelic (Fine Plain). Petty kingdom north of Dublin that included the Hill of Tara, where the *Ard Rí na nÉireann* or High King of Ireland was confirmed in his position.

Breidafjörðr (Bride-ah-fyirth-ur) Norse (Broad Firth). The Moray Firth, Scotland.

Brenn Isles (Brenn). Islands in southern Sweden.

Bretland (Brett-land) Norse name for Wales, based on the true and original name of the Welsh, the Britons. Bretland could also be applied to Ystrad Clud or Strathclyde, a kingdom of the Britons in what is now southwest Scotland.

Brunanburh (Broon-an-burr) Saxon (Bruna's Fort). Possibly Bromborough on the Wirral Peninsula, Merseyside, northwest England. A battle was fought here in 937 in which Causantín mac Áeda, King of Alba and Amlaíb mac Gofraid (Óláfr Guðrøðarson), King of Dublin and their allies were defeated by the forces Æþelstan, King of the Saxons. The report of the battle in *The Annals of Ulster* has it that *uncounted thousands of Northmen fell...and on the other side a multitude of Saxons...* According to *Egils saga,* Æþelstan deliberately prolonged negotiations with Óláfr before the battle to such an extent that greater numbers had time to join his army and tip the balance of the scale in his favour.

Bryneich (Brin-aych) Brythonic (Land of Mountain Passes). A kingdom of the Britons encompassing cross-border territories of Berwickshire, East Lothian and Northumbria, in what is now Scotland and England.

Bute (By-oot) possibly from Gaelic *bót* (fire). An island in the Firth of Clyde. The Norse called it Bót as well as Rothesay.

Carham (Carrum) Anglian (Rocky Steading) from Brythonic *kair* (fortress). The village of Carham-on-Tweed in Northumbria. A battle was fought here in 1018 with Máel Coluim Forranach (Malcolm the Destroyer), High King of Alba, allied with Owain the Bald, King of Strathclyde against Uhtred, earl of Northumbria. Uhtred's army was beaten and Alba's eastern border extended to the River Tweed.

Carn Lugdoch (Carn-Loo-daw-ch) Gaelic (possibly the Injurious Cairn of Lug). Site of battle between Máel Sechnaill mac Máele Ruanaid, High King of Ireland and Máel Gualae mac Donngaile, King of Munster in 858.

Cashel (Cash-al) Gaelic *Caiseal* (Stone Ring Fort). An ecclesiastical province in what is now County Tipperary, Ireland.

Cenn Fuait (Cen-fay) Gaelic (Fuat's Head). Location of *Cath Cinn Fuait* or the Battle of Confey in 917. Either in County Kildare or County Carlow.

Cheshire (Chesh-eer) Saxon *Legeceasterscir* (Shire of the City of Legions). A county in northwest England bordering on Wales.

Chluain Tarbh (Cloon-tarv) Gaelic (Bull Meadow). Clontarf near Dublin.

Cill ua nDaigri (Kill oo-a nDarry) Location uncertain. Site of battle in 868 between Áed Findliath and his enemies – the Uí Neíll of Brega, the Leinstermen and their Norse allies. Áed had the victory.

Cinnbelachoir Gaelic. Palace possibly near Scone, where Cináed mac Ailpín, King of the Picts, died in 858.

Clackmannan (Clack-man-an) Gaelic *Clach Mhanainn* (Manau's Stone). A part of the Brythonic Kingdom of Manau Gododdin in what is now southern Scotland. In current times a small town in the Forth Valley.

Clonard (Clon-ard) Gaelic *Cluain Eraird* (Erard's Meadow). Site of early monastery at the River Boyne founded in 520 by Saint Finnian. The monastery was pillaged in 838 by vikings and the monks massacred. In alliance with the vikings of Waterford, Cellachán King of Munster plundered the abbey in 939.

Clonfert (Clon-fert) Gaelic *Cluain Fearta* (Grave Meadow). A village in what is now County Galway. The monastery there was plundered four times by vikings. In 866 or 867 it was plundered by one Tomrar (Þórir) and his men, who were subsequently defeated by Congal, King of the Ciarraige.

Clonmacnoise (Clon-mac-noy-sha) Gaelic *Cluain Mhic Nóis* (Meadow of the Sons of Nóis). A monastery on the River Shannon in County Offaly, Ireland. It was plundered by vikings about seven times and by the Irish themselves over twenty times.

Clontarf (Clon-tarf) Gaelic *Cluain Tarbh* (Bull Meadow). Site near Dublin of the famous battle in 1014 between the mixed Irish/Norse forces of Brian Bóruma, Máel Mórda mac Murchada and Sihtric Silkbeard.

Coldingham (Cold-ing-ham) Anglian (Village of the Kin of Colud). Site of Coldingham Priory in what was once part of the Anglian kingdom of Bernicia. Now in Berwickshire, Scotland.

Connacht (Con-awcht) Gaelic (A province in the west of Ireland, named after the *Connachta* or descendants of Conn of the Hundred Battles).

Corbridge (Cor-bridge) Anglian for Roman *Coria* or *Corstopitum* in Northumbria. Two battles were fought here in 914 and 918 between Ragnall ua Ímair, King of the Norse Gael and Causantín mac Áeda, King of Alba.

Cork (Cork) Gaelic *Corcaich Mór na Mumhan* (Great Marsh of Munster). A monastic settlement established by Saint Finnbar in 606, later also developing into a trading port for the Norse alongside it. Now a city in the province of Munster, Ireland.

Craig Phadrig (Crayg-fad-rig) Gaelic (Rock of Patrick). Location of hilltop stronghold of Bridei mac Maelchon, King of the Picts, near Inverness.

Crail (Cray-l) Gaelic *Cathair Aile.* A village on the East Neuk of Fife. Some traditions have Causantín mac Cináeda, King of the Picts captured and killed by viking raiders after a battle at Fife Ness, near Crail in 877.

Cruden Bay (Croo-den) Gaelic *Croch Dain* (Slaughter of the Danes). Site of battle in Aberdeenshire where Máel Coluim Forranach (the Destroyer) defeated a Danish army.

Damsay (Damsay) Norse (Pond Island). An island in Orkney where Jarl Erlendr Haraldsson was killed in 1154.

Danelaw (Dane-law) Danish *Danelagen* and Anglian *Dena lagu.* The Viking territory that was to take in most of England, in which settlement commenced in the late ninth century, where Danish law was supreme and English status and laws were inferior. It was composed of fourteen shires – Bedford, Buckingham, Cambridge, Derby *(Djúrabý)*, Essex, Hertford, Huntingdon, Lincoln, Middlesex, Norfolk, Northampton, Nottingham, Suffolk and York.

Dál Riada (Dahl-ree-ada) Gaelic (Riada's Share). Norse *Dalar.* An early Gaelic kingdom of the 6th -7th centuries spanning western Scotland and Ulster. Later applied to Argyll in general.

Degsastan (Deg-sa-stan) Saxon (Degsa's Stone). Unidentified location of a battle in 603 between Áedán, King of Dál Riada and Æþelfrið, King of Bernicia, thought by some to have been in the vicinity of Dawstane in Liddesdale, Scotland. Hering son of Hussa, a Bernician royal exile, was an ally of Áedán in this battle, but Æþelfrið had the victory.

Derry (Derr-ay) Gaelic *Daire* (Oak Grove). A town in Ulster founded by Saint Colum Cille or Columba.

Difeyrar (Diff-ay-rar) Norse name for Banff, a town in what is now Aberdeenshire, Scotland.

Din Eidyn (Deen Ay-din) Brythonic (Fortress of Eidyn). The original stronghold and settlement at what is now Edinburgh, power base of the Gododdin tribe. The Brythonic name *Eidyn* is the original word from which the *Edin* of Edinburgh derives, not from the speculative *Edwin's burh* suggested by some. In Gaelic it is *Dún Éideann.*

Dollar (Daw-lar) Gaelic *Dolair* (Dark, Gloomy) from early Pictish and Gaelic. Small settlement in what is now Clackmannanshire, Scotland. In 875 there was a battle near there in which the Picts were defeated by a viking force with heavy losses.

Donaghpatrick (Donna-pawdrig) Gaelic *Domhnach Pádraig* (Patrick's Church). A village in County Meath. According to tradition, the place was given to Saint Patrick by Conaill, brother of Laoghaire, High King of Ireland. It was raided by vikings in 949 and 996.

Drogheda (Drawch-eeda) Gaelic *Droichead Átha* (Bridge of the Ford). A town in what is now County Louth, Ireland.

Drumomuy (Drum-o-mooy) Gaelic *Druím Dá Maige* (Ridge of Two Plains). Site near River Feegile of battle in 861 in which Máel Sechnaill, High King of Ireland defeated Áed Findliath and the Dublin Norse.

Dubhgall's Bridge (Doo-gawl's Bridge) Gaelic *Droichead Dubhgall.* A bridge across the Liffey in Dublin, Ireland.

Dublin (Dub-lin) from Gaelic *Dubhlinn* (Black Pool), known in modern Irish as *Baile Átha Cliath.* Norse *Dyflin.* From around 841 it was a Norse settlement at the River Poddle, with the Gaelic settlement of Áth Cliath (Aw Klee-ah), Ford of the Hurdles, upriver. Dublin was to become one of the biggest trading centres in the entire Norse world.

Dumbarton (Dum-bar-ton) from Gaelic *Dún Breatainn* (Fort of the Britons). Chief stronghold of the Brythonic Kingdom of Strathclyde.

Dún Ailinne (Doon Ellin-ye) Gaelic. Ancient ceremonial site in what is now County Kildare, possibly once the inauguration site of the Kings of Leinster.

Dunbar (Dun-bahr) Gaelic *Dún Barra* (Stronghold on the Summit). Originally a stronghold of the Brythonic Votadini tribe, it was later absorbed into Northumbria by the Angles and became known as *Dynbaer* in their tongue. It was burnt by Cináed mac Ailpín, King of the Picts, according to the *Chronicle of the Kings of Alba,* and after the Battle of Carham in 1018, Máel Coluim the Destroyer took Lothian from the Angles, and Dunbar became absorbed into the Kingdom of Alba. It is now a town in East Lothian.

Dún Breatainn (Doon-Brettan) Gaelic (Fort of the Britons), originally the main stronghold of the early Brythonic Kingdom of Strathclyde. Now Dumbarton in western Scotland.

Dundalk Bay (Dun-dawlk) Gaelic *Cuan Dhún Dealgan* (Bay of Dalgan's Fort). A bay on the east coast of Ireland near the town of Dundalk in County Louth.

Dungalsbaer (Dun-gals-byre) Norse for Duncansby, a headland in Caithness, Scotland.

Dunkeld (Dun-keld) Gaelic *Dún Chailleann* (Stronghold of the Caledonians) north of what is now Perth. A church was established here by Causantín mac Fergus, King of the Picts and later rebuilt by Cináed mac Ailpin, who had some of the relics of Saint Colum Cille or Columba brought to it from Iona to protect them from viking plunderers.

Dún Másc (Doon-Mask) Gaelic (Fort of Másc). Hillfort and settlement plundered by vikings in 842. Now Dunamase in County Laois.

Dunmore Cave (Dun-more) Gaelic *Dún Mór* (Big Fort). A cave in Kilkenny. Originally referred to as *Dearc Fearna,* among other names, it was the scene of a mass killing in 928, according to the *Annals of the Four Masters,* when *Gofraith ua Ímair, with the foreigners of Áth Clíath, demolished and pillaged Dearc Fearna.* This was Gofraid the grandson of Ímair. The cave was either being used as a place of habitation or shelter by the victims who died in large numbers by the sword and probably by the smoke from fires made to burn them out.

Dún Nechtain (Doon-Nech-tan) Gaelic (Stronghold of Nechtain). Location of a Pictish victory over the Northumbrian Angles in 685. Initially thought to be Dunnichen in Angus, but now believed to be more likely at Dunachton in Badenoch. The Picts, led by King Bridei mac Bili, inflicted a devastating defeat on the army of King Ecgfrið, annihilating the invading forces and destroying Northumbrian ascendancy in northern Britain.

Durham (Durr-um) From Celtic *dun* or fort and Norse *holme* or island, an important settlement in Northeast England. Máel Coluim Forranach (the Destroyer), High King of Alba besieged the town unsuccessfully in 1006. Donnchad mac Crínáin also mounted a disastrous siege of the town in 1039.

Dyflin (Diff-lin) Norse. Dublin, from Gaelic *Dubhlinn* (Black Pool), known in modern Irish as *Baile Átha Cliath.*

Dyraksborg (Deer-aks-borg) Norse for Durrës in western Albania, though *Orkneyinga saga* refers to it as *Bulgaraland* or Bulgaria, presumably because of the high proportion of Bulgarians there.

Dyrnes (Deer-ness) Norse for Deerness, a peninsula in Mainland, Orkney.

Ekkjal (Ek-yal) Norse for Oykel (Gaelic Óiceall). A river forming the boundary between Sutherland and Ross, Scotland.

Engilsnes (Engils-ness) Unidentified ness visited during Jarl Rögnvaldr's voyage.

Ethandun (Eth-an-dun) Saxon. Probably Edington in Wiltshire. Site of a battle between the viking forces of Guþrum and Ælfred the Great. Ælfred was victorious, but an agreement was made whereby the vikings kept possession of northern England, which became known as the Danelaw.

Eyrar (Ay-rar) Norse. (A steading in east Iceland).

Érinn or Éireann (Err-in) Gaelic name for Ireland, along with Ériu, from the matron goddess of the island. *Eireannach* means people of Eireann.

Färlev (Fehr-lev) Norse. A place in Götaland where Haraldr Gilli was defeated by Magnús Sigurðarson in 1134.

Færeyjar (Faye-ray-yar) Norse for Faroe Islands.

Fimm Borginn (Fim-Bawr-ginn) Norse (Five Boroughs) of the Danelaw – Lincoln, Derby, Nottingham, Leicester and Stamford *(Stafnfurðr).*

Fífi (Fee-fi) Norse for Fife (Pictish *Fib,* Gaelic *Fíobha*), originally an important Pictish kingdom. Now the Kingdom of Fife, Scotland.

Flyðrunes (Flith-roon-ess) Norse (Flounder Ness). A farm on Mainland, Orkney.

Fortriu (Fort-ree-oo) Pictish (Fortress People, from the early Verturiones tribe). A kingdom of Pictavia or Pictland corresponding to the territories of Moray and Ross, sometimes used to refer to Pictland in general.

Friðarey (Free-thar-ay) Norse (Fair Isle). Fair Isle in Shetland.

Gaddgeðlar (Gad-geth-lar) Norse for Galloway, Scotland.

Galicia (Gal-liss-ee-a) An autonomous community of the northwest Iberian Peninsula. The name is derived from Greek Καλλαϊκοί and Latin *Callaecia* – terms for the *Gallaeci*, an ancient Celtic tribe that once occupied the area, said to be among Rome's toughest opponents.

Garðaríki (Garth-ah-reeki) Norse (Kingdom of Cities). Realm of the Kievan Rus.

Gáreksey (Gah-rek-say) Norse for Gairsay, a small island in Orkney.

Glen Máma (Glen Mah-ma) Gaelic (Glen of the Gap). *Cath Ghlean Máma* or the Battle of Glen Máma took place between the forces of Meath and Munster on the one side and Leinster and Dublin on the other in the year 999. The location is thought to be beside Ardclough on the border between Dublin and Kildare.

Glen Foichle now ***Gleann Eallaigh*** (Glen of the Cattle) in the Sperrin Mountains, County Tyrone, Ulster. Site of battle in 856 between Áed Findliath and the Norse Gaels. Áed had the victory.

Govan (Guv-an) from Brythonic *Guovan.* An important monastic site in the kingdom of Strathclyde said to have been founded by King Causantín ap Rhydderch under the rule of Saint Columbanus. After Alt Clud or Dumbarton fell to the forces of Ímar and Amlaíb in 870, Govan appears to have risen to greater prominence under Norse Gaelic influence. It would certainly have been of commercial and strategic importance to the vikings.

Götaland (Gyota-land) Norse (Goth Land). Southern territory of Sweden, with Svealand to the north.

Grímsbaer (Greems-byre) Norse for Grimsby in northern England.

Gulberuvík (Gull-beroo-veek) Norse for Gulberwick, a village southwest of Lerwick, Shetland.

Gwynedd (Gwin-eth) Brythonic from Gaelic *fine* (tribe). A territory in northwest Wales settled by Irish from Munster and Leinster, later to become the Kingdom of Gwynedd after the warlord Cunedda of the Gododdin tribe from what is now southern Scotland defeated the Gaelic settlers there, according to the chronicler Nennius. Gwynedd was a target for viking raids and attempted settlement from the 850s on. In 856 Rhodri Mawr, King of Gwynedd defeated a Danish force and killed its leader, Gormr.

Hafrsfjörðr (Hafurs-fyirth-ur) Norse (Male Goat Fjord). A fjord in the Stavanger Peninsula in Rogaland, Norway, scene of the famous battle that resulted in the merging of the various Norse kingdoms under a single monarch, Haraldr Hárfagri.

Hálogaland (How-loga-land) Norse (Land of High Logi, a fire giant).

Hæerri (Haye-ree) Norse (Higher) Harris in the Outer Hebrides.

Hjaltland (H-yalt-land) Norse (Hilt Land) Shetland, known in Irish Gaelic as *Innse Catt* or the Isles of the Cats, the pictish Cat tribe that occupied it before the Norse.

Hjálmundalr (H-yal-mund-al-ur) Norse for Helmsdale in Sutherland, Scotland.

Hoðskuldstaðr (Hith-skoold-stath-ur) Norse. Höðskuld's steading in Laxriverdale, Iceland.

Hornafjörðr (Horna-fyirth-ur) Norse. A fjord in southeast Iceland.

Hólmgarðr (Hoh-lm-garth-ur) Norse (Island Stronghold). Veliki Novgorod, capital of Garðaríki (the states of Kievan Rus). Now the city of Novgorod in Russia.

Höfn (Huf-n) Norse for Hamm, a village in Caithness, Scotland.

Hörðaland (Hurth-a-land) Norse (Land of the Harudes, an ancient northern people). Now a Norwegian county bordering Sogn og Fjordane, Buskerud, Telemark and Rogaland.

Hrossey (H-ross-ay) Norse (Horse Island) Orkney, another name for Mainland.

Hrútafjörðr (H-roota-fyorth-ur) Norse. A fjord in the northwest of Iceland.

Hvammr (H-vamm-ur) Norse (Unnr's steading in Hordudalr, Iceland).

Hvera (H-verra) Norse for River Wear, Northumberland.

Hvítsborg (H-veets-borg) Norse name for Whithorn in Dumfries & Galloway, Scotland.

Imbolum (Im-bol-um) A town in Greece or Asia Minor.

Inbher Boinne Site of a battle in 1032 between Sihtric, King of Dublin and the allied forces of the Conailli, the Uí Tortain and the Uí Meith. Sihtric was victorious.

Inchcolm (Inch-col-um) Gaelic *Innis Choluim* (Coluim Cille's or Columba's Island). A monastic island in the Firth of Forth off the Fife coast. According to tradition, after Macbeth, *Ard Rí* of Alba repulsed a Danish invasion in 1040, the Danes buried their dead on the island after paying a large sum of gold.

Ingólfshöfði (Ing-awlfs-sith-ee) Norse (Ingólfr's Head, a headland on the south coast of Iceland, named after Ingólfr Arnason, the first Norse settler on the island.

Inis Cathaigh (In-is Cah-hay) Gaelic. Scattery Island in the Shannon Estuary. The island was home to Saint Senán but was to become part of the Norse-Irish Kingdom of Limerick, the viking leaders choosing to base themselves there through the 970s because of its strategic position. Ímar, King of Limerick and his sons were killed there by Brian Bóruma in 977.

Innse Gall (Inshah-gawl) Gaelic (Isles of the Outlanders or Foreigners). The Outer Hebrides.

Inverdovat (In-vir-dov-at) Gaelic (Dark River Mouth). A place near the present Newport-on-Tay where Causantín mac Cináeda, King of the Picts is said to have been slain by Norse marauders in 877.

Iona (Eye-oh-nah) Gaelic Í Chaluim Chille, Norse *Eyin Helga.* Small island in the Inner Hebrides where Coluim Cille (Saint Columba) established his famous monastery.

Islandbridge (Island Bridge). Location of a battle in what is now County Dublin between an army of the Uí Ímair led by Sihtric Cáech and an alliance of Irish forces commanded by Niall Glúndub, Overking of the Northern Uí Néill and *Ard Rí* of Ireland. Sihtric gained the victory and Niall died along with five other Irish kings.

Jarlsnes (Yarls-ness) Norse (Jarl's Ness). An unidentified ness in Bretland (Wales).

Jemtland (Yemt-land) Old Norse for Jämtland, a province of central Sweden bordering on Norway.

Jorsalir (Yorsa-leer) Norse for Jerusalem. Also called *Jorsalaland.*

Jórvík (Yor-veek) Norse for Latin *Eboracum* (from Brythonic *Eborakon*), the Viking York. Taken by Ímar in 866, York was the main power base of the Irish vikings in what is now England. The Kingdom of York was ruled alongside the Kingdom of Dublin by the Uí Ímair from 875 to 954.

Katanes (Kata-nes) Norse (Ness of the Cat People). From the early Pictish kingdom known as Catt or Cait, named from the ancient tribe known as the Cats. The Kingdom of Cait comprised Caithness and part of Sutherland (Gaelic *Cataibh*) in what is now modern Scotland. The Gaelic name for it was *Gallaibh* after it became settled by the *Gall* or Norse.

Kells (Kells) Gaelic *Ceannanas* or *Ceann Lios* (Head Fort). A monastery founded about 804 in what is now County Meath.

Kildare (Kill-dare) Gaelic *Cill Dara* (Church of the Oak). Church and monastery founded by Saint Brigid. Now a town in County Kildare, Ireland.

Kilkenny (Kil-kenny) Gaelic *Cill Chainnigh* (Church of Cainnech). A county in Leinster, Ireland.

Killineer (Kill-in-eer) Gaelic. A place in County Louth by the River Boyne, where Carlus, son of Amlaíb Conung died in battle against Áed Findliath in 868.

Kilmallock (Kil-mal-ock) Gaelic *Cill Mocheallóg* (Church of Mocheallóg). Location of a battle between the vikings of Waterford and the vikings of Limerick. Now a town in County Limerick.

Kincora (Kin-cawra) Gaelic. A settlement in the sub-kingdom of Tuadmumu in north Munster, Ireland, birthplace of Brian Bóruma. Now County Clare.

Kinghorn (King-gawrn) Gaelic *Ceann Gronn* (Head of the Marsh). Macbeth mac Findláech, High King of Alba is said to have repulsed a Danish invasion here in 1040.

Kintyre (Kin-tyre) Gaelic *Cinn Tíre* (Headland). A peninsula in Argyll, once part of Dál Riada and ruled by the Cenél nGabráin.

Kirkjuvág (Kirk-yoo-vahg) Norse for Kirkwall in Orkney.

Kjarrekstaðir (Kyar-ek-sath-eer) Norse (Kjarrek's Steading). A farm on Mainland, Orkney. Now Cairston.

Kjolen Mountains (K-yolen) Norse (Keel). The range of mountains along the border between Norway and Sweden.

Kunnaktir (Kunn-ak-teer) Norse name for Connacht, a western province in Ireland.

Liffey (Liff-ay) Gaelic *an Life,* the river flowing through Dublin, Ireland.

Limerick (Lim-erick) Gaelic *Luimneach,* Norse *Hlymrekr.* A Norse Irish kingdom along the banks of the Shannon Estuary and rival of Dublin. Now a city in County Limerick, Ireland.

Lochlann (Loch-lann) Gaelic name applied to Norway, Loch Land, but also to the Norse areas of Scotland and the Isles. *Lochlannach* was a term for Norsemen.

Lothian (Lo-thee-an) Early Brythonic *Luguduniana* (Land of the Stronghold of Lugus), Middle Brythonic *Lleuðinyawn.* An eastern Lowland region of what is now Scotland. It was originally named after the Celtic god Lugus and ruled as a kingdom of the Cymric-speaking tribe of Britons known as the Gododdin, with their main stronghold based at *Din Eidyn* or Edinburgh. It later became absorbed by the Anglian kingdom of Bernicia. English control of territories in what is now Scotland was severely weakened after the decisive Pictish victory over the Angles at the Battle of Dún Nechtain in 685. During the reign of Indulfr an Ionsaighthigh (Indulfr the Aggressor) Gaelic *Ildulb mac Causantín,* King of Alba from 954 to 962, Edinburgh was taken under Scottish control, and in 1018 after the Battle of Carham, Lothian was absorbed by the Kingdom of Alba.

Loch Cuan (Loch Coo-an) Gaelic (Loch of the Havens). The older name of Strangford Lough (from Norse *Strangrfjörðr* or Strong Firth) in the present County Down.

Loch Gabhair (Loch Gav-ar) Gaelic (Goat Loch). In the present parish of Ratoath, County Meath.

Lough Foyle (Loch Foil) Gaelic *Loch Feabhail* (Loch of the Lip). An estuary of the River Foyle in Ulster.

Lough Owel (Loch Owl) Gaelic *Loch Úll.* A lough in Westmeath, Ireland.

Lough Ree (Loch Ree) Gaelic *Loch Rí* (Loch of the King). Second largest lough on the River Shannon.

Lundey (Lun-day) Norse (Puffin Island). Lundy Island, off the Devon coast.

Magh Luirg (Moy Loorg) Gaelic (Shin-Shaped Plain). Early kingdom of Connacht. Known as *Magh Luirg an Dagda* (Plain of the Dagda's Track), after the god Dagda.

Maigue (My-g) Gaelic *An Mhdigh* (River of the Plain) in what is now County Cork.

Manegid (Mann-eh-gith) Brythonic. Unidentified location of a battle in which Rhodri the Great, King of the Britons defeated the vikings.

Mann (Man) Isle of Man. *Ellan Vannin* (Manx) *Manau* (Irish Gaelic) *Manaw* (Brythonic). Traditionally named after the Irish god Manannán.

Mar (Marr) Gaelic *Márr.* A mormaerdom in Northeast Scotland.

Marselia (Mar-sell-ee-a) Marseilles, France.

Máeyar (My-ahr) Norse for Isle of May in the Firth of Forth.

Meath (Mee-th) Gaelic *Midhe* (Middle or Centre). Royal seat of the High Kings of Ireland.

Meginland (Megin-land) Norse (Mainland, the main island of Orkney).

Melkorkastaðr (Mel-korka-stath-ur) Norse (Melkorka's steading at Salmon River Dale, Iceland).

Melrose (Mel-rose) from Brythonic *Mailros.* Gaelic *Maolros* (Bald Moor). Anglian *Magilros.* An early monastery east of the present town of Melrose in the Scottish Borders, at a bend of the River Tweed connected with Saint Cuthbert when the area was part of Northumbria. It was captured by Cináed mac Ailpín, King of the Picts during one of his frequent invasions.

Mercia (Mer-see-ah) Anglian *Miercna rice* (Kingdom of the Border People). A powerful Anglian kingdom that was preeminent among the English realms south of the Humber from around the year 600 until the invasion of the Great Heathen Army resulted in a large proportion of it being taken under Danish rule. By 879 what remained of it was under the control of the Saxon kingdom of Wessex.

Midhe (Meeth) Gaelic (Middle or Centre). Seat of the *Ard Rí* or High King of Ireland. Now County Meath in the province of Leinster.

Miklagarðr (Mikkla-garth-ur) Norse (Great City). Constantinople.

Mocetauc (Mawk-eh-tawk). Brythonic. Probably Mugdock in Stirlingshire. Site of battle between Picts and Britons, in which Talorgan, brother of Óengus mac Fergus was slain in 750.

Monasterboice (Man-aster-bawk-ya) Gaelic *Mainistir Bhuithe* (Monastery of Buithe). Early monastic settlement in what is now County Louth established in the late 5th century.

Moray (Mur-ray) Gaelic *Moireibh* (Sea Settlement). Norse *Mýrhæfi.* A powerful northern kingdom comprising the present territory of Moray as well as Ross, Caithness and Sutherland. The rulers, belonging to the House of Loairn, were often at odds with the Jarls of Orkney over control of land as well as being rivals to the Mac Ailpín dynasty ruling Alba to the south.

Mórthlach (Mawrt-la-ch) Gaelic. An ancient parish in Moray, Scotland.

Munster (Mun-ster) Gaelic *an Mhumhain* (Land of Mumha's Men), from the goddess Mumha or from Eochaidh Mumho, an early king. A southern province of Ireland.

Mæren (Maye-ren) Norse. Mære, a village in Trøndelag County, Norway, an important heathen centre in early viking times.

Mön (Munn) Norse name for Isle of Man or Mann.

Mýræfi (Meer-aye-fee) Norse. From the Gaelic *Moireabh* - Celtic *Mori* -sea/*treb* -settlement. Moray, a mormaerdom or Pictish Gaelic kingdom in Northern Scotland.

Niðarós (Neeth-ar-oss) Norse (Nid River Mouth). Old name of Trondheim, Norway.

Njorfasund (Nee-yorfa-soond) Norse for Straits of Gibraltar.

Nordmøre (Nord-mirr) Norse. A district in what is now Møre og Romsdal, Norway.

Normandy (Nor-man-dee) from Norman French *Normaundie.* A duchy in northern France founded in 911 and originally settled by Northmen, hence *Normans,* possibly from the Norse *Norðmaðr.* These settlers intermarried with Franks and Gallo Romans to create a French speaking expansionist feudal society dominated by the heavily armoured knight. In 1066 they conquered England under Duke William and later invaded Wales and Ireland, where many are said to have become *more Irish than the Irish.* The first Normans in Scotland were refugees taken in by Macbeth. Norman culture and settlement in Scotland then began on a significant scale under King David I (1124-1153). Although intermarriage took place between Normans and the Gaelic and Brythonic nobility, they were more often than not culturally and militarily at odds with native British and Gaelic dynasties and the Norse Gaelic rulers of the Isles.

Northumbria (North-umbree-ah) Anglian *Norþanhymbra rice.* Norse *Norðimbraland* (North-imbra-land). Translates as *North of the Humber.* An early kingdom of the Angles stretching from what is now northern England to the southeast of Scotland. It was at first formed of the former Brythonic kingdoms of Bryneich and Deifr, that then became Bernice (Bernicia) and Dere (Deira), the former to the north and the latter to the south of the River Tees. They were later to merge in 654. The Great Heathen Army invaded Northumbria in 866 to 867 and the Anglian kings Ælla and Osberht were slain in the conflict, after which the vikings took York. By 919 York was under Norse Gaelic control and part of the Kingdom of Dublin.

Norðreyjar (North-ray-yar) Norse. North Isles – Orkney & Shetland.

Orkneyjar (Ork-nay-yar) Norse for the Orkney Islands.

Osraige (Ossory) Gaelic (People of the Deer). An early kingdom that took in the best part of present County Kilkenny and the west of County Laois.

Papey Meiri (Pap-ay Mehri) Norse. Big Island of the *Papar,* or Irish hermit monks - Papa Westray, an island in Orkney.

Papey Minni (Pap-ay Mini) Norse. Little Island of the *Papar,* or Irish hermit monks - Papa Stronsay, a small island in Orkney.

Péttlandsfjörðr (Pyett-lands-fyirth-ur) Norse (Pentland Firth, a strait separating the Orkneys from Caithness, named after the Picts (Old Norse *Péttr*).

Pictavia (Pict-ay-vee-ah) Latin for Pictland, which comprised the bulk of what is now Scotland – all the territory north of the Firth of Forth and east of the Grampians. Originally composed of seven sub-kingdoms – Fib (Fife), Fotla (Atholl), Círcinn (Angus & the Mearns), Cé (Mar & Buchan), Fidach (near Inverness), Fortriu (long considered to be Strathearn & Mentieth, though recent studies have suggested Moray and Ross instead) and Cait or Catt (Caithness and Sutherland). Orkney and Shetland were also Pictish and with a piratical reputation before the arrival of the Norse. The Pictish realm came to be divided into a northern kingdom and a southern one, with rivalry between the two. This was to continue after Pictland became Alba CE 900, with the Pictish-Gaelic dynasties of Ailpín in the south and Loairn in the north competing for supremacy.

Raumsdalr (Rawms-dal-ur) Norse. District in what is now Møre og Romsdal, Norway.

Rauðabjörg (Row-tha-byirg) Norse (Red Stonghold-Shaped Headland), Roberry, Caithness, Scotland.

Rechru (Rech-roo) Gaelic. Either Rathlin Island off the Antrim coast in Ulster or the island monastery of Lambay off County Dublin.

Ror (Rawr) Norse. Probably *Røros* in Trøndelag County, Norway.

Ross (Rawss) Gaelic (Headland). A territory of Northern Scotland that once formed part of the kingdom of Moray.

Sandvík (Sand-veek) Norse (Sand Bay) Sandwick on west coast of Mainland, Orkney.

Saxland (Sax-land) Norse for Saxony in Germany.

Sátíri (Sat-eer-ee) Norse name for Kintyre, a peninsula in the west of Scotland. A part of the old Gaelic kingdom of Dál Riada ruled by the powerful *Cenél nGabráin* kindred. It became part of the *Suðreyjar* or South Isles when the Norse settled it in turn.

Scíath Nechtain (Skee-ah Ne-ch-tahn) Gaelic (Shield of Nechtain). Site of battle in 848 near what is now Castledermot, County Kildare, in which Lorcán mac Cellaig and Ólchobar mac Cináeda defeated the vikings and their leader Jarl Tomrair was slain.

Sekker (Sekk-ur) Norse. Probably Sekken, an island in Molde Municipality, Møre og Romsdal, Norway.

Seley (Sel-ay) Norse – Selja, a small island in Sogn og Fjordane, Norway.

Serkland (Serk-land) Norse for Land of the Saracens.

Shannon (Shan-on) Gaelic *an tSionainn.* Longest river in Ireland named after *Sínann,* a goddess, granddaughter of the sea god Lir. Used by vikings to access monasteries for plunder.

Skáney (Skawn-ay) Norse. Probably Skania, the southernmost province of Sweden, once part of the Kingdom of Denmark.

Skiðam⊠rr (Skith-a-meer) Norse for Skitten, a place near Wick, Caithness, Scotland.

Skotlandsfjörðr (Scotlands-fyirth-ur) Norse (the Minch, a strait dividing the northwest Highlands and the northern Inner Hebrides from Lewis and Harris in the Outer Hebrides).

Skýey (Skee-ay) also *Skíð, Skujö.* Norse (Cloudy or Misty Isle) – Skye, the biggest and most northern island of the Inner Hebrides. In Gaelic tradition the Isle of Shadows or Scaíth, presided over by the Pictish-Gaelic warrior goddess Scáthach, similar to the Norse goddess Skaði. Both of their names translate as *shadow.*

Sligo (Sly-go) Gaelic *Sligeach* (Shell Rich), a coastal town in what is now County Sligo, Ireland.

Stainmore (Stayn-more) Anglian (Stone Moor). An area bordering Cumbria, Durham and North Yorkshire. Eiríkr Blóðøx is said to have been killed here by a certain Maccus son of Óláfr, probably a Norse Gaelic jarl.

Stamford Bridge (in Old Norse *Stafnfurðubryggja* – staff-n-firth-oo-brig-ya) in Yorkshire, location of the famous battle in 1066 between the forces of Haraldr Harðráði and Harold Godwinson.

Stiklarstaðir (Stik-lar-stath-eer) Old Norse for Stiklestad, a village in Verdal in Nord Trøndelag, Norway, the site of a famous battle in 1030 between the forces of King Óláfr Haraldsson (the Saint) and the so-called Peasant Army loyal to Knútr the Great. Óláfr was slain.

Strathclyde from Brythonic *Ystrad Clud* (Strath of the Clyde). A kingdom of the Britons stretching from what is now southern Scotland to northern England, probably established by the Damnonii tribe, with the stronghold of Alt Clud or Dumbarton as its capital. Early sources, in particular the Irish Annals, record conflicts of the Strathclyde Britons with the Gaels of Dál Riada, the Picts and the Northumbrians. In 870 Ímar and Amlaíb Conung besieged Alt Clud with a large fleet and army, taking a great number of Britons, Picts and Angles captive to Ireland. The captives included the then King of Strathclyde, Arthgal ap Dyfnwal, who was assassinated in 872 at the instigation of Causantín mac Cináeda, King of the Picts, apparently to put Arthgal's son Rhun, husband of Causantín's sister, on the throne of Strathclyde. Both the Kingdom of Alba and the Norse Gaels appear to have significantly involved themselves in the politics and rule of Strathclyde thereafter. In 1018 Owain the Bald, King of Strathclyde was an ally of Máel Coluim the Destroyer, High King of Alba when he defeated the English at the Battle of Carham. Strathclyde appears to have become a client kingdom of Alba some time during Máel Coluim's reign (1005-1034), as his grandson Donnchad came to rule there as King of the Cumbrians.

Straumey (Stremm-ay) Norse (The Island in the Current), now called Stroma, two miles off the north coast of Caithness, Scotland.

Sulcoit (Sool-cot) from the Gaelic *Sulchóid Bheag* (the present-day townland of Soloheadbeg in County Tipperary). Site of battle in 968 between the Dál gCais and Ímar of Limerick's viking forces. Brian Bóruma, together with his brother Mathgamain mac Cennétig, had the victory. Mathgamain plundered and burned Limerick before noon following the day of the battle.

Sunnmøre (Sun-mirr) Norse (district in what is now Møre og Romsdal, Norway).

Suðreyjar (Sooth-ray-yar) Norse (South Isles). The Hebrides, the islands of the Firth of Clyde and the Isle of Man.

Suðrland (Suth-ur-land) Norse (Southern Land). Old name for the region of Northern Scotland now known as Sutherland. Part of the kingdom of Moray, it was fought over by the Orkney Norse and the Picto-Scottish mormaers.

Svínafell (Sveen-ah-fell) Norse (A homestead in Öræfi, Iceland).

Syllingar (Sillin-gar) Norse for the Scilly Isles, off the coast of Cornwall.

Tara (Tah-rah) Gaelic *Teamhair* or *Teamhair na Rí* (Tara of the Kings). The seat of the high kings of Ireland at the River Boyne, County Meath, Ireland.

Torfness (Torf-ness) Norse (Turf Ness). Tarbat Ness in Easter Ross, Scotland, from Gaelic *tairbeart* (isthmus) and Norse *ness* (headland).

Tweed (Tweed) A border river between Scotland and England.

Tyninghame (Ty-ning-hame) Anglian (Hamlet on the Tyne). Originally a monastery and village founded by Saint Bealdhere or Baldred in the mid 700s. Sacked by Amlaíb mac Gofraid (Óláfr Guðroøðarson) in 941. Now a village in East Lothian.

Tyrconnell (Teer-conn-ul) Gaelic *Tír Conaill* (Land of Conall). Now County Donegal, Ireland.

Ulaztír (Ool-az-teer) Norse for the province of Ulster, Ireland.

Ulfreksfjörðr (Ool-freks-fyirth-ur) Norse (Ulfrek's Firth – *Lough Larne,* in Ireland).

Valland (Vawl-land) Norse for Gaul or Continental Celtica. The *val* of Valland comes from Proto-Germanic *Walhaz* or *foreigner,* deriving from the powerful Celtic tribe known as the *Volcae* and later applied to Gauls and Romans in general. The term *Walhaz* was later to give rise to the term *Welsh,* (again meaning *foreigner*) and applied, possibly without seeing the irony, by the Anglo-Saxons to the Britons, the people whose land they had invaded. The Norse correctly referred to the inhabitants of Wales, Strathclyde and Lothian as *Brettar* or Britons.

Vatnsfjörðr (Vat-ns-fyirth-ur) Norse for Loch Vatten on the Isle of Skye.

Veradalr (Verra-dalr) Norse (Ver River Dale). Now Verdal, a municipality in Trøndelag, Norway.

Verbon (Ver-bawn) Possibly Narbonne in southern France.

Vík (Veek) Norse (Inlet, Cove). Now a municipality in Sogn og Fjordane, Norway.

Waterford from Norse *Veðrafjörðr,* a Norse Irish kingdom with its settlement established in 853. A rival of the Kingdom of Dublin and ally of Brian Bóruma at the Battle of Clontarf in 1014. Now a city in Munster, Ireland.

Wexford from Norse *Veisafjörðr* (Mud Flat Inlet), a viking settlement and city state established in 800. Now a town in County Wexford, Ireland.

Wicklow (Wick-low) possibly from Norse *Víkingr-ló* (Viking Meadow) or alternatively Bay Meadow. Gaelic *Cill Mhantáin* (Church of the Toothless One). A town in the present County Wicklow, south of Dublin. The vikings used Wicklow as a base from the middle of the 9th century.

Þingvöllr (Thing-vull-ur) Norse for Dingwall in northern Scotland.

Þórsá (Thor-so) Norse (Þórr's River). Thurso in Caithness, Scotland. Originally Celtic *Tarvedubron* (Bull River).

Þrasnes (Thras-ness) Norse (Raging Ness) - unidentified ness, possibly on Spanish coast.

Þrasvík (Thras-veek) Norse. Now Freswick, small hamlet in eastern Caithness, Scotland.

Þussasker (Thoos-ask-ur) Norse for Gaelic *An Tuscar* (Tuskar Rock, off the coast of County Wexford, Ireland).

Þvatt River (Th-vatt) Norse. A river in Iceland.

Terms

Ard Rí (Ard Ree) Gaelic (High King). *Ard Rí na hÉireann* (Ard Ree nErin) High King of Ireland; *Ard Rí Alban* (Ard Ree Alapan) High King of Scotland.

Creach Ríg (Creh-ch Ree) Gaelic (Royal Prey or King's Prey). A customary raid on enemy territory by a new chieftain or king to demonstrate his power.

Drengr (Dreng-ur) Norse (Brave, gallant man).

Ealdorman (Ee-aldor-man) Saxon (Elder Man). An official and chief magistrate appointed by the English king over a shire or group of shires.

The title was also given to rulers of smaller kingdoms that were absorbed into greater ones.

Eyraþing (Ay-ra-thing) Norse. The *Eyraþing* was an important yearly gathering at Niðaróss. In *Orkneyinga saga* Magnús Óláfsson is recognised as ruler of Norway during this assembly.

Heiðinn (Hee-th-enn) Norse (Heathen).

Hirð (Hurth) Norse (Warrior retinue, *húskarlar*).

Húskarlar (Hoos-karl-ur) Norse (House men, personal bodyguards of a king or the armed following of a jarl).

Jarl (Yarl) Norse (Earl). A Norse leader or chieftain ranking next below a king.

Karl (Kahr-l) Norse (Freeman), the typical northern warrior farmer.

Lagmann (Lag-man) Norse (Law Man). Also Icelandic *lögsögumaðr.* The lawman or lawspeaker presided over the þing or legal assembly, recited the law and acted as an arbitrator between conflicting parties. The *lagmann* later became absorbed in the Gaelic *breitheamh* (lawman or judge) throughout the Hebrides. The Norse Gaelic Clann mac Gille Mhoire or Morrisons were hereditary lawmen for the Lords of the Isles. Another name for the clan was *Clann na Breitheamh.*

Longphort (Long-fort) Gaelic (Long Ship Camp). Fortified coastal camps used for defence and trade by vikings in Ireland.

Gjald (Gy-awld) Norse term for compensation, usually for a killing.

Lughnasadh (Loon-nasah) Gaelic (Assembly of Lugh). Irish harvest festival in honour of the god Lugh.

Mormaer (Mawr-myre) Pictish/Gaelic (Sea Lord or Great Steward). The ruler of a province in early Scotland. In the sagas, they are usually referred to with the Norse title *jarl.*.

Muckle (Muck-ul) Scots from Norse *mikill* (big), used to refer to large things in general – *he had a muckle great head on him.*

Ogam or ***Ogham*** (Aw-mm) Gaelic (possibly from Irish *og-úaim* or point cleft, the cleft made through carving by knifepoint). An early Irish alphabet used for esoteric and everyday purposes, for example on memorial stones. In mythology it was invented by the god Ogma (Continental Celtic Ogmios).

Peedie (Peedy) Norse term for anything small.

Rune (Roon) Norse *rúnar* and Gaelic *rún* (mystery, secret). An ancient alphabet used for esoteric and everyday purposes by the Norse and known as *fuþark* after the first six characters. It is closely associated with the god Óðinn or Odin in early mythology and features frequently in the sagas as a carved script used in magical spells. It was also utilised in an everyday sense for things such as love messages and traders' slogans. See *The Viking Runes* by the author.

Skáld (Skaw-ld) Norse. A court bard who composed and recited praise poetry in honour of kings, warlords and heroes for reward.

Skatt (Skat) Norse. Icelandic *skattur.* Tax or tribute. The word *scot* (as in tax or payment) derives from this and the term *scot-free* means not having to pay *skatt.*

Skrud (Skrood) Norse term for fine cloth.

Toíseach (Tee-shaw-ch) Gaelic (Leader, Chieftain). Modern Irish *Taoiseach.* From the Proto-Celtic *towissākos.*

Uðal (Ooth-ul) Norse from Icelandic óðal. A freehold or steading held by allodial right, free of bonds or liabilities or written title deeds, originating from the first settler's land claim. Norse udal law was established at an early period in Orkney and Shetland, the Isle of Man and some parts of Scotland and still exists to this day. Udal law covers shore ownership as well as farmland. Later a payment of *scatt* (tax or tribute) was paid to a jarl or king to ensure a farmer's uninterrupted possession without charter. The ōþala (o-thala) rune from the Elder *fuþark* refers to inherited estate as well as blood descent, an indication of how closely linked land and family was.

Þing (Thing) Norse. A legal assembly presided over by the lawspeaker at which claims involving *mangeld* for example could be settled and chieftains elected. According to Icelandic saga tradition, the þing also appears to have been an occasion for socialising, arranging marriages and pastimes such as *hestavígs* (horse fights). Place names attesting to the existence of these assemblies in Ireland, Scotland and the Isles include the Þingmote, a raised assembly mound at Dublin, Tynwald on the Isle of Man, Tingwall on Orkney and Shetland, Dingwall in the Highlands and Tinwald in Dumfries and Galloway (from Norse þingvöllr place of the assembly). The present national parliament of Iceland is the *Alþingi.*

Þriðjungr (Thri-th-yung-ur) Norse (a third, as in a share).

Þræll (Thr-aye-ull) Norse (slave).

Old Norse Pronunciation

The Á or á like *ow* as in *cow*

The Ð or ð with a *th* sound as in *mother*

The É or é pronounced like *yeah*

The Í or í pronounced as *ee*

The J is pronounced with a *Y* sound

The Ó or ó pronounced *oh* as in *low*

The Þ or þ with a *th* sound as in *thorn*

The Ú or ú pronounced *oo* as in *moo*

The Ý or ý pronounced *ee* as in *wee*

The Æ or æ pronounced *y* as in *my*

The Ö or ö pronounced *u* as in *curve*

The Ø or ø pronounced *ih* as in *bird*

Old Irish Gaelic Pronunciation

The Á or á (accompanied by no other vowels) pronounced *ah*

Æ or æ pronounced *y* and *my*

Ái or ái pronounced *a* as in *and*

Ai or ai pronounced *ee* as in *cheese*

Ó or ó (accompanied by no other vowels) pronounced *oh*

Óe or óe pronounced *ay* as in *lay*

Ú or ú pronounced *oo* as in *moo*

É or é pronounced *ay* as in *lay*

Í or í pronounced *ee* as in *cheese*

Bibliography

Saga, Myth & Folklore

Aðalsteinsson *A Piece of Horse Liver: Myth, Ritual & Folklore in Old Icelandic Sources* Haskolautgafan 1998

Auden & Taylor (tr.) *Norse Poems* Faber & Faber 1981

Black (ed. by Thomas) *County Folklore vol.3: Examples of Printed Folklore Concerning the Orkney & Shetland Islands* Folklore Society 1903

Bromwich *Trioedd Ynys Prydein: The Triads of the Island of Britain* University of Wales Press 2017

Crockatt (ed.) *Crimsoning the Eagle's Claw: The Viking Poems of Rögnvaldr Kali Kolsson, Earl of Orkney* Arc Publications 2014

Dasent *Brennu-Njáls Saga* (The Story of Burnt Njál) 1861 Cornell University Library 2009

Davidson *Myths & Symbols in Pagan Europe* Syracuse University Press1988

Davidson & Söderberg *Nordens gudar och myter* Prisma, Stockholm 1993

Dooley & Roe *Tales of the Elders of Ireland: A Translation of the Irish Acallam na Senórach* Four Courts Press 1998

Dunford *Táin Bó Flidhais* Fádo Books 2008

Edwards & Pálsson *The Words of Odin: Hávamál* Lockharton Press 1998

Grimm *Teutonic Mythology* R.A. Kessinger Publishing Co. 2003

Guðmundsson *Orkneyinga saga* Hid Islenzka Fornritafelag 1965

Hjaltalin, Goudie, Anderson (trs.) *Orkneyinga saga* Edmonston & Douglas, Edinburgh 1873

Kinsella *The Tain* OUP Oxford 1969

Mackenzie *Teutonic Myth & Legend* Gresham Publishing Company 1912

Magnusson & Morris (trs.) *The Saga of Gunnlaug the Worm Tongue & Raven the Skald* Abela Publishing 2012

Magnusson & Pálsson (tr.) *Njals Saga* Penguin 1960

Magnusson & Pálsson (tr.) *King Harald's Saga* Penguin 1966

Magnusson & Pálsson *Laxdaela Saga* Penguin 1975

Marwick *The Folklore of Orkney & Shetland* Birlinn 2000

Morrisson *The Viking Runes: Runes, Lore, Saga* Sídh Chailleann Press/ Amazon 2015

Morrisson *The Celtic Heroic Tradition in Myth & Legend* Sídh Chailleann Press/ Amazon 2016

Nasstrom *Freyja, the Great Goddess of the North* Almquist & Wiksell 1995

Nennius *Historia Brittonum* Forgotten Books 2008

O' Donoghue *Skaldic Verse & the Poetics of Saga Narrative* OUP 2005

Pálsson & Edwards (tr.) *Egil's Saga* Penguin 1976

Pálsson & Edwards (tr.) *Orkneyinga Saga* Penguin 1978

Pálsson & Edwards (tr.) *Eyrbyggja Saga* Penguin 1989

Pálsson (tr.) *The Book of Settlements: Landnámabók* University of Manitoba Icelandic Series 2007

Pálsson *Legendary Fiction in Medieval Iceland* (Islenzk fraeði) University of Iceland, Faculty of Liberal Arts and the Icelandic Cultural Fund 1970

Saxby *Shetland Traditional Lore* Grant & Murray 1932

Simpson *Icelandic Folktales & Legends* Tempus 2004

Ström *Diser, Nornor, Valkyrjor; Fruktbarhetskult ok sakralt Kungadome I Norden* Almquist & Wiksell 1954

Ström *Nordisk Hedendom; Tro och Sed I Forkristen Tid* Akademiforlaget, Goteburg 1993

Sturluson (tr. Faulkes) *Edda* Everyman Paperback Classics 1995

Sturluson *Heimskringla: Chronicle of the Kings of Norway* CreateSpace 2014

Sveinnson *Brennu-Njáls saga* Hid Islenska Fornritafelag 1954

Todd *Cogadh re Gaedhel re Gallaibh: The War of the Irish with the Foreigners* Cambridge University Press 2012

History

Adamnan *The Life of Saint Columba: Founder of Hy* Ulan Press 2012

Anderson *Kings* & Kings*hip in Early Scotland* John Donald Short Run Press 2011

Anderson *Early Sources of Scottish History A.D. 500 to 1286* HardPress Publishing 2013

Bannerman *Studies in the History of Dalriada* Scottish Academic Press 1974

Batey, Jesch & Morris (ed.) *The Viking Age in Caithness, Orkney & the North Atlantic* Edinburgh University Press 1995

Binchy (ed.) *Críth Gablach* Dublin Institute for Advanced Studies 1941

Broun *The Irish Identity of the Kingdom of the Scots in the Twelfth & Thirteenth Centuries: Studies in Celtic History* Boydell Press 1999

Burne *The Norn Language of Orkney & Shetland* The Shetland Times 1998

Byrne *Irish Kings & High Kings* Harper Collins 1973

Cannan *Scottish Arms & Armour* Shire Publications 2009

Cannan & Ó'Brógáin *Galloglass 1250-1600 Gaelic Mercenary Warrior* Osprey 2010

Carver *Surviving in Symbols: A Visit to the Pictish Nation* Birlinn 1999

Christansen *The Vikings & Viking Wars in Irish & Gaelic Tradition* Oslo / Dybwald 1931

Clarke & Johnson (ed.) *The Vikings in Ireland & Beyond: Before and After the Battle of Clontarf* Four Courts Press 2015

Crawford *Scandinavian Scotland* Continuum International Publishing 1987

Crawford *Earl & Mormaer: Norse-Pictish Relationships in Northern Scotland* Groam House Museum Trust 1995

Cross & Sherbowitz-Wetzor *The Russian Primary Chronicle* Medieval Academy of America 2012

Cunningham *The Annals of the Four Masters: Irish History, Kingship & Society in the Early Seventh Century* Four Courts Press 2014

Donaldson *A Northern Commonwealth: Scotland & Norway* Saltire Society 1990

Downham *Viking Kings of Britain & Ireland: The Dynasty of Ívarr to AD 1014* Dunedin Academic Press 2008

Duffy *Brian Boru and the Battle of Clontarf* Gill & Macmillan 2014

Dumville *The Chronicles of the Kings of Alba* in *Kings, Clerics & Chronicles in Scotland 500-1292: Essays in Honour of Marjorie Ogilvie Anderson on the Occasion of her 90th Birthday* (ed.) Taylor Dublin 2000

Ellis *Macbeth* Frederick Muller 1980

Enright *Lady with a Mead Cup: Ritual, Prophecy & Lordship in the European War Band from La Tène to the Viking Age* Four Courts Press 1995

Farmer (tr.) *The Age of Bede* Penguin Classics 1983

Fenton & Pálsson (ed.) *The Northern & Western Isles in the Viking World: Survival, Continuity & Change* John Donald 1983

Fitzpatrick *Royal Inauguration in Gaelic Ireland c. 1100-1600: A Cultural Landscape Study* The Boydell Press 2004

Foote & Wilson *The Viking Achievement* Book Club Associates 1970

Fordun (edited by Skene) John of Fordun *Johannis de Fordun Chronica Gentis Scotorum* Andesite Press 2017

Fraser *The Pictish Conquest: The Battle of Dunnichen 685 and the Birth of Scotland* NPI Media Group 2000

Gerald of Wales (tr. O'Meara) *The History and Topography of Ireland* Harmondsworth, Penguin 1982

Graham-Campbell *The Viking Age Gold & Silver of Scotland* National Museum of Scotland 1995

Graham-Campbell *The Viking World* Frances Lincoln 2001

Graham-Campbell & Batey *Vikings in Scotland: An Archaeological Survey* Edinburgh University Press 1998

Grant *The Province of Ross & The Kingdom of Alba* in *Alba: Celtic Scotland in the Medieval Era* John Donald 2012

Gray *Sutherland & Caithness in Saga Time (or the Jarls & the Freskyns)* Oxon Printed by W.R. Rendall, Stromness / Oliver & Boyd 1922

Griffiths *Vikings of the Irish Sea* The History Press 2010

Clarke *Ireland & Scandinavia in the Early Viking Age* Four Courts Press 1998

Hennessy & McCarthy (trs.) *The Annals of Ulster* Dublin 1887-91

Hjardar & Vike *Vikings at War* Casemate Publishers 2016

Hudson *Kings of Celtic Scotland* Praeger 1994

Hudson *Viking Pirates & Christian Princes: Dynasty, Religion & Empire in the North Atlantic* Oxford University Press 2005

Hudson *Irish Sea Studies: 900-1200* Four Courts Press 2006

Jakobsen *Dialect & Place Names of Shetland* T.J. Monson, Lerwick 1897

Larsen *The Vikings in Ireland* Viking Ship Museum 2001

Mac Airt & Mac Niocaill *The Annals of Ulster (to AD 1131)* Dublin Institute for Advanced Studies 1983

Mackay *History of the Province of Cat* Peter Reid & Co. Ltd., Wick 1914

Mackenzie *Scotland: The Ancient Kingdom* Blackie 1930

MacShamhráin *The Vikings: An Illustrated History* Dublin 2002

McCarthy *The Irish Annals: Their Genesis, Evolution & History* Four Courts Press 2008

McGettigan *The Battle of Clontarf Good Friday 1014* Four Courts Press 2013

Magnusson *Hammer of the North* Orbis 1976

Magnusson *The Vikings* Tempus 2003

Marsden/Gregory/Green *The Illustrated Life of Columba* Floris Books 1995

Marsden *Alba of the Ravens: In Search of the Celtic Kingdom of the Scots* Constable 1997

Marsden *Gallowglas: Hebridean & West Highland Mercenary Warrior Kindreds in Medieval Ireland* Tuckwell Press 2003

Morrison *The North Sea Earls: The Shetland/Viking Archaeological Expedition* Gentry Books 1978

Ó' Corráin *Brian Boru & the Battle of Clontarf* in Liam de Paor (ed.) *Milestones in Irish History* Mercier Press 1993

Ó'Donovan (tr.) *The Annals of the Kingdom of Ireland by the Four Masters* Dublin 1848-51

Ó'Rahilly *Early Irish History & Mythology* Dublin Institute for Advanced Studies 1964

Owen & Dalland *Scar: A Viking Age Boat Burial in Orkney* Tuckwell Press 1999

Owen *The Sea Road: A Viking Voyage Through Scotland* Birlinn 1999

Petersen *De Norske Vikingesverd* Jacob Dybwad, Kristiana 1919

Pleiner *The Celtic Sword* Clarendon Press 1993

Rixson *The West Highland Galley* Birlinn 1998

Saxo Grammaticus (Hans-Jürgen Hube tr.) *Nordische Mythen und Geschichte Gesta Danorum* Marix Verlag 2004

Shetelig & Brøgger *Vikingskipene* Dreyers Forlag 1971

Skene *Celtic Scotland: A History of Ancient Alban vol.1 of 3* Forgotten Books reprint of 1886

Skene *Chronicles of the Picts, Chronicles of the Scots & Other Early Memorials of Scottish History* Forgotten Books 2018

Smyth *Celtic Leinster: Towards an Historical Geography of Early Irish Civilisation AD 500-1600* Blackrock 1982

Smyth *Scandinavian Kings in the British Isles 850-80* Oxford University Press 1978

Smyth *Scandinavian York & Dublin: The History & Archaeology of Two Related Viking Kingdoms* Templekieran Press 1975

Smyth *Warlords & Holy Men: Scotland AD 80-1000* Edinburgh University Press 1989

Stokes *Annals of Tigernach* Llanerch Press 1993

Whaley *The Poetry of Arnórr Jarlaskáld (Westfield Publications in Medieval and Renaissance Studies)* Brepols N.V. 2002

Runes & Ogam

Barnes *The Runic Iinscriptions of Maeshowe, Orkney* Institutionen för nordiska språk, Uppsala universitet 1994

Barnes, Hagland & Page *Runic Inscriptions of Viking Age Dublin* Royal Irish Academy 1997

Holman *Scandinavian Runic Inscriptions in the British Isles: Their Historical Context* Skrifter Norges Teknisk-aturvitenskapelige Universitet, Senter for Middelalderstudier / Tapir Academic Press

Kermode *Manx Crosses* Pinkfoot Press, Angus 1994

McManus *A Guide to Ogam* Maynooth 1991

Morrisson *The Viking Runes: Runes, Saga & Lore* Sídh Chaillean Press/ Amazon 2015

Spurkland *Norwegian Runes & Runic Inscriptions* Boydell Press 2005

Reference

Cleasby & Vigfusson *An Icelandic – English Dictionary 2nd ed.* Clarendon 1957

Jamieson *Jamieson's Dictionary of the Scottish Language* William P. Nimmo Edinburgh 1867

Mackillop *Dictionary of Celtic Mythology* OUP Oxford 2016

Maier *Dictionary of Celtic Religion & Culture* Boydell Press 2000

Watson *The Celtic Place Names of Scotland* Birlinn 1986

Zoëga *A Concise Dictionary of Old Icelandic* University of Toronto Press 2004

Papers

Androshchuk *Viking Swords: Swords & Social Aspects of Weaponry in Viking Age Societies (Studies 23)* Stockholm, Swedish History Museum 2014

Broderick (PhD) *Tynwald: A Manx Cult Site & Institution of Pre-Scandinavian Origin?* Universität Mannheim

Chadwick *The Story of Macbeth: A Study in Gaelic & Norse Tradition* Scottish Gaelic Studies vol 6 1949 & vol 7 1953

Clouston *Two Features of the Orkney Earldom* The Scottish Historical Review, Edinburgh University Press/JSTOR 2014

Downham *The Battle of Clontarf in Irish History & Legend* History Ireland 13, number 5 2005

Downham *Hiberno-Norwegians and Anglo-Danes: Anachronistic Ethnicities & Viking Age England. No Horns on their Helmets? Essays on the Insular Viking Age. Celtic, Anglo-Saxon & Scandinavian Studies series (vol.1).* The Centre for Anglo-Saxon Studies & The Centre for Celtic Studies, University of Aberdeen 2013

Duffy *Irishmen & Islemen in the Kingdom of Dublin & Man 1052 – 1171* Ériu 43 1992

Duffy *Ostmen, Irish & Welsh in the Eleventh Century* Peritia 1995

Epstein *War Goddess: The Morrigan & Her Germano-Celtic Counterparts* University of California 1998

Ewing *The Birth of Lugh: Óðinn & Loki among the Celts* Sinsear 8 Department of Irish Folklore, University College, Dublin 1995

Forsyth *The Ogham Inscriptions of Scotland: An Edited Corpus* Harvard University (Ann Arbor: UMI 1996)

Fotheringham *Orkney Charms: Notes & Queries series 1 vol. 10* from the Traills of Westray 1848

Hines *Old Norse Sources for Gaelic History* Quiggin Pamphlets on the Sources of Medieval Gaelic History 5, Cambridge 2002

Hudson *Cnut and the Scottish Kings* English Historical Review 1992

Jennings *An Historical Study of the Gael and Norse in Western Scotland from c.795 to c.1000* University of Edinburgh 1993

Mac Gonagle *Celtic Chainmail* www.academia.edu/3891226/Celtic_Chainmail

MacShamhráin *The Battle of Glen Máma, Dublin & the High Kingship of Ireland* Medieval Dublin 2 2000

Megaw *Norseman & Native in the Kingdom of the Isles: A Reassessment of the Manx Evidence* Scottish Studies 20 1976

Ní Mhaonaigh *Cogadh Gáedhel re Gallaibh & the Annals: a comparison* Ériu 47 1996

Ní Mhaonaigh *A Neglected Account of the Battle of Clontarf* Zeischrift fur Celtische Philologie 59 2012

Ó Corráin *The Vikings in Scotland & Ireland in the Ninth Century* Department of History, University College, Cork / Chronicon 2 1998

Ó Corráin *High Kings, Vikings & Other Kings* Irish Historical Studies 21 1978-9

Ó Corráin *The Second Viking Age in Ireland* (Three Studies on Vikings & Christianisation) Rindal (ed.) KULTs skriftserie 28 Oslo 1994

O'Mahony *A History of the O'Mahony Septs of Kinelmeky and Ivagha* Journal of the Cork Archaeological and Historical Society 1906-10 Cork: Guy & Co. 1912

Ó Murchadha *Lagmainn, Lögmenn* Ainm 2 1987

Peterson *Old Norse Nicknames* Háskóli Íslands Íslensku-og menningardeild 2012

Scott *Old Norse Forms of Early Irish Names* www.ellipsis.cx/-liana/names/drafts/irish-norse.html

Speidel *Berserks: A History of Indo-European Mad Warriors* Journal of World History vol.13 no.2 2002

Webpages

Ard-Mhúsaem na hÉireann (National Museum of Ireland): *https://www.museum.ie/Archaeology/Exhibitions/Current-Exhibitions/Viking-Ireland*

Battle of Clontarf: *dh.tcd.ie/Clontarf/*

Celtic Ireland & Scotland *on Facebook*

Dublinia: *www.dublinia.ie*

Every Ogham Thing on the Web: http://www.evertype.com/standards/og/ogmharc.html

Nationalmuseet (National Museum of Denmark): *https://natmus.dk/museer-og-slotte/*

National Museum of Scotland: *https://www.nms.ac.uk/national-museum-of-scotland/things-to-see-and-do/scottish-history-and-archaeology/*

Nordic Names: www.nordicnames.de

Pictish Nation: *halfmoon.tripod.com/pict2.html*

Sveinbjörn Beinteinsson: *https://web.archive.org/web/20091027105907/http://geocities.com/odinistlibrary/OLArticles/Articles/Sveinbjorn.htm*

UiO: Kulturhistorisk Museum: *http://www.khm.uio.no*

Viking Answer Lady: *www.vikinganswerlady.com*

Viking Ireland & Scotland *on Facebook*

Viking Rune: *www.vikingrune.com*

Viking Sword: *www.vikingsword.com*

Vikings/The Swedish History Museum: *http://historiska.se/utstallningar/vikings-2/*

Museums

Ard-Mhúsaem na hÉireann (National Museum of Ireland), Kildare Street, Dublin 2

Dublinia, St Michael's Hill, Christ Church, Dublin 8

Govan Stones, Govan Old Church, 866 Govan Road, Glasgow G51 3UU

Meigle Sculptured Stone Museum, Dundee Road, Meigle, Perthshire PH12 8SB

Museum nan Eilean, Stornoway, Isle of Lewis HS1 2BW

National Museum of Scotland, Chambers Street, Edinburgh EH1 1JF

Nationalmuseet (National Museum of Denmark) Ny Vestergade 10, Prinsens Palæ DK-1471 København K

Orkneyinga Saga Centre, Gyre Road, Orphir KW17 2RD

Orkney Museum, Tankerness House, Broad Street, Kirkwall, Orkney KW15 1DH

Shetland Museum & Archives, Hay's Dock, Lerwick, Shetland ZE1 0WP

UiO: Kulturhistorisk Museum & Vikingskipshuset, Frederik's Gate 2 0164 Oslo

Vikings/The Swedish History Museum, Narvavägen 13-17, 114 84 Stockholm

ABOUT THE AUTHOR

Páll Thormod Morrisson has an enduring fascination with early literature and mythology, in particular Norse, Irish, and Far Eastern traditions. He has blood links with the Pictish Gaelic Mac Ailpín dynasty, the Norse Gaelic Clann Mac Gille Mhoire and the Clann Suibhne *gallóglaigh* kindred of Ulster. As well as T*he Viking Saga in Ireland, Scotland & The Isles,* he is the author of *The Viking Runes, The Celtic Heroic Tradition in Myth & Legend and Dionysos in Myth, Drama & Comedy: Bacchic Elements in Greek & Celtic Culture.*

Printed in Great Britain
by Amazon

69455477R00159